Ecology, Spirituality, and Cosmology in Edwidge Danticat

ENVIRONMENT AND RELIGION IN FEMINIST-WOMANIST,
QUEER, AND INDIGENOUS PERSPECTIVES

Series Editor

Gabrie'l Atchison

Environment and Religion in Feminist-Womanist, Queer, and Indigenous Perspectives is a series that explores the subject of ecofeminism from feminist-womanist, queer, and indigenous perspectives. The governing assumption of the series is that ecofeminism is not only a mode of scholarly discourse and analysis, but also a hub for social formation and action. What distinguishes this series in particular is that it focuses on ecofeminism as a disciplinary matrix through which the voices of women, particularly women of color, and indigenous peoples can speak from their religious and spiritual traditions and practices to address the environmental challenges and concerns of the age. Volumes in this series will attend to the environmental and ecological issues that impact women, people of color, and indigenous populations, as these communities are, in almost all respects, the most immediately threatened by contemporary climate and ecological changes and catastrophes. Works in the series will focus on the history; scholarly resources and perspectives; constructive practices; religious, spiritual, and natural traditions from which these voices speak; and how these can provide alternative narratives, illuminate hidden agendas, and generate resistance to environmental and religious racism and exploitation.

Titles in the series

Ecology, Spirituality, and Cosmology in Edwidge Danticat: Crossroads as Ritual, by Joyce White
Re-Indigenizing Ecological Consciousness and the Interconnectedness of Indigenous Identities, edited by Michelle Montgomery
Ecotheology and Love: The Converging Poetics of Sohrab Sepehri and James Baldwin, by Bahar Davary
Ecowomanism at the Panamá Canal: Black Women, Labor, and Environmental Ethics, by Sofía Betancourt
Mapping Gendered Ecologies: Engaging with and beyond Ecowomanism and Ecofeminism, edited by K. Melchor Quick Hall and Gwyn Kirk
In the Name of the Goddess: A Biophilic Ethic, by Donna Giancola

Ecology, Spirituality, and Cosmology in Edwidge Danticat

Crossroads as Ritual

Joyce White

LEXINGTON BOOKS
Lanham • Boulder • New York • London

Published by Lexington Books
An imprint of The Rowman & Littlefield Publishing Group, Inc.
4501 Forbes Boulevard, Suite 200, Lanham, Maryland 20706
www.rowman.com

86-90 Paul Street, London EC2A 4NE

British Library Cataloguing in Publication Information Available

Library of Congress Cataloging-in-Publication Data

Names: White, Joyce, 1975- author.
  Title: Ecology, spirituality, and cosmology in Edwidge Danticat :
    crossroads as ritual / Joyce White.
  Description: Lanham, Maryland : Lexington Books, [2023] | Series:
    Environment and religion in feminist-womanist, queer, and indigenous
    perspectives | Includes bibliographical references and index. | Summary:
    "Returning to the cosmological and ontological center of Africana
    spirituality, 'Ecology, Spirituality, and Cosmology in Edwidge Danticat:
    Crossroads as Ritual' explores the ways in which Danticat texts awaken
    Africana consciousness and clarify identity and subjectivity"-- Provided
    by publisher.
  Identifiers: LCCN 2022041788 (print) | LCCN 2022041789 (ebook) | ISBN
    9781793646637 (cloth) | ISBN 9781793646644 (ebook)   Subjects:
  LCSH: Danticat, Edwidge, 1969---Criticism and interpretation. |
    Ecology in literature. | Spirituality in literature. | Cosmology in
    literature. | LCGFT: Literary criticism.
  Classification: LCC PS3554.A5815 Z96 2023 (print) | LCC PS3554.A5815
    (ebook) | DDC 813/.54--dc23/eng/20220926
  LC record available at https://lccn.loc.gov/2022041788
  LC ebook record available at https://lccn.loc.gov/2022041789

This book is dedicated to Mama, Inell White, who was and will always be my first and greatest teacher and now my Ancestor. Until we meet again.

Contents

List of Figures

Acknowledgments

Without the love, support, and encouragement from my friends and family this undertaking would not be possible. My gratitude must start with my parents who created a world full of vivid dreams and imparted the discipline to pursue those dreams. To my sisters and brothers (Donna, David, Mary, and Marvin) who keep me grounded and laughing. To my nieces and nephews who give me hope and joy. A special acknowledgment is given to my extended family whose love and support keep me sustained.

Words cannot begin to express my appreciation for my husband, Johnny Johnson, whose continued love, support, and unceasing listening ear have seen me through this project and beyond. I am deeply grateful for your unbelievable belief in this project.

I am also deeply grateful for my scholarly sisters and brother (Black School of Thought) Drs: Kyle Fox, La' Niece Littleton, and Courtney Terry. I am indebted to the three of you for providing me with an academic family, words of encouragement and comfort, and confidence. The success of this project depended on my cohort's support. To my other sister scholar, Maythee Rojas, whose guiding voice is always with me. And to the many others who have been advocates and supports, thank you.

I am deeply grateful for my academic mentors and teachers. In particular, I would like to thank Dr. Daniel Black for his instruction, guidance, and vision. I am thankful for his faith in this project and continued support. I offer a special note of thanks to Drs. Ligon and Sears for pushing and challenging me every step of the way. Without their collective and keen insight and in depth reading, the enclosed thoughts would still be in draft form. The comments and encouragement from the three of you propelled this project far beyond my wildest dreams.

Introduction

Home Is Where the Healing Is: Ritual Pathways to Home

Edwidge Danticat, in the grand and communal Haitian literary tradition of the *maître conte*—professional and master storytellers—invokes the imperative call of the storyteller; *Krik?*, as her readers and critics, alike, enthusiastically respond *Krak!*, and with bated breath wait for the story to unfold, listening for the voice of the storyteller as they read her texts.[1] The transformative work of Edwidge Danticat—who has either won or been nominated for the National Book Award, The American Book Award, The National Book Critics Circle Award, The Ansfield-Wolf Book Award, The Lannan Book Fellowship, and the coveted MacArthur Fellowship—is undeniable. Early on in her career, Danticat's works received tremendous scholarly attention and found place in lay book clubs across the nation, including Oprah's famous list. Hailed as "One of the best books of the year" by *The Chicago Tribune*, *The New York Times*, and *People's Weekly*, Danticat's *The Farming of Bones*, winner of the American Book Award in 1999, cements Edwidge Danticat into the academy of writers and, in particular, Haitian and Africana writers.

The start of critical and literary analysis of Danticat's works began in 2000. In particular, in 2001 the *Journal of Haitian Studies* published a Special Issue dedicated exclusively to the works of Edwidge Danticat. Markedly, the subtitle of the special edition "Crossing Waters and Remembering," clearly references the transnationalistic and diasporic readings and renderings of Danticat's work. The edition included critical essays, reviews, and book analyses along with an interview of Danticat by Renee Shea. Interestingly, in the interview Danticat discusses a series of short stories that would soon comprise her ground-breaking novel *The Dew Breaker*.[2] Acclaimed for her storytelling prowess and the beauty of her prose, Danticat's work ostensibly floats in the liminal space between her prolific record of publication and her insistence that history, found within the lived experiences and narratives that are often oral and/or mythic, of the diasporic experience provides the greatest context for the contemporary diasporic narrative. Indeed, all her works explore the complexities of history, tradition, and ancient culture that inform the current literary and transnationalist moment.

Edwidge Danticat, as a writer, is oftentimes difficult to place within a specific genre of writing, as the intersection of places and spaces she occupies complicate designation attempts. Martin Munro, in his introduction to *Edwidge Danticat: A Reader's Guide*, clearly articulates the complexity of attempts to situate Danticat within a given border or boundary of identity. Questions abound about origin, migration, literary tradition, among other categories. And, with no one clear definition, Munro describes Danticat and her work within the tradition of her Haitian literary foremothers who have, "mapped out 'new territories of the imagination.'"[3] Danticat, as Munro further explores, "is free from many of the constraints of and expectations that direct, unambiguous attachments bring. Danticat can and does write freely, in a style that is unmistakably hers."[4] Consequently, Munro utilizes his discussion of Régine Michelle Jean-Charles's approach to Danticat, which includes her in the company of other Africana women writers, to envision Danticat's place(s), not too narrowly, within the literary landscape. By broadening the borders and boundaries assigned to Black women writers, Jean-Charles,[5]

> argues that the contemporary definition of an African American woman writer is itself fluid and expansive and that Danticat makes an important contribution to this broadening and diversification of the tradition. To include Danticat in the African American women's literary tradition is to acknowledge the "diasporic nature," of blackness in the United States and to contribute to the reworking of the notion of Americanness to include all the peoples and nations of the Americas, as well as those like Danticat who spend time moving between different sites within the Americas.[6]

The broadening fluidity of spaces held by Africana women writers is particularly apt when examining Danticat and her work through an African diasporic perspective because it allows her, as well as other writers, mobility and mutability within and outside of a given text and context. Place and space become sites of exploration rather static fixed landscapes and national identities. Edwidge Danticat, herself, argues that, "Home is not a place anymore but an idea, an attitude, and ideal."[7] Whether a landscape or book genre, home remains a fluid construct that flows and moves like the ebb and the flow of water. As the quote implies, the examination of textual topography—how a text can extend beyond the boundaries of physical realities and landscapes to cross the threshold of spiritual realities, or the liminal, locating the missing, replacing the displaced, and moving the immovable—is more important than distinct and defined physical locations. Danticat's discussion of home is punctuated by Carol Boyce Davies, In *Black Women, Writing, and*

Identity: Migration of the Subject: "Re-negotiating of identities . . . [remains] fundamental to migration."[8] Davies's quote, like Danticat's work, centers the renegotiating of cultural disruption and dislocation often entrenched in nationalistic discussions. Instead, for Danticat globalization is a means of creating a "bridge" between here and there. To the extent that she argues that global migration of the Diaspora has also changed the scope of the idea and notion of a "National Literature."[9] In an interview with Nancy Mirabal, Danticat credits technology for the modern-day connection of the Diaspora, differing from the way the Diaspora connected when she was a child, positing that technology acts as a "bridge."[10] Danticat's writing also acts as a bridge, crossing borders, languages, and cultures instinctively creating intersectionalities of lived experiences that recover and reaffirm subjectivity. Indeed, Danticat's fiction utilizes technology too.

The primacy of home for the Diaspora remains a constant and lived trauma that continually seeks reconnection to distant and ancient lands and peoples, many of which have been compromised or obliterated by the dusty finger of hatred, greed, and white supremacist ideology. Instinctively, as novels act as containers for stories, peoples, and lands, Danticat's fiction dares willing participants to step into and occupy diasporically-centered spaces, where barriers like land, sea, and languages fade into oblivion and the construction of a new and symbolic homeland derived from textual inscriptions that, to quote Danticat, "Create Dangerously," boldly, and lovingly emblazoned edifices of existence and identity.[11] Danticat's novels are spaces that live and breathe and are buttressed by the words of the text. Words speaking into existence the pain and trauma of the displaced, once functioning as misarticulated inaccuracies, stripped bare, down to the bones, and wounds long covered by bandages are given salve and (ad)dressed. Not only does Danticat's work bring one back to the way, she intimates, "We are seeing ourselves as what we might have as pre-Columbian people," but it also demonstrates the migratory process of African cosmology and its modern articulation through textual signification.[12] For, as Danticat's quote reveals, if one can return to visions, articulations, and transmissions of oneself in one's own image and space, the journey's aim is to restore what was stripped, land and body. Boundaries and borders, language, and nationality, which often occupy nationalistic literary discourse, especially when trying to negotiate the Africana self of the Diaspora, are, thus, expanded. The strength and beauty of Danticat's fiction lies in the potentiality and possibilities of providing a literary pathway to healing the traumas that no official state apology or decree can heal.

Through the use of myth and folklore, Danticat is able to recast landscapes in a multiplicity of space, place, and time and reconnects the Diaspora with a symbolic, liminal, home and land that reveal the method(s), individually and collectively, needed to heal the traumas against land and body the Africana Diaspora historically and contemporarily experience. Hence, this book examines Danticat's work as a project of cosmological reclamation, with the overall purpose to demonstrate the presence and function of ritual, through the scope and lens of Kongo Cosmogram in four Danticat novels—*The Dew Breaker, The Farming of Bones, Claire of the Sea Light,* and *Breath, Eyes, Memory.* Specifically, this book will examine the ways in which her texts provide a means and method to heal and clarify, through narrative pathways within textual topography, Africana diasporic consciousness and subjectivity by returning to origins.

Reading Danticat's fictional work through a cosmological lens centers the liminality of the crossroads' transtopography and creates spaces for the contemplation of diasporic subjectivity. Her work carves out pathways through the crevices and cracks of false images and narratives, reclaiming time and space free from the ubiquitous occidental gaze. Danticat's writing stands at the intersections, somewhere between here and there, and, like the myths and folklore she often employs in her novels, attends to the historical intermediacy of the Diaspora. The interaction between the lived experiences, history, and time and space in Danticat's fictional work hinges upon the novel acting as a repository for the cosmological technology rampant in her works. Ritual, and in particular the crossroads via the Cosmogram as processional ritual, permeates Danticat's works and demands critical examination.[13]

A predominant structural choice in Danticat's fiction, the crossroads is traceable through her body of works. Particular to this text, the examination of the crossroads in Danticat's *The Dew Breaker*, *The Farming of Bones*, *Claire of the Sea Light*, and *Breath, Eyes, Memory* demonstrates the import of the crossroads in Danticat's Oeuvre, as well as thematically traces the evolution of the crossroads within these texts. Danticat's works under examination could be read in the same counterclockwise motion or movement of the cosmogram. Framing Danticat's work in this way renders a cosmographic framework for interpreting the cosmogram in each individual work and collectively, creating a cosmogram of a cosmogram, the ultimate crossroads, whereby ritual becomes the form and function of the body of work, the container where each of the works is inscribed. A conceptual framework and container of interpretation, combining the image of the cosmogram with the symbolic structure of ritual engenders a textual format to "read" ritual within a text. The cosmogram serves as an important ritual symbol in Africana religion and in Haiti, especially because of the concentration of West Africans from Bantu and Bakongo regions.[14] Like the processional cross used in Catholic services, the cosmogram functions as a ritualized processional symbol and carries with it the symbolic nature of ritual. The crossing from one realm to the next, one position to the next, one moment to the next, illustrates the processional motion of the cosmogram and its inherent ritual structure.

Employing Robert Farris Thompson's cosmogram image, the cosmogram is a cruciform that illustrates the symbolic movement of a soul through the four phases of existence, the four points of "Yowa," or the four phases of the sun—Tukula, LuVemba, Musoni, and Kala.[15] Tukula is the highest point or the zenith of human existence.[16] Having achieved the highest point of existence in the physical, one's life source must follow the directional force of the cosmogram, like the tide, life too ebbs and flows between the realms. Achieving the highest level of existence or consciousness moves a soul to the next point, LuVemba, death, or sunset. The LuVemba position represents a passing of a person from the physical realm into the spiritual realm. Musoni corresponds to the midnight of one's journey. The Musoni position of the cosmogram is where one travels through the spiritual womb of rebirth and travels upward through the birth canal of Kalunga. When the sunrises the soul is delivered back into the land of the living. As such Kala represents birth and sunrise. Figure 0.1 provides a graphic image of the cosmogram.

The cross that the cosmogram forms separates the two spheres or realms of existence. The top half of the sphere, Nseke, is the land of the living, the physical realm, or "the mountain of the living."[17] The bottom half of the sphere, Mkempa, is the land of the dead, "white clay." Separating the land of the living from the land of the dead is the Kalunga Ocean, the primordial waters of the great beyond. The point in the middle of the cosmogram, where the vertical and horizontal lines intersect and form a cross, is the "crossroads . . . the point of intersection between the ancestors and the living."[18] The four quadrants of the cosmogram, as the arrows on figure 0.1 demonstrate, work in a continuous manner suggestive of the cycle of life. The continuous circle, either surrounding or directly in the middle of the cosmogram, is indicative of the sun and the soul's movement within the quadrants. It is the points between the graph that are the directional force and movement of the cosmogram, " . . . it is the 'knowledge between the lines' that does the work."[19] Teresa Washington's diagram of the "Interrelated Domains and Dominion of Àjé," brilliantly illustrates the lines at work in between the four quadrants of the cosmogram.[20]

The crossroads give the planes of intersection between the physical and the spiritual realm and provides form and structure within Danticat's novels. It shapes ritual by providing a clear pathway of ritual's trajectory. The intersections of the roads lend directionality to the text, characters, and readers, while providing space and place for the realms to exist simultaneously. The crossroads provides a panoramic view of the world the characters live in while centering ritual within the core of this world. Not only does this provide the characters the ability to exist in multiple spaces at once, but it also

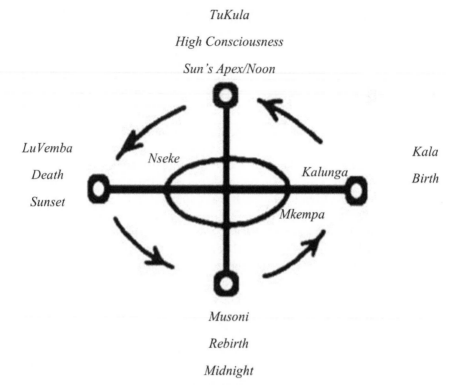

TuKula

High Consciousness

Sun's Apex/Noon

LuVemba   *Kala*

Death   *Birth*

Sunset

Nseke

Kalunga

Mkempa

Musoni

Rebirth

Midnight

Figure 0.1. A Visual Representation of the Kongo Cosmogram. Source: Image of the Cosmogram was adapted from Robert Thompson's *Flash of the Spirit: African and Afro-American Art and Philosophy* (1984, 109).

provides space conducive for ritual to occur. Thus, the crossroads textualizes ritual, and invites the intermingling and communication between the spiritual and physical realms. It marks the meeting point of the realms and initiates the need for ritual to occur. In Danticat's novels under examination, death, trauma, prayer, or even an inscription to the divine act as invocation for ritual. As the beginning position of all the novels under examination, and of this book, the LuVemba position (death) opens the cosmographic analysis of ritual occurrences. Death opens the realms ritually by asserting the death of dis(ease) or the problem plaguing the person or community and initiates the necessity of ritual. It marks the beginning of the movement between the four positions, or moments of the sun, the cosmogram represents. The Musoni position rebirths the issue that plagues a character, transforming it through communication between the realms. Realm communication both initiates and necessitates a ritual occurrence. Thus, Kala births structure and form to that which has been rebirthed. As ritual is an act to restore balance and order, its performance, even textually, teaches and reinforces the form and structure of ritual, birthing complete transformation. Once the cycle is complete, the novel and characters reach the highest state of consciousness, Tukula, which signals that transformation has occurred and order has been restored. This position of the sun signifies growth and the success of the ritual.

Via the great roads, the intersection of intersections, the crossroads leads to the point where the terrestrial and superterrestrial converge, creating transtopography, a domain birthed out of the liminal place where the realms converge. The import of the crossroads in Danticat's works looms large, and her novels are a space where textualized ritual can occur. Thus, Danticat's fiction fashions a home, a "Quisqueya," Mother of the Earth or Mother of all Lands, a symbolic superterrestrial womb where the Diaspora can return to an organically conceived indigenous space and be rebirthed as autonomous selves. This symbolic birth allows the diaspora to exist within two spaces at once, physical and liminal, forming a duality of existence free from the fragmented identity politics of postcolonial studies or nationalistic ideations. As Danticat argues: "We cross borders to reach a neutral space."[21] Reversing sail, as Michael Gomez's text of the same title intimates, going back to the place from whence one came, a reverse middle passage which crosses land, time, and space and creates a structural route for the Diaspora to traverse. Erasure of the past is not the aim, but, rather, reconnection. Or in Danticat's words, " . . . history is not something in the past, but . . . people carry it forward . . . they live in it . . . they claim it . . . So I'm interested in the gaps in history."[22] However, to traverse the space between the present and the past requires both a mode and a medium to bridge the space between the two points, or in this case a ritual via the crossroads. What African people did in ritual communal spaces, Edwidge Danticat does on the written page and through the written word. Her texts invoke spirit and create a dialogue between the reader and the invisible characters who, then, together function to create spaces of healing and wholeness. What Africans were doing in ancient communities, Danticat does through novels in order to connect or reconnect diasporic citizens to their sacred, healing roots. Danticat's texts become sacred text, like the Ifá, that provide healing. These spiritual texts utilized by Danticat reconnect the Diaspora to a liminal home and engenders a pathway to the ancestors and ancestral ways of being and living.

The power of Danticat's work is its ability to bridge diasporic communities and trace their intersecting lines back to the lines of historical origin, like the navigational routes mapping a ship's voyage. The crossroads allows the global diasporic community to exist within liminality, where a character, place, or community can remain grounded in both a physical and memorial landscape. For example, through spoken memories, photographs, or audio tapes Martine sends back home to Haiti in *Breath, Eyes, Memory*, she is able to stay connected and exist as a "present" family member while living abroad in the United States. Similarly, as Martine exists somewhere between her physical existence in the United States and her re-membered existence in Haiti, Danticat's works create an origin and beginning point, a positionality that allows characters, and, most importantly readers, to create a historical and subjective rendering of their life and reimagine it through their voice and image somewhere between here and there, that crosses physical boundaries and barriers that, as she argues, " . . . Poses a challenge" for the Diaspora. A problem, I argue, she seeks to solve through her fiction.[23] Her fiction solves challenges for the Diaspora, through cultural restoration, by going back to the origin of origins and the cosmological and ontological locating of a people, centering the Diaspora in the signs and symbols of sacred language and in the processional ritual of the crossroads. Danticat's works create pathways for the Diaspora to go back to its historical origins to reimagine, reconstruct, and renegotiate the ontological questions of identity and subjectivity.

The remaining chapters in this book, employ the cosmogram as a framework to engender spaces within the novel structure where the contemplation of Africana consciousness occur. Utilizing the principles of the cosmogram to extend the textual landscape, I argue that four Danitcat novels work together in reconstructing the points or positions on the cosmogram. Each novel is representative of a point or moment of the cosmogram and their combined textual movement leads to the fourth point, the apex of their collective meaning, higher consciousness—*The Dew Breaker* (death), *The Farming of Bones* (rebirth), *Claire of the Sea Light* (birth), *and Breath, Eyes, Memory* (higher consciousness). Thematically, death unites these four novels because death alters the landscape in both realms and serves as an intersection for the convergence of realms to occur. The funerary rites and text of death creates ritualized space within the texts for the characters and plots to move through. Within the larger cultural scope, death allows for the demise of preconceived notions and positionalities of Africana identity and subjectivity within a hegemonic construct. Moreover, in death, the healing and clarifying of Africana consciousness is rebirthed within a cultural milieu of ancient practices and beliefs that still have modern articulations and significance, like the cosmogram. Death illuminates the pathway a soul or consciousness traverses to reach the fourth and highest position of the cosmogram, Tukala. While these four novels individually work to heal and clarify Africana consciousness, collectively they also work to transform. However, the ability to sift these select texts by Danticat through the theoretical framework of the cosmogram requires a building of spiritual and conceptual framework and edifice from the ground up, as no template exists and the majority of what the project depends upon is ancient, ensconced, and entrenched ideas.

Chapter 1, "They Did Not Come Alone: Towards a Theoretical Framework," constructs the framework for the analysis of the four novels. The chapter examines the cultural retentions of Africans in the Americas. Utilizing nature as text, the chapter theoretically postulates how Africans were able to read the landscape, and, through the natural elements and inherent signs and symbols, form a sacred language of ritual received and translated by ancestors and the divine. Creating a call and response between ancestors, ancestral land, and knowledge, the Africana Diaspora returned to indigenous beliefs, practices, and values. Intrinsic in the myth and lore, the building blocks of the literary tradition, the return to the mother of mothers and motherland, centralizes the role of Africana women writers in the preservation of indigenous belief and practices, even contemporarily, as cultural bearers and producers.

Chapters 2 through 5 analyze four of Danticat's novels to examine the use of the crossroads as a representation of ritual occurrences and explores the ways in which one of West Africa's potent cultural retentions, the cosmogram represented by the crossroads, functions within her texts. By returning to the ontological and cosmological center of African consciousness, this book will examine how Danticat writes and creates the liminal space of the cosmogram where ritual is textually performed and transformations of diasporic consciousness occurs.

Chapter 2, "At the Crossroads: Rituals of Death in Danticat's *The Dew Breaker*," creates a ritual structure through the utilization of the oral tradition, vis à vis Osiris's myth. This particular myth symbolizes the crossroads and a soul passing from one realm to the next—Osiris is killed, rebirthed by Isis's re-membering, birthed as a divinity, and represents the communion with God through the principles he and his myth represent. Through the ritual structure embedded in retelling the myth, ritual is textually performed. Each chapter functions as testimonial and lead reader and character alike to the crossroads. The crossroads function as a divine entrance on the road to healing for those traumatized by the harm the Dew Breaker inflicts, and also is at the ultimate crossroads where the Dew Breaker's fate will be weighed on the great scales of MAAT.

Chapter 3, "Lót Bót Dlo (The Other Side of the Water): Examining the Cosmogram in Danticat's *The Farming of Bones*," argues that Danticat creates a textual crossroads by paralleling the spiritual and physical realms through the doubled-voiced narrative and narration of the main character, Amabelle Desir. The crossroads provides a medium for Amabelle to exist in the past and the present, space, and place, and the physical and spiritual realms simultaneously. The cross intersections of Amabelle's existence provide a medium and method for the collection of the forgotten and erased narratives of the 1937 massacre, for which Amabelle's physical body becomes a repository. While *The Farming of Bones* chronicles Amabelle's movement through the crossroads, her body, acting as a repository of narratives, becomes a crossroads too.

Chapter 4, "A Seat at the Table: Constructing Identity in Danticat's *Claire of the Sea Light*," examines how Claire physically disappears for the majority of the novel, but spiritually exists in the retelling and memories of her birthdays. Claire exists between her physical reality and the alternative world her invisibility denotes. The text and Claire's existence creates a crossroads for Claire to exist and to negotiate. The transtopographic space of her existence, both seen and unseen, allows Claire a space to negotiate her fate, and enables the deities, who exist on the precipice of life and death, to convene and help guide Claire through the crossroads and to perform self-recreation through ritual.[24]

Chapter 5, "May These Words Bring Wings to Your Feet": Re-membering Ancestral Healing in *Breath, Eyes, Memory*," utilizes Brigitte Ifé as a living embodiment of an ancestor re-membered in the flesh. Brigitte, as her name suggests, is able to provide the Caco women a "bridge" to the ancestral and spiritual realm needed for healing. Traversing the gaps perceived between past and present, ancestor and progeny, Guinea and Haiti, the novel creates a complete life cycle, moving from death (Luvemba) to high consciousness (Tukala). Although Brigitte's conception and birth are associated with pain, and, in particular, a historicized pain, her birth is the announcement and pronouncement of the cosmographic healing found in the movement through the four points of the sun—death, rebirth, birth, and high consciousness.

NOTES

1. Diane Wolkstein and Elsa Henriquez, *The Magic Orange Tree: And Other Haitian Folktales* (New York: A.A. Knopf, 1978), 2–9.

2. Haitian Studies Association, and University of California, Santa Barbara. Center for Black Studies. *Journal of Haitian Studies* 7, no. 2 (Fall 2001): 1–10.

3. Martin Munro, *Edwidge Danticat: A Readers Guide* (Charlottesville: University of Virginia Press, 2010), 3.

4. Ibid., 4.

5. "Danticat's work, like Kincaid's, often resonates as well with that of the community of black women writing in the United States." Henry Louis Gates Jr. and Valerie A. Smith, general editors, *The Norton Anthology of African American Literature.* Third Edition. Volumes Two (W.W. Norton, 2014), 923.

6. Munro, *Edwidge Danticat*, 5–6.

7. Ginetta E.B. Candelario, Edwidge Danticat, Loida Maritza Perez, Myriam J.A. Chancy, and Nelly Rosario, "Voices from Hispaniola: A Meridians Roundtable with Edwidge Danticat, Loida Maritza Perez, Myriam J. A. Chancy, and Nelly Rosario." *Meridians: Feminism, Race, Transnationalism* 5, no. 1 (2004): 72.

8. Carole Boyce Davies, *Black Women, Writing, and Identity: Migrations of the Subject* (London: Routledge, 1994), 3.

9. Nancy Raquel Mirabal, "Dyasporic Appetites and Longings: An Interview with Edwidge Danticat." *Callaloo* 30, no. 1 (2007): 30.

10. Ibid., 30.

11. Edwidge Danticat, *Create Dangerously: The Immigrant Artist at Work* (Princeton: Princeton University Press, 2010), 1.

12. Candelario, "Voices from Hispaniola," 72.

13. Ritual practices will be thoroughly discussed in Chapter 1.

14. For further discussion of West African continuities, cultures, and religious practices in Haiti, see Robert Farris Thompson, *Flash of the Spirit: African and Afro-American Art and Philosophy* (First Vintage Books. New York: Vintage Books, 1984).

15. Although the entrance into the Cosmogram begins with rebirth, for thematic and structural choices salient to this study, I read the cosmogram as beginning with death and following the other points respective to the counterclockwise motion— rebirth, birth, and higher consciousness. I reference Sharon Holland's description of how the positionality of death lends liminality for diasporic people and writers to explore subjectivity in *Raising the Dead Readings of Death and (Black) Subjectivity*: "Speaking from a site of familiarity, a place reserved for the dead . . . [creates] a plethora of tensions *within* and *without* existing cultures. Embracing the subjectivity of death allows marginalized peoples to speak about the unspoken—to name the places *within* and *without* their cultural milieu where . . . they have slopped between the cracks of language." Sharon Patricia Holland and Donald E. Pease, *Raising the Dead Readings of Death and (Black) Subjectivity* (Duke University Press, 2000).

16. Thompson, *Flash of the Spirit,* 109.

17. Ibid., 109.

18. Ibid., 109.

19. Grey Gundaker, "The Kongo Cosmogram in Historical Archaeology and the Moral Compass of Dave the Potter." *Historical Archaeology* 45, no. 2 (2011): 180.

20. Teresa Washington, *Our Mothers, Our Powers, Our Texts: Manifestations of Àjé in Africana Literature* (Bloomington: Indiana University Press, 2005), 40.

21. Candelario, "Voices from Hispaniola," 72.

22. Mirabal, "Dyasporic Appetites and Longings," 35.

23. Ibid., 29.

24. I will refer to deities that are on the precipice of life and death, like Oya as crossroads deities. Here I am merely asserting a positionality between, or intertwined within, realms. I am not asserting that these deities are like Esu Legba, who is the orisha of the crossroads.

Chapter 1

They Did Not Come Alone
Towards a Theoretical Framework

The disruption of identity and community entering the "New World" forced enslaved Africans to reimagine their cosmological perspective as "the scene of history shifted from the Old World to the New."[1] However, the cultural disruption slavery intended for the enslaved inadvertently created proximity for the African to nature and rekindled a reconnection to African-ness that the enslavers could not fathom or anticipate. Henry Louis Gates Jr., in *The Signifying Monkey,* elucidates the power and will to remember the Africans forced to endure the Middle Passage performed, and the treasure trove found in the contents of those memories:

> The black Africans who survived the dreaded "Middle Passage" from the west coast of Africa to the New World did not sail alone. Violently and radically abstracted from their civilizations, these Africans nevertheless carried within them to the Western hemisphere aspects of their culture that were meaningful, that could not be obliterated, and that they chose, by acts of will not to forget: their music (a mnemonic device from Bantu and Kwa tonal languages), their myths, their expressive institutional structures, their metaphysical systems of order, and their forms of performance.[2]

Gates's quote explores the greater notion of the ontological and cosmological ideology of an African people that survived those ships and illustrates the cultural retentions of Africans in the Americas.[3] Gates argues that Africans brought with them more than simply the scope of their physical bodies and knowledge of flora and fauna. The invisibility of these vital elements traveled with and within the enslaved during the Middle Passage to the New World. In essence, contrary to popular arguments of the slavocracy, the complete erasure of indigenous African culture did not occur. Indeed, such is impossible, for people carry within themselves the DNA of their cultural identity. While location, freedom, or status can be changed, the memory of cosmological and ontological identity of a people cannot be erased, as "Human mobility does not remove a person's original connection to the birthplace. Your footprints still lead back to the place where you began."[4] Consequently, it is a misnomer to assert that dislocation equates to the erasure of cultural location or locator. As traumatic as the Middle Passage was, Africans still retained their systems, beliefs, and practices. And, most important to this study, Africans retained signs and symbolic cues of those systems, practices, and beliefs. Harkening back to Gates's quote, Africans brought with them the essence of the cosmology vital to the nature of their ontology. The retention of their cosmological and ontological identity provided Africans with the survival skills necessary to transmute the trauma they endured on death marches, Middle Passage(s), and plantations.[5] Thus, as Gates posits, the "African 'read' a new environment within a received framework of meaning and belief."[6] But what did Africans "read"? Through what system did they read? And how did the memories they traveled with help them survive the trauma of both the Middle Passage and slavery through a given framework?

The ecological landscape offered many similarities to home that the displaced Africans in the Americas could utilize and ground indigenous systems and practices within. The landscape enabled Africans to re-member their ontological nature topographically. Isidore Okpewho in the introduction to *The African Diaspora: African Origins and New Identities*, elaborates:

> Deracination must have seemed a little easier to bear the moment the Africans discovered that the environment looked amazingly similar to home. In time, this familiarity encouraged them not only to resume skills (e.g., herbal arts) they had practiced in Africa . . . Memory of Africa, a sense of roots, therefore served these exiles well, especially when conditions became simply intolerable.[7]

Through nature's signs and symbols, memory becomes realized and transmissible. Nature, then, becomes the text displaced Africans read as a means of reconnection to their indigenous practices and identity.

Reading a new environment, as Gates's aforementioned quote suggests, reconnects Africans in the New World with indigenous land and reimagines the African subject within an African context. Although time shifts, nature does not submit to the constraints of man-made notions of time and space, but, rather, occupies a transitional space that surpasses the sensory limitations of physical reality. Anissa Wardi's *Water and African American Memory: An Ecocritical Perspective* explores nature's, specifically water, function as "sites of memory" for the Diaspora:

> Though there is no dispute that the human brain stores memory . . . other kinds
> of memory which transcends individual lived experiences [exist, too] . . . recov-
> ery of the past is frequently conterminous with a literal or symbolic return to the
> originary waters of the Atlantic Ocean. . . . The underwater bones, marking the
> journey from Africa to America, are a material carrier of memory, one in which
> both the body and the ocean water are transformed.[8]

From the ecological and literary perspectives of Wardi's text, water re-members the African bodies within its liquid tomb, while also reconstructing the shared consciousness those bodies carried inside them within the ebb and flow of waterways between Africa and the Americas. The materiality of nature functions as a conduit to the materiality of consciousness that extends to the shores of departure and arrival.[9] While Wardi's text attends to water as the central element of memory for the Diaspora, central to this study are the location and destination the fluid passageways, Wardi beautifully re-members, lead to and fro. In other words, as water is the conduit between where the Middle Passage begins and ends, the physical boundaries of land punctuate water's "constant and fluid movements between shores."[10] The reverberation of water's flow between the shores of Africa and the Americas creates a call and response between Africa and Africans in the Americas and harkens the literal or symbolic return Wardi's text examines.[11] Thus, memory and movement between Africa and the Americas, as the water illustrates, become essential to the cosmology and ontology of Africans in the Americas, especially because they are not physically, but metaphysically and cosmo-logically, connected to indigenous land: "To re-member relates not so much to the cognitive acts of recalling events as to the ability to reconnect with and reclaim what had been dismembered from one's psyche, soul, and/or identity."[12] Africans not only carried within their bones the memory of those who rest within the watery tombs of the Atlantic, but also the memory of the physical landscape they would not return to. While physical death occurs within both the landscape, via death marches, and waterways, the physical absence of the Africans forced into the Transatlantic Slave Trade creates a corporal and spiritual void that can be read as death by those remaining within the African landscape and those removed from the landscape and moving toward the Americas. Their arrival, then, acts as a rebirth of indig-enous ontology in the New World. This transtopographic existence occupies a liminal space between here and there, life and death, and the physical and spiritual for Africans in the Americas. As the site of departure for Africans enduring the Middle Passage, and where the reverberating waters return to, Africa functions as the referent of the water's flow of memory and memo-rial, punctuating the relationship between displaced progeny and ancestors, ancestral knowledge, and ancestral land. Thus, nature textually lends itself to Africans in the New World.

From a traditional West African perspective, nature functions as text through the signs and symbols found within the natural world. One engages the text of the natural world through elements of nature, as the natural world brings one closer to the nature of one's ontology, especially through the act of ritual. According to Malidoma Somé, in *The Healing Wisdom of Africa*, nature's elements—fire, trees, water, mineral, and earth—signal and direct the human psyche to the pathway needed to traverse the spiritual grounds often associated with ritual. These pathways lead to the specific healing for the individual or community. Somé further explores the meaning of nature's elements and their specific healings for the Dagara people: "[Fire's] healing . . . comes from becoming the other, the totem animal" and directs those involved to seek the essence of their animal totem to change or "disrupt" energy not indigenous to their nature. While trees "as our guardians, commissioned by our Mother the earth to provide safety and comfort as we travel though life emphasi[ze] . . . homecoming, recognizing in words the long separation, which has caused so much loss." The cleansing spirit of water ritual is "a sacred purifying act that brings everyone closer to the beauty and bounty of Mother Nature." When earth rituals are performed, "we are trying to remember how to be grateful to our Mother for standing at our side all these years without expecting anything in return from us." Mineral rituals provide "the food [that] nourishes our bodies while the clay, which contains particles of stone, nourishes the bones of our body by keeping memory alive. Memory is the food of our connection with ourselves and our purposes." These natural elements act as sign and symbol for the human psyche to understand and connect with the natural world while providing a healing for the problems or issues suffered by the individual or the community. So, the elements of nature not only connect or reconnect participants with nature, but also act as a conduit to communication between the physical and spiritual worlds. Or, as Somè posits: "Symbols are the doorway to ritual. Just as our bodies can't survive without nourishment, our psyches cannot sustain themselves without symbolism."[13] In direct relationship to the way nature feeds the community on a physical and spiritual level in traditional West African societies, like the Dagara, nature also creates the text for the African in the Americas to read and interpret for clarification and healing. Nature is a linguistic conduit and container as its signs and symbols are consistent and recognizable no matter where the African finds themselves, as "all living things (and dead things, too) are interwoven into innumerable ecological communities."[14] In other words, nature provides a consistent, organic, and readable landscape that is translatable regardless of location and provides a continuity of cosmological and ontological beliefs and practices.

The natural world and the elements previously discussed provide Africans with the signs and symbols necessary for the health and vitality of a community when such are off kilter. As a practice entrenched in cosmological and ontological beliefs, rituals are central to the health and livelihood of an African community. So much so, that without ritual a community's very existence is untenable at best. Malidoma Somè elaborates on the import of ritual in African communities: "A true community begins in the hearts of the people involved. . . . A community that doesn't have a ritual cannot exist."[15] Indeed, rituals are so central to African life and culture that Africans in the Americas could not have imagined themselves without ritualistic practice. To be sure, a ritual is a collective communal gathering of like-minded people who seek knowledge or insight greater than what their humanity affords. It is the combining of spirit with humans and nature to create an epistemological space wherein complex questions are answered and difficult healings occur. According to scholar Teresa Washington, in "Mules and Men and Messiahs: Continuity in Yoruba Divination Verses and African American Folktales," ritual is "a holistic system that includes science, epistemology, astronomy, cosmology, ontology, physics, mathematics, philosophy, and medicine."[16] As Washington argues, ritual integrates all human senses and all non-human energy. It merges sight with insight, physical with invisible, and the living with the extra-living. Thus, ritual encompasses all of what the African consists of and who the African is.

Ritual is a process that brings the invisible to light and provides the revelation needed for transformation and healing. Creating a landscape within a landscape, where the intersection of the spiritual and physical realms meet and exist, rituals construct a space for African consciousness to be reformed and explored. This is especially vital for Africans in the Americas existing within the incongruent ecology of the New World. Ritual becomes the essential element to their very survival because it connects to the epic memory of cultural consciousness. The cultural uncertainty of displaced Africans is derived from the lack of physical connection with indigenous land, which creates, as John Mbiti contends, a psychological breach.[17] However, ritual provides the cultural apparatus for one to reconnect with indigenous consciousness for healing. Nature creates a connection between ancestral presence, knowledge, and land for people of African descent in lands not indigenous to them. Pointing towards the integral relationship between nature and ancestors, ritual connects one to the ontology of beingness because, as Theodore Jennings argues in "On Ritual Knowledge," "ritual does not depict the world so much as it founds or creates the world."[18] Rituals enable the spatiality of the indigenous to be reimagined in a nature conducive to their natural ecology and in an ecosystem that is responsive to their wellbeing. Utilizing elements found in nature, rituals connect the individual and community to landscapes, which themselves are spiritually endowed, through the presence of ancestors, ancestral knowledge, and manifested natures necessary for human whole- ness. Consequently, the relationship between nature and Africans engenders an interconnection between the spiritual and secular realms, and ritual acts as the epoxy that binds together two realms—often thought of as separate—into a singular space and ecology suitable for healing.

Multiple levels of conversations and communications between realms are inherent in ritual practice. The vibrations of ritual transcend time and locale and exist in the liminal spaces shared by all participants, living and non-living, spoken and unspoken, natural and supernatural. The multidimen- sional practice of ritual is difficult for an untrained consciousness or eye to perceive. Seemingly chaotic, the multilateral structure of ritual is a highly organized system and practice. Central to its organization is the commonality of knowledge and spiritual sensibility shared by its participants. Ritual, for the community engaged, reinforces the shared values, beliefs, and virtues of its members. For Africans in the Americas, as Barbara Christian argues in "Ritualistic Process and the Structure of Paule Marshall's: *Praisesong for The Widow*," "the body might be in one place and the mind in another, is characterized not as fragmentation but as a source of wisdom, stemming from a history of the forced displacement of blacks in the West."[19] In other words, ritual practice is also a continued communication and affiliation with ancestors, ancestral knowledge, and ancestral land. Echoing the notion of the call and response between Africans in the Americas and Africa, a community must maintain active and substantive communication with the ancestors in order to maintain balance and harmony in the physical realm. To exist in a ritualized landscape for displaced Africans reifies the importance and cen- trality of ritual practice and the positionality of ancestors in the lives of the Diaspora. Or, as Somé contends, "not to participate [in ritual] can also pollute one's life because the living cannot live peacefully until the dead are really dead, gone to the realms of the ancestors."[20] Disconnection between the spiri- tual and physical realms, especially the lack of ancestral veneration, invites chaos and imbalance. Neglected ancestors may disturb communal order or trouble people's consciousness as they seek to find positionality and remain connected to communities and families. Thus, a relationship between ances- tors and progeny is integral to the health and vitality of a community just as ancestral veneration is an imperative of ritual. In *The Grasp That Reaches Beyond the Grave: The Ancestral Call in Black Women's Texts,* Venertria Patton explores the significant role of ancestors in traditional African com- munities: "Ancestors are seen as sources of ancient wisdom, which forms the backbone of the community."[21] Ancestral veneration stands as the connector between the living and the "just lived." Through ritualistically calling upon or acknowledging an ancestor by name, community members can traverse the liminal space between the physical and spiritual realm in order to connect with spirits and God. Thus, ancestors function as the intercessor of realms and as active participants in community and family life and livelihood. Although they dwell in the spiritual realm, they still participate in the physical lives of their living relatives and community.[22]

Ancestral veneration also reflects the elevated status of elders, who physically demonstrate the importance of a community's connection with ancestors, ancestral knowledge, and land. Patton argues: "The elder is an ancestor in the making."[23] Because of their proximity to the spiritual realm, elders, like ancestors, serve as important teachers, preservers, and repositories of ancient wisdom and values. While ancestors function as spiritual repositories, in Western terms, elders are "living libraries." Somè adds: "Respect owed to the elder derives from the perception that the elder is at the critical junction where the natural meets the supernatural and where the ancestors and the divine intersect with humans."[24] As nature is "read" by Africans, both traditionally and in the New World, nature also functions as the text ancestors read in order to interpret the need of their progeny as ritual indicates. The very essence of breathing the air in and out, seeing trees grow, and hearing the water's ebb and flow because of the moon, become the essence of existence for diasporic people attempting to communicate with ancestors for healing from issues centered around cultural disruption. Through the multilingual tongue of ancestors, the natural world—landscapes, water, stars, trees, sun, and moon—connects one to home. Nature's elements function as the signs and symbols of the scared language that ancestors and their progeny utilize to communicate.

Benedict Anderson, in his seminal text *Imagined Communities,* argues that ancient societies envisaged communal identity through the shared language of signs and symbols. Specifically, Anderson argues: "All the great classical communities conceived of themselves as cosmically central, through the medium of a sacred language linked to a superterrestrial order of power."[25] The concept of ritual, as it relates to West African articulations, fits squarely into the cosmological emanations of community building that Anderson illustrates. For ritual to ensue, communication between the terrestrial and the superterrestrial must occur. The conversation between the physical and spiritual realms necessary for the occurrence of ritual begs the question of how the two realms communicate with each other. What language is spoken? "Sacred languages," as Anderson intimates, stretch far beyond secular languages because the understanding of symbolic expression creates cosmological belonging, it creates "a community out of the signs, not sounds."[26]

The import of signs and symbols in ritual practices cannot be understated. In fact, they remain essential to ritual. This is counter to the way Anderson describes contemporary Western practices. He argues: "Yet if the sacred silent

languages were the media through which the great global communities of
the past were imagined, the reality of such apparitions depended on an idea
largely foreign to the contemporary Western mind: the non-arbitrariness of
the sign."[27] Intriguingly, signs and symbols remain vital to African nations
and for practices of ritual.[28] In spite of ineluctable temporal evolution, ritual's
sacred language continues to be symbolically performed. Not even the forced
migration of Africans to the Americas severed or altered the language of
ritual. Instead, the signs and symbols spread with the Diaspora creating communities still liminally connected to a place of origin and sharing membership
through a sacred language where signs supersede sounds.

The "imagined communities" of Anderson's text prevail in the Diaspora.
As a result of migration, diasporic communities continue to build, form, and
expand into continuous versions of themselves. Sacred language functions as
the connective tissue holding the body of the Diaspora together. And like the
body with its vast systems, blood flows to all its parts nourishing while connecting each of the twelve systems of the body to one purpose, homeostasis:
the idea of the body maintaining optimal function and existence regardless of
changes. Landscapes and environments change, but the body must maintain
and survive. This is the essence of human existence; this is the essence of
the Diaspora. Practices, locations, and languages may differ. However, as
the circulatory system, the first system in the body to develop, carries the
life-sustaining blood from the mother to the fetus, sacred language connects
the Diaspora to its origin and maintains the Diaspora by umbilically connecting to the origin.[29] The heart is the central organ in the circulatory system and
pumps the essential life substance, blood, through to all parts of the body. As
the heart it also the symbol for Sankofa, which represents reaching back to
the place from whence one has come (origin) to inform where one is (present)
and is going (future), the heart functions as a scared symbol and sign of the
continued circulation of blood from the source of origin to its progeny. Thus,
the Diaspora, regardless of locations, remains indigenous unto itself. The
loss Anderson describes for the West is the import of sacred language to its
identity as a community. The loss for the Diaspora is not sacred language or
knowledge, but is the physical origin where the body exists. Thus, the import
for the Diaspora is not the physicality of origin and existence, but rather, how
origin and existence within an alternative landscape is reimagined and reconstructed through signs and symbols.

Nature as a sign and symbol of ancestors, ancestral knowledge, and land
function as "embodied sites where memory and history converge."[30] Because
time in traditional African societies connects historical events and memory
as a recollection embodied in oral and narrative creation, myth and lore utilize the liminal spaces of memory and non-linear time to create a cultural
and historical continuum for Africans, particularly for the Diaspora. Lena

Brøndum in "The Persistence of Tradition" contends: "Mythmaking empha-sizes a remaking of tradition. In this context, I define myths as a story to explain or give meaning to aspects of human life or a culture's origins and identity."[31] Myths and lore orally enabled Africans to rewrite the disruption of slavery not only as a disconnection or dispossession, but also as a narrative of reconnection and possession of an ancestral memory and knowledge. As Brøndum's quote implies, myths reiterate the cosmological and philosophical beliefs of a people. Whenever and wherever, myth is told, it reifies ontol-ogy. Myth reconnects Diaspora to their origins through a retelling of those origins and the beliefs and practices indigenous to those origins. Returning to the origin of origins, myths recreate creation or perform "metacreation," endowing Africans in the Americas with the ability of creation.[32] The dynam-ics of creation and the ability to transform through the connection of spiritual and physical realms align myth and ritual. And what is myth if not a writ-ten record of ritual? Although the physical landscape changed for Africans enslaved in the Americas, the ecology of their expression remained intact through the retention of oral lore and later oral characteristics in written language. Toni Morrison explores the function of myth and lore in her novel *Song of Solomon*. For Morrison, the novel was successful in that it " . . . blend[ed] the acceptance of the supernatural and a profound rootedness in the real world at the same time . . . [and] is indicative of the cosmology, the way in which Black people looked at the world."[33] From a cosmological perspec-tive, myth and lore create a framework for Africans to create and analyze oral expression and narratives. Reconnecting the enslaved back to their place of origin through cosmological expression and belief, myth establishes a continuous flow from one side of the water to the other—primordial, cosmic, memorial, locale.

Re-ordering the world through an African ecologically conducive worldview reifies the function of natural spaces for diasporic survival. Double-tongued narratives, like spirituals and myths, carried communal messages and existed beyond the physical chaos of bondage, becoming an essential component of the healing and expression of diasporic consciousness. Molefi Asante con-tends that, "the creation myths of Africa remained intact for most Africans, and therefore the practical myth dealt with questions of geographical and cultural alienation, conflict with a hostile society, and separation of technol-ogy and nature."[34] Like rituals function to heal and resolve conflict within the human condition, "myth becomes an explanation for the human condition and an answer to the problem of psychological existence in a racist society."[35] Signs and symbols in nature function as literary devices of storytelling, for, "healing, by definition, is this process of coming closer to nature—to the nature around us as well as the true nature within."[36] As Africans preserved the practices, beliefs, and systems that were indigenous to their natural ecology within the storehouse of their ontology, oral literature became the repository for the rituals used to exercise said practices, beliefs, and systems: "It is of paramount importance to note that Ifa and its Odu are grounded in written communication, but this writing differs from Western counterparts in that it conveys both verbal and spiritual messages."[37] The act of defining the signs and symbols of the natural world in spoken word through myth and lore, as a performance ritual, creates embodied landscapes that manifest indigenous cosmology and ontology in the physical and spiritual realms simultaneously.

Through the utterance of words, the inanimate is spoken into dynamic action or animation. Defined as nommo, the process can be understood in as simple of terms as the belief that talking to plants will promote growth and as complex, as Janheniz Jahn explains, as "a creature which is sharply distinguished from the animal and has its place in the community of men is produced, not by the act of birth, but by the word-seed: it is designated."[38] In other words, state of being is modified by the way it is defined orally. For example, in traditional African societies, and even to some extent today, a newborn is not officially part of the living community until named. The defining and classifying element of nommo is imperative to ritual because nommo is the heartbeat of ritual calling into focus that which is indistinguishable, defining what is undefined, endowing, through composition, the narrative of ritual. Accordingly, Barbara Christian in her article, "Ritualistic Process and the Structure of Paule Marshall's: *Praisesong for The Widow*," argues that nommo "is also essential to the ritual, for in African cosmology it is through *nommo*, through the correct naming of a thing, that it comes into existence."[39] Hence, nommo is the procreative and "the generative power of the spoken word."[40] Through nommo one can transcend one's condition or state of being. Nommo is the transference of energy via word from one realm to the next creating harmony and unity, orchestrating communication that transcends time and space and produces form and structure.

Nommo speaks on behalf of all realms, participants, and solutions. Further, Jahn argues that nommo, or "word-seed," plants the kernels of definition or classification to all things, images, and, even, god(s).[41] This is precisely the reason nommo, the power of the word, plays such a vital role in ritual, myth, and lore. For, it is through the word that energy is transferred, gods are called upon, and beings are transformed. Nommo calls into action all forces necessary for ritual to occur and be successful. Nommo provides the conduit between realms and establishes an open and vacillatory dialogue. Molefi Asante opines:

> When we speak of the African community, we are speaking of the *living* and the *dead* . . . and of *nommo* as a collective experience; in fact, without the participation of the ancestors, *nommo* cannot be completed, since the dead are the agents

who continue to energize the living. They assure us that the discourse of life will not be chaotic, and we take this, in whatever society we live, as a permanent expression of rebirth.[42]

Nommo rearranges the ontology of being creating a symbiosis of ritual elements that provide the code of transcendence. Inscribed within the regenerative word of nommo, then, is the text of ritual written across realms, beings, and nature.

The framework of this study up to this point examines the manner in which African culture is rebirthed through retention in the Americas primarily through the convergence of nature, ritual, and nommo. The framework also emphasizes how the process of diasporic reading and interpretation of nature developed through shared principles and ideology wholly connected to cosmological and ontological perspectives through signs, symbolic cues, and language. Hence, the examination of Africana consciousness and expression requires a certain level and standard of understanding, a foundational center of knowledge. Vévé Clark in "Developing Diaspora Literacy and Marasa Consciousness" surmises the imperative of an Afrocentric methodology when examining Africana cultural productions, especially literary discourse: "Diaspora literacy is the ability to read and comprehend the discourses of Africa, Afro-America, and the Caribbean from an informed, indigenous perspective."[43] Thus, the theoretical framework of this book employs an Africana-centered content analysis through the employment of Afrocentricity, Africana Humanism, and Africana Womanism. Utilizing these three approaches reasserts those subjects usually positioned at the margins of traditional Western humanistic inquiry as the center of both the framework and methodology. Specifically, these three approaches augment the research and theoretical landscape of humanistic inquiry by placing Africa, Africans (continental and diasporic), and Africana worldviews as centralized subjects for the employment of research methodologies specific to the discipline of Africana studies.

Molefi Asante's concept of Afrocentricity calls for humanistic scholars to consider the relevance and justification of an Africana centered methodology for critical examination in the discipline of Africana/Black studies. Through an Afrocentric perspective, the African is viewed through the African's own perspective, value and belief system, and discourse. Evaluations of cultural production, history, and narratives are not prescribed or dictated by a dominant cultural perspective, but are formulated, researched, and discussed through the African's worldview. Afrocentricity is a theoretical infrastructure and philosophical stance with clear consequences to the discipline of Africana studies if research and theory development is not Afrocentered. This is of particular import when the study, as is the case here, primarily deals with Africana subjects.[44]

While some scholars have discounted the validity[45] of Asante's theory, the value of this approach for the purposes of this study is best postulated by Gay Wilentz in the introduction to *Binding Cultures: Black Women Writers in Africa and the Diaspora*: "As a critic of African/African-American and ethnic women's literature, I find it imperative to use a literary criticism which is neither racist, patriarchal, nor Eurocentric. The difficulty arises in finding a comprehensive criticism not grounded in white male Western Christian hegemony."[46] Foundational to the humanistic concern of Afrocentricity as a methodology is the central question of why an Afrocentered scholar conducting research on an Afrocentered subject matter must employ an Afrocentered methodology for critical evaluation. As the approach contends, Afrocentricity centralizes that which is African and pushes the boundaries of critical examination and discourse by providing new lenses and perspectives that are not available or utilized in traditional Western humanistic methodological approaches, moving what is typically at the center of humanistic inquiry and discourse to the margins and removing the persistent urge of hegemony to define within specified and dictated positions. Afrocentricity's cultural milieu utilizes quintessential constructs of cultural identity in order to analyze and substantiate culturally specific philosophy: Cosmology (How the African interfaces with the world), Epistemology (How the African defines truth and knowledge), Axiology (What is of value to the African), and Aesthetics (What constitutes art and beauty to the African). Afrocentricity engenders a culturally specific and appropriate viewpoint for the examination of Africana works and, particular to this book. Vévé Clark furthers this perspective: "[Characters and authors] represent mnemonic devices whose recall releases a learned tradition. This type of literacy is more than a purely intellectual exercise. It is a skill for both narrator and reader which demands a knowledge of historical, social, cultural, and political development generated by lived and textual experience."[47] As Afrocentricity lends a particular cultural perspective and worldview to the examination of Africana texts, Africana Humanism lends a particular cultural perspective to the interrogation of culture and cultural retentions within texts. Wilentz highlights the need for an Africana humanistic approach: "Moreover, the task of exploring works of cultures suppressed by the dominant culture needs an interdisciplinary approach to criticism, an examination of the literature's historicity and social significance, attention to its oral/folkloric inheritance, and an understanding of the writer's commitment to reflect and often reform the culture that literature represents."[48]

In an Africana context and study such as this, humanistic inquiry provides a way for communal knowledge to be examined through the evaluation and assessment of works based solely from Afrocentered and Africana communal perspectives. Valeria Harvell, in "Afrocentric Humanism and African American Women's Humanizing Activism," provides such a lens for evaluation: "We must reach into the past; recover its richest lessons, most instructive models and best practices and put them in service of the present and future."[49] Quoting Maulana Karenga, Harvell focuses Africana humanism through the lens of Sankofa, utilizing Africana history, communal understanding, and traditions as foundations for healing and transformation. The inclusion of community is an important distinction to make at this juncture. As a core value of Africana humanism, community stands as the central vanguard of an Africana worldview. The community's centrality in the lives of Africana people speaks to the collective and shared consciousness, continental and diasporic, as Karenga's quote explores. As community shapes the ideation of Africana humanism, Harvell centers the role of Black women as cultural antecedents within the community. Drawing on Patricia Hill Collins, Harvell's article asserts:

> This article discusses a particular type of vision, one deeply rooted in the culture of African people, frequently referenced by many Afrocentric scholars and consistently manifested in Black women's thoughts and practices: the humanistic vision. Drawing connections between the humanistic principles articulated by many Afrocentric scholars and Black women's humanizing sociopolitical activities, the article sets forth the proposition that African American women have been the most ardent promoters, defenders, and practitioners of the humanistic vision within the Black community.[50]

A concept that positions Africana values at the center of existence and human interaction, which combines Karenga's call for culturally specific values and mores with Collin's focus on Black women's role in shaping community, Harvell's Africana humanism centralizes Black women as the progenitors of Black liberation, endowed with cosmological and ontological belief and expression utilized in their liberatory aims.[51] Thus, Harvell's text coalesces around the communal understanding and values the work of Black women activist promotes and reifies them as a central cultural apparatus of Africana freedom. While community remains central to this study and is representative in all three methodologies employed here, the humanistic inquiry of Africana women's activism as cultural apparatus demands an additional lens when applied to literary productions and works.

The examination of texts demands a methodology adept to the particular theoretical and philosophical approach of Africana culture, and the role Africana women play in the preservation and transmission of Africana culture. As a communally based theory, Africana Womanism lends the same subjectivity Africana women utilize to self-define to the greater community. Africana Womanism expands the ground where the Africana woman is the subject of her own discourse. This theory when utilized as methodology also centralizes the Africana woman as cultural producer and endows her with the power to define the terms and turf of her own, and by extension communal, existence. From this approach, Africana women can reimagine and recreate self through the intrinsic value of their own subjectivity and consciousness in a landscape ecologically conducive. By providing subjectivity to the subject, the Africana woman is not studied as an object of Western construction but is able to provide the context and content to answer humanistic questions of her lived experiences through an Africana perspective. Thus, through the liberatory perspective of Africana Womanism, the community can autonomously negotiate identity, subjectivity, and consciousness birthed from Africana women as cultural producers.[52] Bernice Regaon's study of the African Diaspora for the Smithsonian Institute reinforces the centrality of Africana women's work in the preservation of traditional practices in the modern world:

> There is the element of transformation in all of their work. Building communities within societies that had enslaved Africans, they and their people had to evolve in at least dual realities. These women are best seen as a central part of community structure and process. Their role was to resolve areas of conflict and to maintain, sometimes create, an identity that was independent of a society organized for the exploitation of natural resources, people, and land.[53]

Reagon explores Africana diasporic women and their work and maintains that they represent "the story of an evolving or rebirthing" community and culture that reaches beyond the national boundaries they exist within.[54]

This framework attends to Clenora Hudson-Weems's concept of Africana Womanism because of the emphasis on both the communal and spiritual aspects of the theory. In her outline of the characteristics of Africana Womanism, Hudson-Weems accentuates several areas of cultural retentions integral to the understanding of the theory, and also to the Africana communal and cultural understanding at large: Naming (nommo), self-defining, male inclusive, communal, valuing elders, and spirituality (ancestral).[55] Of spirituality's role, Hudson-Weems posits: "A natural phenomenon, spirituality cannot be omitted from the character of Africana women . . . she bears witness to, either consciously or subconsciously, this aspect of African cosmology . . . she frequently goes back to folk medicine and spiritual healing [and] is often spiritually guided by those of that world."[56] Fundamental here is the return to ancient and traditional beliefs, values, and practices intrinsic to spirituality in an Africana Womanist perspective. Similar to Harvell's discussion of

Karenga's call to return and Collin's focus on women as cultural liberators, Africana Womanism contemporarily functions as a call and response between the Diaspora and Africa through the communal and spiritual work of Africana women. Hudson-Weems's employment of the philosophical tenets of community and spirituality inherent in Africana Womanism applies to Africana women writers and characters within their texts through the return to indigenous origins.

Akin to the way Africans in the Americas built a framework to "read" their new environment by returning to indigenous practices and beliefs, Africana women's literature utilizes the communal and spiritual underpinnings of Africana culture. Describing the contemporary period of Black literature, Henry Louis Gates outlies six key characteristics that define the period. Of particular import is the third element that Gates provides: "the emergence of black women writing."[57] Further exploring the focus and aim of Black women writers, Gates postulates:

> In a society ordered by social hierarchies of power based on race, class, and gender, no one is more powerless . . . than a poor black girl. . . . In a sharp departure from many of their male precursors . . . their female contemporaries did not focus on the traumatic encounters of blacks and whites.[58]

As with Harvell's earlier references to the liberatory work of Black women, Gates also aligns Black women's writing to the cause of Black liberation. By centering the defenseless in an oppressive system, Black women and girls, true liberation is defined through the way in which Black women depict and construct their lives, whether fictional or not. As a part of their lived experiences, the community functions as a referent within these texts and, "Black women throughout the diaspora have kept their heritage alive."[59] Departing from the racialized and binary landscape of Black and white dynamics, Black women writers, instead, returned their focus to landscapes conducive to explore Africana consciousness.[60] Reimaging and re-creating sites of oppression, like the landscapes of the 19th century, Wilentz expands this notion: "We see Black American women focusing on Africa not only as historical ancestor, political ally, and basis for ideological stance but as part of a continuum in which Black women, before the slave trade and since, have recorded cultural history and values through their stories."[61] Thus, even if a fictional text, Black women's literature returns to the site and origin of Africana literary tradition. Referring to Harriet Wilson's *Our Nig*, in the introduction of the pivotal text *Conjuring: Black Women, Fiction, and Literary Tradition*, Marjorie Pryse asserts that, "Gates is correct in calling the book a 'missing link' between the tradition of black autobiography and the "slow emergence of a distinctive black voice in fiction. . . . The transformation of the black-as-object into the black-as-subject."[62] Texts like Wilson's distinctly inform contemporary Black women's literature and stand as a beacon not only for Black women's literary tradition, but for the Black literary tradition as a whole: "Those nineteenth-century 'mothers' who preserved biological lineage and connection by telling their stories as autobiographies or slave narratives made fiction writing possible for black women."[63] Bernice Regaon offers a critical point of clarification when discussing mothers within this context: "Mothering here does not refer to biologically having babies out of your body. These women . . . are nurturers and holders, womblike, of a people, of a birthing community in a strange land."[64] Autobiographical form and structure function, then, as a site of reclamation in the literature of Africana women and return to origins that speak to the ontology and cosmology inherent in Africana belief systems and practices within the literary tradition. A return to origins must return to the mother, as "Movement away from the mother—'thrusting her aside'—is movement away from Africa."[65] The literary lineage Africana women writers create conjures, as Pryse signifies on in her introduction to the text of the same name, the powerful images of spiritual entities like ancestors, conjure women, priestesses, and deities that endow the pages of Africana women's texts with the power and force of the word, nommo.

Revisiting sites of oppression and trauma for the Black body, like slavery, the mother symbol positions Black bodies in direct connection and communication with sites of healing and transformation, such as indigenous spaces, practices, and beliefs. Reordering sites of oppression and trauma according to the viewpoint of Africana women recreates a world centralized in the lived experiences of Black women and to the understanding of the world. The world is not only created but viewed through their vision. Thus, as a significant trope for Africana women writers, the mother as sign and symbol creates textual landscapes capable of rebirthing the Africana subjects and consciousness: "For African and African-American women writers, generational and cultural continuity—'to look back through our mothers'—is seen as a woman's domain."[66]

Pryse's discussion of Alice Walker's *The Color Purple* provides a salient example of how the spaces occupied by Black women in texts offer healing and transformation of Africana consciousness.

In *The Color Purple* Walker moves folk heritage further forward, into a context in which loving women becomes the most successful 'conjure' of all. And she does so by simultaneously moving backwards, taking for her narrator a woman whose incorrect spelling and broken syntax place her firmly within the nineteenth-century tradition.

As Celie begins to write letters to her sister instead of God, she "manages to redefine her own concept of "God" as stars, trees, peoples, sky, and "Everything." Celie's redefinition of God and spirituality centers nature, even the nature of women, as the manifestation of God and the divine. Through the love Celie and Shug Avery realize and share, Africa, in the form of Celie's long-lost sister and family, returns. Walker's text demonstrates the return to nature is also a return to the mother, and, hence, the motherland and represents "Everything" Black women's literature accomplishes from the oral tradition to the tradition of letters.[67]

As Pryse demonstrates "the way back" to the ancient and supreme power of mothers in the literary tradition of Africana women, Teresa Washington signifies upon one of Alice Walker's foremothers, Zora Neale Hurston.[68] Here, Washington explores the power inherent within the work of Africana women's literary tradition. Specifically, Washington examines how Hurston's return to the mother led to Washington's own return, or as Pryse so poignantly describes "the way back" to the ancient power of Africana women:

> Hurston's works became artistic and critical roots that moved stones of Western ideology out of my path. She also lent me her shoes with the sky-blue bottoms so I could fly to Nigeria and better understand the power inherent in Africana women that makes it a forgone conclusion that they will create and recreate and texture, color, and enliven nearly everything they touch no matter where they are . . . She knew there was something deeper, larger—there was a Yewáj o bí—a Mother of all Òrì s à (Gods) and life forms. Her name is disremembered, but Her visage is only a clear lake away. Overlooked and ignored, She is the ink of the text, and She is the framing reflective margin. She wears an Afro like Queen Tiye. She is as vain as Erzulie but as shy as Odù. Her arms are as long as Yeye Muwo, and She smells just like creation. . . . She had shrines all over Europe until Constantine dismantled some and whitewashed others in 333 c.e. Yet she survived this and slavery, colonialism, and imperialism. She is the red earth we till—that which soaks up the blood of lynching victims. It is in Her womb that the ancestors are reborn. And although She smiles when you do it, She begs you on her knees not to call Her out of Her name.[69]

While a lengthy quote to be sure, the value of Washington's example of the powerful lineage of Africana women, which is divinely known as Ajé, is most necessary. The lineage from Hurston back to the "Mother of all," reconstructs the power inherent in the voice of Africana women. Her lineage begins at creation, and, thus, places her progeny, Africana women, squarely within the tradition of creation. Within the very being of Africana women resides the divinity that her writing harkens back to. As the "Mother of all," ancient or modern, Africana women writers stand on the cultural precipice of life and death. It suffices to say that Africana women, in particular, play a primary and dominate role in the creation of textual space that examines Africana consciousness and subjectivity through an Africana-centered lens. Precipitated by the subjugated position of Black subjects within the hegemonic stratification of race and class, and heightened by the further subjugation of gender, Africana women exist on the margin of the margins as the other of others, a subjugated crossroads that Cherríe Moraga defines as a "theory in the flesh," a coalescing of lived intersectionalities that forges a "politic of necessity." Africana women's position, then, necessitates alternative ground to contemplate their identity and subjectivity and harkens back to a fundamental building block of a culture's communal existence—storytelling.[70]

Myriam Chancy in *Framing Silence: Revolutionary Novels by Haitian Women* discusses the revolutionary role of stories within the cannon of Haitian women writers, arguing: "When a population is considered so insignificant that its existence goes undocumented, storytelling becomes, necessarily, a source of retrieval; a story must be imagined, a fiction, created that will stand the stress of devaluation."[71] Chancy emphasizes the imperative of self-creation in Haitian women's writings. Chancy utilizes Gloria Anzaldua's sentiments on the imperative act of self-creation in *Borderlands: La Frontera* to insist that for Africana and Third World women, in particular, storytelling remains a vital act of revolution that liberates voices relegated to a gendered and historical silence. Anzaldua intimates:

> I want the freedom to carved chisel my own face, to staunch the bleeding with ashes, to fashion my own gods out of my entrails. And if going home is denied me then I will have to stand and claim my space, making a new culture—*una cultura mestiza*—with my own lumber, my own bricks and mortar and my own feminist architecture.[72]

Stories provide the essential building materials for revolutionary Africana women who dare to create a space and place not only to exist but to live. A space and place where borders and boundaries merge into dreamscapes of fertile lands, and where the contemplation of consciousness and subjectivity lead to dynamic and tangible transformation. Thus, for these revolutionary women, stories build, within the crevices of their real and lived experiences, a new ground. Stories set what is off kilter straight, or, rather, they set what is straight off kilter, reordering the order of subjugation and creating a chaos indicative of the crossroads where the four corners of the earth meet and the winds of change blow from all directions simultaneously. Or as Mary Kolawole quotes Patricia Waugh in *Womanism and African Consciousness*, "metafiction unveils how the meanings and values of the world have been constructed and how, therefore, they can be challenged or changed."[73] Storytelling is a revolutionary act of creation that positions Africana women at the crossroads of the divine and mundane. Mary Kolawole's own argument about African women as textual architects is salient to this point:

> Literature becomes useful as its own metalanguage and this is useful for declaring the writer's ideological position. The self-referential process is therapeutic, as it allows direct self-commentary by unveiling temporarily the veil of fiction. . . . This is central to the process of self-definition and self-healing. Metafiction therefore enhances self-awareness and self-definition.[74]

As creative devices, metalanguage and metafiction refer to the process of language creating fiction as a genre. But, just as Africana women employ metafiction and metalanguage as modes of self-definition and self-healing, the function of metalanguage and metafiction serve as a device in that very aim. In other words, metalanguage and metafiction define and heal both the terms and turf Africana women use to create stories that define and heal their own consciousness and subjectivity. Inherent in the use of metalanguage and metafiction, then, is the employment of traditional uses of language and genre, fiction in this case, as a container which holds a new language and a new fiction that Africana women are creating. The new space craved out by Africana women is one void of restraints of traditional ideas and identity construction. The void is a new space where creation can occur simultaneously within a real and lived experience. Kolawole's sentiments are echoed by Chancy who contends the following:

> The project of recovering the roots of Haitian women's self-definition is made possible only through the evaluation of narrative forms. In fact, writings by women of color in the United States as well as in the third world reveal that the creation of identity in the face of imperialist and colonial oppression begins with the transmutation of the personal into the creative, into modes of self-empowerment that in and of themselves create a theory of self-determination.[75]

Seemingly in plain view, metalanguage and metafiction create hidden crevices. By virtue of the reconceptualization of communal space, and the renegotiating of communal belonging, Africana women's texts also function as a container for a recreated collective consciousness for all its residents and reshapes, recreates, and transforms a space conducive to holding within its parameters a place for the ideation of Africana women writers' visions. Kolawole furthers: "The process of writing oneself is also the process of re-writing the collective self. So, the communal values that inform the unconscious also emerge in the literary production."[76] Indeed, both the self and the community are reflected.

Symbolic of nature's fecundity, Africana women writers utilize fiction as a communal womb to rebirth conducive narrative spaces to self-define and also reorder the community. Karla Holloway contends in *Moorings and Metaphors*: "Language restructures the community."[77] Africana women's fiction (re)defines social norms as does ritual: "Storytelling becomes a significant means of revising traditional historiography, because it gives authority to the spoken word as historical record. In other words, storytelling disrupts the discursive history of hegemony."[78] These texts lend their narrative spaces to engender the transformation of an ostensibly fixed traditional and societal form like history, gender, class, and race. In *Woman, Native, Other,* Minh-Ha asserts:

> Storytelling, the oldest form of building historical consciousness in community, constitutes a rich oral legacy, whose values have regained all importance recently, especially in the context of writings by women of color. She who works at un-learning the dominant language of "civilized" missionaries also has to learn how to un-write and write anew. And she often does so by re-establishing the contact with her foremothers, so that living tradition can never congeal into fixed forms, so that life keeps on nurturing life, so that what is understood as the Past continues to provide the link for the Present and the Future.[79]

Thus, Africana women's position within the community necessitates a re-envisioning of the community and communal vision in order to maintain and reestablish the community's epic memory. This process of creation births into existence a new space to place a transformed Africana consciousness beyond the hegemonic grip of subjugation and engenders a space for an Africana-centered contemplation of consciousness beyond the persistent occidental gaze, all the while resembling communal and collective existence.

Karla Holloway reverberates Brøndum's points in her exploration of the imperative of communal renewal in the works of Africana women and contends that, "The vision of the community is critical in literature by Africans and African Americans [because] Communal generation is historically a part of black culture."[80] Holloway's discussion of Zora Neale Hurston provides a realized textual examination and example of the ways in which Africana women reorder the world through their storytelling and create textual landscapes conducive to self-definition and the contemplation of Africana consciousness. In her discussion of Zora Neale Hurston's literary work *Moses,* Holloway argues that "its historical events and people and her linguistic revisioning of the oral text are recirculations of story, an appeal to the ritual of an ocular word that centers and grounds literate text."[81] In Holloway's estimation, Hurston accomplishes this in three ways. First, the essence of the story centers upon the performance of language and words and not plot and positions Hurston's voice as the creator and teller of the story. Holloway contends: "Hurston's authorial voice is certainly the primary structuralist of this story; but it is not an individuated voice."[82] Holloway's point is indicative of the aforementioned role Kolawole suggests metalanguage plays in African women's texts. The language the writers deposit into the text positions their voice as the central narrative and narrator. Second, the emphasis on language and not plot restores the community and communal space through the familiarity that language creates. The language reflects the community and communal spaces. Holloway argues: "Here Hurston's emphasis on positioning words in places where they have the potential to direct and redirect action . . . can change events through language."[83] Here again, Kolawole's use of metafiction proves useful because the text functions as the container of the writer's voice. Third, the combination of Hurston's narration and textual space births a new place that is the writer's vision, or as Holloway posits that "voice and text are linked and reestablish a relationship to God (and metaphorically to creation)."[84] While Hurston literally reenvisions the myth of Moses, the steps Holloway utilizes to demonstrate Hurston's recreation also reveals how, through myth, Africana women writers build place and space to self-define, heal, and to contemplate consciousness. Lena Brøndum establishes the connection between storytelling and myth and how they disrupt traditional historical discourse. Brøndum argues:

> In much the same way that storytelling serves to disrupt the representation of history by revising it, so mythmaking emphasizes a reworking of tradition. In this context, I define a myth as a story that seeks to explain or give meaning to aspects of human life or a culture's origins and identity. Contemporary African American [and diasporic] women's writing of stories that function as myths of origin and identity differs from the traditional notion of the mythical as something that points back to a distant historical time. In actuality, African American women's use of myth is another disruption of dominant discourse: first, by valuing myth in contrast to "history" and, second, by the writer's sense of agency and subjectivity in the discussion of a communal historic past.[85]

Myth as a living history transcends time and space limitations. It records and creates the vision and words of the people represented within them. The remembering of events and ceremonies place the past firmly in the present and provide a vehicle for the future. Myth takes us, as Julie Dash recounts, "inside our collective memories."[86] It rewrites, or as Minh-Ha argues "writes anew," the gaps in identity and subjectivity and gives voice to the voiceless. In this context, myth possesses a regenerative power and the textual language and container creates a narrative continuum. This is not an act of disconnection or dispossession but is an act of creation and transformation. In other words, myth performs ritual. Myth creates a living history, disrupts the dominant discourse, and constructs a narrative body representative of the people within the myth. The retelling of narratives taps into a people's memory and creates a collective consciousness. Social norms, values, and morals maintain a presence. Ancestors are venerated. Divinities are honored. And the history of a people resides in perpetuity.

In continuum with Holloway, Chancy discusses the usage of a theory she calls "culture-lacune."[87] Through the combination of the term lacune, which denotes a negative absence, and culture, which denotes a positive existence, she posits that "Lacune can be read into the texts as a space of 'nothingness' that is transformed and affirmed by the politics of representation revealed in each [of its definitions]."[88] Chancy's theory hinges on the gaps and voids in existence that Haitian women writers, and I argue Africana women writers, utilize to create a textual landscape fertile for the germination of self-expression and self-definition. Chancy illustrates:

> Haitian women represent the ultimate lacune in Haitian society: they are the absence that completes the whole. Working with these various definitions of lacune: simultaneously, it becomes possible to apprehend the diverse levels of Haitian women writers' visions: these visions describe a culture within a culture, one that embraces its own silencing even as it contests it. This is the essence of culture-lacune, a theory that positions the margin as its own center and, paradoxically, as a tool not only for subversion but also for self-expression.[89]

The culture-lacune relies on the simultaneous adoption of the four definitions of lacune: "1) as an empty space within the body; 2) A textual interruption; 3) That which is missing to complete a person, place, or thing; and 4) The absence of a level of soil in a stratigraphic sample."[90] Expanding on Chancy's representational theory of the culture-lacune, I assert that the theory is a mimesis of the Kongo cosmogram's four moments of the sun. As the beginning point, death, representative of absence, sets in motion the creation of space for Africana women's narrative.[91] This creation of space lends itself to the insertion of voice or a rebirth of subjectivity and identity via Africana women's narratives. The insertion of voice disrupts the traditional inclusion of voices and interjects voices relegated to the margins and deemed unnecessary. The narrative disruption or the insertion of Africana women's narratives births a space and place conducive for the new narrative voices to be birthed, creating a new point, a new ground where higher consciousness is contemplated.

The culture-lacune rearticulates the voids and gaps in representation of Africana women's voices within their lives and lived experiences. Similar to Kolawole's metalanguage (terms) and metafiction (turf) and Holloway's rendition of Hurston's creation through the recreation of myth, the emptiness of lacune is embodied with the beingness of culture. The absence creates a space for recreation and a narrative rendition of creation. A liminal space, culture-lacune creates a world within a world, a space within a space, a place within a place that Africana women can utilize to self-create and self-define. The gaps and voids do not disconnect or separate Africana women from their culture or community, but, rather, it reconnects by filling what was empty and transforming what was static, hence, producing a cosmological shift where voices excluded from the dominant discourse become the voices of representation. As the crossroads marks the intersection of the physical and spiritual realms on the cosmogram, Chancy's culture-lacune crosses the borders and boundaries of representation and existence where women writers negotiate individual and communal subjectivity and identity and create a new ground— a crossroads. In the center of the crossroads, within the container of the cosmogram, Africana women and their narratives exist nestled in the primordial waters of the Kalunga: "the empty circle of existence before creation."[92] What Chancy's culture-lacune offers, in terms of an empty space embodied with life, is the cosmological perspective the cosmographic symbol of the Kalunga represents as an empty space where the lives and lived experience of Africana women fill the void. In the midst of the crossroads, the intersection

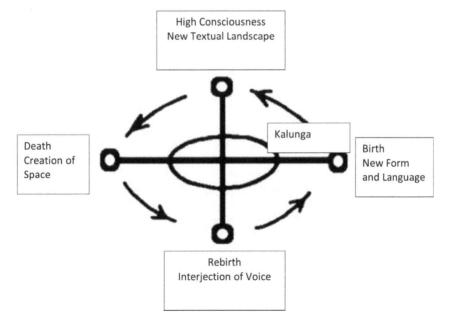

Figure 1.1. A Visual Representation of the Culture-Lacune as a Cosmogram. Source: Image of the Cosmogram was adapted from Robert Thompson's *Flash of the Spirit: African and Afro-American Art and Philosophy* (1984, 109).

of intersections, the primordial water of the Kalunga allow the comingling of the spiritual and physical self to negotiate the four points of the cosmogram and the dynamic intersections between them. Africana women are, thus, on the edge of existence and their narratives symbolize the movement through the four phases of the cosmographic and liminal existence of both the cosmogram and Chancy's culture-lacune. See Figure 1.1 for a graphic description of the culture-lacune.

NOTES

1. Lawrence W. Levine. *Black Culture and Black Consciousness: Afro-American Folk Thought from Slavery to Freedom.* 30th ed. (New York: Oxford University Press, 2007), 88.

2. Henry Louis Gates. *The Signifying Monkey* (New York: Oxford, 1988), 4.

3. "One of the effects of the eighteenth- and nineteenth-century disruptions was the dispersal of millions of Yoruba peoples over the globe, primarily to the Americas—Haiti, Cuba, Trinidad, and Brazil—where their late arrival and enormous numbers ensured a strong Yoruba character in the artistic, religious, and social lives of Africans in the New World. That imprint persists today in many arts and in a variety of African American faiths that have arisen not only in the Caribbean and South America, but also in urban centers across the United States. Yoruba philosophical, religious, and artistic tenets, ides, and icons have transformed and continue to transform religious beliefs and practices and the arts of persons far beyond Africa's shores" Henry John Drewal, et al. *Yoruba: Nine Centuries of African Art and Thought* (Center for African Art in association with H.N. Abrams Inc., Publishers, 1989), 4–5.

4. Malidoma Somé. *Ritual: Power, Healing, and Community: The African Teachings of the Dagara.* African Teachings of the Dagara (New York: Penguin/Arkana, 1997), 39.

5. "Survival here does not simply address the questions of staying alive but in fact addresses the need to survive beyond the narrow definitions afforded by slave and post-slave structure. To function as slaves within the society would be much too narrow to ensure that a people would prosper. There was a need to establish a structure and system with its own content that would allow an improved situation for survival beyond the confines of carrying out the required functions as slaves." Bernice Johnson Reagon. "African Diaspora Women: The Making of Cultural Workers." *Feminist Studies* 12, no. 1 (1986): 79.

6. Gates, *The Signifying Monkey,* 4.

7. Isidore Okpewho, Carole Boyce Davies, and Ali A. Mazrui. The African Diaspora: African Origins and New World Identities (Bloomington: Indiana University Press, 2001), xv.

8. Anissa J. Wardi. *Water and African American Memory: An Ecocritical Perspective.* (Gainesville: University Press of Florida, 2011), 5–7.

9. Wardi, *Water,* 7.

10. Ibid., 8.

11. For further examination of the Vernacular see Henry Louis Gates, Jr. and Valerie A. Smith, general editors. *The Norton Anthology of African American Literature.* Third Edition. Volumes One and Two (W.W. Norton, 2014).

12. This quote is taken from note 3 of the text. Teresa Washington. "Mules and Men and Messiahs: Continuity in Yoruba Divination Verses and African American Folktales." *Journal of American Folklore* 125, no. 497, 2012: 283.

13. Malidoma Somé. *The Healing Wisdom of Africa* (New York: Putnam, 1998), 259–264.

14. Wardi, *Water*, qtd. Allister, 20.

15. Somé, *Healing*, 52–53.

16. Although Washington is specifically referring to Ifa, I am including this religious practice in the scope of ritual. Washington, "Mules," 264.

17. While I acknowledge the breach, I am arguing a return to origins soothes the breach. John S. Mbiti. *African Religions & Philosophy* (New York: Praeger, 1969), 26–27.

18. Theodore W. Jennings. "On Ritual Knowledge." *The Journal of Religion* 62, no. 2, (1982): 116.

19. In her discussion of ritual here, Christian is referring to *Praisesong for the Widow* by Paule Marshall. Barbara Christian. "Ritualistic Process and the Structure of Paule Marshall's *Praisesong for the Widow.*" In *Black Feminist Criticism: Perspectives on Black Women Writers* (Pergamon Press, 1985), 150.

20. Malidoma Somé. *Ritual: Power, Healing, and Community: The African Teachings of the Dagara.* African Teachings of the Dagara (New York: Penguin/Arkana, 1997), 78.

21. Venertria Patton. *The Grasp That Reaches Beyond the Grave: The Ancestral Call in Black Women's Texts* (New York: State University of New York (SUNY) Press, 2013), 9.

22. For an in-depth description of the formation and manifestation of ancestors see Fu-Kiau, Kimbwandènde Kia Bunseki. *African Cosmology of the Bântu-Kôngo: Tying the Spiritual Knot: Principles of Life & Living.* 2nd ed. (Brooklyn: Athelia Henrietta Press, 2001).

23. Patton, *The Grasp that Reaches Beyond the Grave*, 9.

24. Somé, *Ritual*, 125.

25. Benedict R Anderson. *Imagined Communities: Reflections on the Origin and Spread of Nationalism.* Rev. ed. (London: Verso, 2006), 13.

26. Ibid., 13.

27. Ibid., 14.

28. Drewal's aformentioned quote in footnote 3 regarding the result of forced migration demonstrates the presence and impact of cultural retentions.

29. Further, discussing cultural retentions, Gay Wilentz in *Binding Cultures: Black Women Writers in Africa and the Diaspora*, references a return to the mother and motherland. Gay Alden Wilentz. *Binding Cultures: Black Women Writers in Africa and the Diaspora* (Indiana University Press, 1992), XX.

30. Wardi, *Water*, 6.

31. Lena Brøndum. "The Persistence of Tradition." In *Black Imagination and the Middle Passage*, edited by Maria Diedrich, Henry Louis Gates, and Carl Pedersen (W.E.B. Du Bois Institute. New York: Oxford University Press, 1999), 156.

32. Although metacreation is a computational musical term that refers to the endowment of machines (technology) to create or recreate, I apply it here in terms of indigenous technology inherent to Africans in the Americas. Philippe Pasquier, Arne Eigenfeldt, Oliver Bown, and Shlomo Dubnov. "An Introduction to Musical Metacreation." *Computers in Entertainment* 14, no. 2 (2016): 1–14.

33. Toni Morrison. "Rootedness: The Ancestor as Foundation." In Gates, Henry Louis Jr. and Valerie A. Smith, general editors. *The Norton Anthology of African American Literature.* Third Edition. Volume Two (W.W. Norton, 2014), 1069.

34. An example of the myths Asante describes here is the Flying African. Molefi K. Asante. *Afrocentricity, the Theory of Social Change* (Buffalo, NY: Amulefi Publications, 2003), 110.

35. Asante, *Afrocentrictiy*, 110.

36. Somè, *Healing*, 272.

37. Teresa Washington. "Mules and Men and Messiahs: Continuity in Yoruba Divination Verses and African American Folktales." *Journal of American Folklore* 125, no. 497 (2012): 265.

38. Janheinz Jahn. *Muntu: The New African Culture* (New York: Grove Press, 1961), 125.

39. Christian, Barbara. "Ritualistic Process," 157–58.

40. Asante, *Afrocentrictiy*, 202.

41. Jahn, Janheinz, *Muntu,* 125.

42. Asante, *Afrocentrictiy*, 111.

43. VèVè A. Clark. "Developing Diaspora Literacy and Marasa Consciousness." *Theatre Survey* 50, no. 1 (2009): 9.

44. Asante, *Afrocentrictiy*.

45. Gates, *Norton*, 921.

46. Wilentz, *Binding Cultures,* xii.

47. Clark, "Developing Diaspora," 9.

48. Wilentz, *Binding Cultures*, xiii.

49. Valeria G Harvell. "Afrocentric Humanism and African American Women's Humanizing Activism." *Journal of Black Studies* 40, no. 6 (2010): 1053.

50. Ibid., 1053.

51. Ibid., 1056.

52. While this study employs Alice Walkers's second of four all-encompassing definitions of womanism, the use of Africana Womanism squarely fits the scope of the project, which centers a communal and spiritual component. Powerful in her own right, Walker defines a womanist as,

A woman who loves other women, sexually and/or nonsexually. Appreciates and presser women's culture, women's emotional flexibility . . . and women's strength. Sometimes loves individual men, sexually and/or nonsexually. Committed to survival and wholeness of entire people, male *and* female. Not a separatist, except periodically, for health. Traditionally universalist. . . . Traditionally capable (Walker, Alice. *In Search of Our Mothers' Gardens* (Harcourt, 1983), xi)

53. Bernice Johnson Reagon. "African Diaspora Women: The Making of Cultural Workers." *Feminist Studies* 12, no. 1 (1986): 79.

54. Reagon, "African Diaspora Women," 79.

55. Clenora Hudson-Weems. *Africana Womanism: Reclaiming Ourselves*. 4th rev. (Troy: Bedford, 2004), 55–73. Condensed list.

56. Ibid., 70.

57. Gates, *Norton*, 914.

58. Ibid., 919.

59. Wilentz, *Binding Cultures*, xx.

60. "Writers in the contemporary period have seen [slavery] as a way of understanding the present" (Gates, *Norton*, 917).

61. Wilentz, *Binding Cultures*, xiii.

62. Marjorie Pryse, and Hortense J. Spillers. *Conjuring: Black Women, Fiction, and Literary Tradition* (Indiana University Press, 1985), 6.

63. Ibid., 3.

64. Reagon, "African Diaspora Women," 88.

65. Although Cartey is referring to African autobiographies here, the idea is a salient on for this discussion. Wilfred Cartey. *Whispers from a Continent: The Literature of Contemporary Black Africa* (Random House, 1969), 3–4.

66. Wilentz, *Binding Cultures*, xiv.

67. Pryse, *Conjuring*, 17 (qtd. Walker).

68. Pryse, *Conjuring*, 2.

69. Teresa Washington. *Our Mothers, Our Powers, Our Texts: Manifestations of Àjé in Africana Literature* (Bloomington: Indiana University Press, 2005), 56.

70. Cherríe Moraga, and Anzaldúa Gloria. *This Bridge Called My Back: Writings by Radical Women of Color*. Fourth (Albany: State University of New York (SUNY) Press, 2015), 19.

71. Myriam J. A. Chancy. *Framing Silence: Revolutionary Novels by Haitian Women* (New Brunswick: Rutgers University Press, 1997), 15.

72. Chancy, *Framing Silence*, qtd. Anzaldua, 22.

73. Mary E. Kolawole. *Womanism and African Consciousness* (Trenton: Africa World Press, 1997), 169.

74. Ibid., 167–168.

75. Chancy *Framing Silence*, 6.

76. Kolawole, *Womanism and African Consciousness*, 169.

77. Karla F.C. Holloway. *Moorings & Metaphors: Figures of Culture and Gender in Black Women's Literature* (New Brunswick: Rutgers University Press, 1992), 97.

78. Brøndum, "The Persistence of Tradition," 156.

79. Trinh, T. Minh-Ha. *Woman, Native, Other: Writing Postcoloniality and Feminism* (Bloomington: Indiana University Press, 1989), 149.

80. Holloway, *Moorings and Metaphors*, 94–95.

81. Ibid., 94.

82. Ibid., 96.

83. Kolawole, *Womanism and African Consciousness*, 97.

84. Holloway, *Moorings and Metaphors*, 98.

85. Brøndum, "The Persistence of Tradition," 156.

86. Julie Dash. *Daughters of the Dust: The Making of an African American Woman's Film* (New York: New Press, 1992), 31.

87. Chancy, *Framing Silence*, 16.

88. Ibid., 16.

89. Ibid., 16–17.

90. Ibid., 16.

91. To reiterate an earlier point, death is the entry point for the purposes of this study. Traditionally, the Cosmogram begins with rebirth. See Introduction of this book for more explanation.

92. Molefi K. Asante, and Ama Mazama. *Encyclopedia of African Religion* (Thousand Oaks: Sage, 2009), 361.

Chapter 2

At the Crossroads

Rituals of Death in Danticat's
The Dew Breaker

The Dew Breaker is a novel about a seemingly ordinary man and his family. However, the eponymous titular character, the Dew Breaker, refers to not only his role in the Duvalier regime but also his shadow-like, trailing past. On the surface, the stories and chapters seem loosely related, but, by novel's end, it becomes apparent that even when the Dew Breaker is not physically present within the narratives, his spirit is present on the periphery of each tale. The stories are in limbo, and like the Dew Breaker appear and disappear throughout the text. Each of the nine chapters recounts multiple traumas in the lives of Haitian and Haitian Americans as a result of the Duvalier regime.[1] Of particular interest to this inquiry is the special force of the Duvalier's regime, the Tonton Macoute, who committed decades of atrocities against the citizens of Haiti and of whom the Dew Breaker in this novel belongs.

The novel is predicated upon the Dew Breaker's confession to his daughter, Ka, that he is an imposter. That he, and by extension his wife, Anne, has buried his true identity. Significantly, in Ancient Kemet, Ka represents the spirit of a person, and the double entendre of Ka's name suggests that the Dew Breaker is not only confessing to his daughter, but he is confessing to his own spirit. Ka is a sculptor who carves images of her father as the prisoner she believed him to be during the Duvalier regime. However, at the close of the first chapter, "The Book of the Dead," the Dew Breaker reveals that he was a member of the feared and reviled Tonton Macoute and is, "the hunter . . . not the prey."[2] The next seven chapters of the novel consist of related allegoric tales of multi-generational Haitians that are connected to the Dew Breaker and his actions during the Duvalier regime. The legacy of violence, loss, and displacement permeate through the chapters like a thread in a finely woven garment. The last chapter, broken into thirteen parts, like Osiris's body in

Ancient Kemetic mythology, pieces together the narrative body of the Dew Breaker and fills in the gaps in his story.[3]

The myth of Osiris is an example of Ancient Kemet's belief and understanding of the cycle of life—death, rebirth, birth, and creation. Similar to the structural function of the Kemetic myth within the novel, *The Dew Breaker's* own vacillation between structural forms, not necessarily a novel or a short story collection, mimics the ancient papyri found in the chambers and tombs of Kemet that retell the dead's story. The scripts found in ancient tombs are at once the story of the deceased and the myth of Osiris. In the end, Osiris and the dead become one as the recently departed assumes the name Osiris: "thus, in the Book of Vindication, the resurrected one declares, 'I die and I live for I am Osiris.'"[4] Concomitant stories construct the foreground and obvious structure of the book, but present in the background is the continual repetition of one of the earliest myths and texts—the myth of Osiris in *The Book of the Dead*.[5] The looping repetition of the myth recited throughout the novel from different perspectives tightly bind *The Dew Breaker* together. In addition, the encompassing indirection of this mythical retelling creates narrative passageways where holistic recollections of the Dew Breaker's life can traverse beyond his physical existence, creating the narrative body that the Dew Breaker will carry with him into the afterlife like the Ancient Egyptians he admires in the novel. The tightly woven threads of the fabric of the overlapping mythic narratives create the multilayered and intersectional nature of *The Dew Breaker*. Thus, the novel explores many themes and threads from forced migration, hauntings, and multi-generational trauma, to disconnection, loss, dispossession, and death. Of all themes listed, death undoubtedly is the most central to this text. The novel begins and ends with death, and death concurrently runs through all the stories, literally and symbolically. The first chapter is aptly titled "The Book of the Dead," and, similar to the structure in Danticat's previous novel *The Farming of Bones*, bears witness to the atrocities inflicted by the Dew Breaker or someone like him. Reminiscent of the mythical bogeyman figure the Tonton Macoute are named for, *The Dew Breaker* hauntingly pieces together, as Isis completes with Osiris's body, the narrative which exists somewhere between the fact and the fiction of the titular character's existence. Danticat's use of the Osiris myth as the backstory of *The Dew Breaker* renders the text a funerary tale, and performs the rites of death for the title character, while simultaneously assembling a new container for his narrative body to reside in by resembling the scattered pieces of his story, like the limbs of Osiris.[6] Thus, it can be argued that the nine narratives in *The Dew Breaker* function as a divine container that houses the Dew Breaker and his narratively reconstructed body to formulate a living and oral history of how his role in the Duvalier regime shaped him and multiple generations of Haitians.

The repetitious orality of Osiris's myth in the nine chapters, inscribes a funerary text and harkens back to the concept of nine affinities of man necessary, according to Ancient Kemetic beliefs in *The Book of the Dead*, to eternal afterlife. Each of the nine human affinities correlates with one of the nine chapters of the novel and create doubles, or Kas, of each other. The following is a list of the nine inseparable affinities of man and the correlating chapters in the novel: "(a) natural body ["The Book of the Dead"], (b) spiritual body ["Seven"], (c) heart/ab ["Water Child"], (d) double/ka ["The Book of Miracles"], (e) soul/ba ["Night Talkers"], (f) shadow/khaibit ["The Bridal Seamstress"], (g) ethereal casing or spirit ["Monkey Tails"], (h) form/sekhem ["The Funeral Singer"], and (i) name ["The Dew Breaker"].[7] As the novel closely traces the nine affinities of man, the number nine is also the number of divinities forming the Ennead who sit in the Great Hall of Maat and hear the confessions of those seeking immortality. The confessions of the deceased are represented by the heart and weighed against Maat's feather, as "The Maatian concept of afterlife or immortality and the theology that undergirds and informs can be discussed under five headings: (1) resurrection, (2) ascension, (3) judgment, (4) acceptance, and (5) transformation."[8] Described as the five phases of vindication, these headings are representative of the cycle of life previously mentioned and are represented in the myth of Osiris—death, rebirth, creation, and transformation. Each of the nine narratives and affinities within *The Dew Breaker* undergoes one of the phases of vindication and the novel completes a life cycle to prepare a divine container for the Dew Breaker and his Ka. Thus, the nine narratives that form the Dew Breaker's body speak to the fullness and quality of his embodiment of the nine affinities of man and is measured and must traverse the phases of vindication required of eternal life. As such, the nine narratives represent the phases respectively.

Encased in his own narrative body, and accompanied by a funerary text, the novel provides the structure, mode, and method the Dew Breaker utilizes to traverse the physical and spiritual realms, and ultimately the Great Hall of Maat, to face his day of reckoning. Using ritual structure—invocation, opening, dialogue, repetition, and closing—the novel is transformed into a ritualized space respectively imbued with the Maatian principles of eternal afterlife—resurrection, ascension, judgment, acceptance, and transformation.[9] Thus, this chapter will demonstrate how the nine affinities of man create a textual body through the corresponding nine chapters of the novel and traverse the cosmogram through ritual structure. Utilizing ritual structure, *The Dew Breaker* explores the junctions between the cosmogram and the nine affinities of man, blurring the lines between the physical and spiritual realms, creating a literary crossroads that perform a complete cycle of the soul. Invocation begins ritual structure and is responsible for initiating communication between the realms. Intercessory in nature, invocation represents the meeting point or the intersection of the realms, the crossroads.[10]

Symbolic of the journey the soul takes to get to the afterlife, the first narrative of the novel, "The Book of the Dead," begins with the performance of the Dew Breaker's funerary rites and preparation of an empty vessel for him to exist within. The opening line of the novel "My father is gone," signals the Dew Breaker's absence and foreshadows his narrative absences and, ultimately, his death.[11] His disappearance startles Ka, and she cannot comprehend why he has left, where he has gone, or why he took the sculpture she carved in his image. As Ka tries to explain to the police officer and hotel manager why her father may have disappeared, she realizes that "I had never tried to tell my father's story in words before now."[12] The Dew Breaker's disappearance forces Ka to consider her father's image in concrete terms and words. However, the only image of her father that Ka has been able to see is the one she creates and recreates of him, "naked, kneeling . . . his back arched . . . his downcast eyes," never true to his likeness.[13] When asked by the hotel manager and police officer for a recent photo of her father, Ka realizes that she does not even have a pictorial image of her father showing his entire face. Comprehending the constraints of a descriptive identifier, Ka is unable to identify her father. Her father's disappearance symbolizes the fleeting image of her father that Ka attempts to recreate in words for the hotel manager and police officer. Moreover, it creates a separation between father and daughter, image and identity, and physical and spiritual realms. The Dew Breaker's disappearance also creates a liminal space and a duplicity of existence within the text. While he cannot be physically found, spiritually his presence is felt. On some level he exists. However, exactly where his existence resides is undefined until he physically returns to the hotel.

Ostensibly the entire novel occurs during a trip to and from Florida, where Ka and her father travel to deliver a sculpture to a famous Haitian American actress. Ka carves a piece of mahogany wood in what she envisions as her father's image. Ka explains that it is her, "first completed sculpture of him . . . but it is my favorite of all my attempted representations of my father. It was the way I had imagined him in prison."[14] As a sculptor, Ka attempts to create what she believes is the natural body, or raw form, of her father. Even the wood, which she describes as "naturally flawed," mimics the physical blemish of the scar on the side of his face. Ka envisions herself to be a natural extension of her father, his double in nature: "Like me, my father tends to be silent a moment too long during an important conversation and then say too much when less should be said."[15] The Ancient Kemites believed that the ka was a smaller version, in form and structure, of the person. In other words, a person's ka reflects a person's form or natural body. Further, the idea of a person's ka also exemplifies the father daughter relationship at play here, as

Ka thinks of herself as another version of her father. However, Ka's depiction of her father is always flawed because she is not privy to his true form and instead sculpts an inaccurate likeness or a false idol.

The construction of her father's persona in wooden form mimics the artificiality of the man-made tropical paradise of Lakeland, Florida. The man-made garden where the Dew Breaker destroys Ka's statue is indicative of the man-made image Ka tries to create for him. However, the lushness of the landscape symbolizes an elevation of spiritual consciousness akin to the deceased in *The Book of the Dead*.[16] In an Eden-like setting with a submerged likeness of self, the Dew Breaker's act of confession within the landscape reveals his "natural body" and ultimately sets Ka free. As he is trying to explain himself by making a comparison between himself and the Ancient Egyptian statues he visits at the museum, Ka dismisses her father, laughing at him and waving her hands wildly. He grabs hold of her wrist almost crushing her bone. Ka commands him to "let go," and her father responds, "I'm sorry . . . I did not want to hurt you. I did not want to hurt anyone."[17] In this instance, Ka is set free and the Dew Breaker exposes his natural body through his seemingly natural actions.

Ultimately, this is the story of Osiris. The Dew Breaker is a Set archetype who throws his counter image, Osiris, into the river.[18] Ka finally sees her father, and his textual composition begins. Osiris is the giver of life, and Set is the taker, and Ka is left to imagine the statue of her father broken into pieces at the bottom of the pond, swollen with water. Like Set, the Dew Breaker tries to usurp the rites and reign of the innocent, as the exploitation of the Tonton Macoute often document. The Dew Breaker, in the novel, takes ownership of others' land, womanizes, and terrorizes the community. He even usurps a new persona. Within this context, the image Ka constructs of her father collides with the Dew Breaker and exposes his natural body serving as a catalyst for the Dew Breaker confession: "You see, Ka your father was the hunter, he was not the prey."[19] It is for this reason that he takes the statue, and later Ka, to a man-made lake to destroy the man-made image he created of a mild, quiet, and distant barber enthralled by Ancient Egyptians. He destroys the statue and its representative ka. Ka's, his daughter, purpose as his "good angel" aligns with the sculpted version of her father and not the natural body he reveals at the lake. By confessing, the Dew Breaker attempts to sculpt his narrative body back together, like the scattered pieces of Osiris. The ensuing narratives of the novel chisel out the Dew Breaker's existence and reveal not only his natural body but also his true ka.

Proceeding the exposition of the Dew Breaker's natural body in "The Book of the Dead," the next chapters, "Seven" and "Water Child," explore and examine the ritualization of his spiritual body and heart/ab. Following the counterclockwise motion of the cosmogram, the novel shifts from the crossroads to the Luvemba position, or the point of death, and represents the transitioning of the Dew Breaker from the physical realm to the spiritual realm. Utilizing the ellipsis as rhetorical device, the chapters "Seven" and "Water Child" signify upon the gaps in time and the liminal space between the realms. The opening ellipsis in the chapter "Seven," allows the embedding of ritual into the text and specifically "The Opening of Mouth and Eyes Ritual." An imperative ritual for the deceased in Ancient Kemet, "The Opening of Mouth Ceremony," prepares and purifies the dead for the transition from the physical to the spiritual realm. The ritual was performed on the funerary statue of the deceased, shedding the natural body through the process of mummification and preparing a representative sculpture to house the ka.[20] This ritual act is imperative to the survival of the Dew Breaker in the afterlife. Although he has prepared a container for his natural body, the container is empty. Without a ka, the afterlife is nonexistent.

Traditionally, the ritual is typically performed by the eldest child of the deceased. Ironically, in the novel, Ka's unsuccessful attempt to sculpt the likeness of the Dew Breaker's natural body alleviates her from this role, and, with no other children or options, the task seems to rest upon the Dew Breaker alone. Just as the Dew Breaker invokes his natural body through the act of confessing, he must also sculpt a funerary statue for his new ka and deliver a ka suitable to his true identity.[21] The natural body "The Book of The Dead" exposes in turn reveals the Dew Breaker's spiritual body underneath. With the form and structure of his outer body constructed, the underbelly of his spiritual identity is given shape in the proceeding chapters.

To emphasize the sanctity and the interconnection of the natural body and the spiritual body, the chapter "Seven" utilizes the motif of marriage and union. Specifically, "Seven" examines the dissolution of a marriage because of time and distance and demonstrates the transformation and transition from the physical body to the spiritual body. Specifically, the chapter explores the marriage of an unnamed young Haitian couple who enter a hurried union. The husband relocates to the United States a few days after the marriage, hoping that his wife will be able to join him shortly after he saves the money for her visa. However, it takes seven years for the couple to reunite. When the wife finally arrives in the United States, the couple is instantly consumed by the seven years of penned up lust, so they make love seven times representing each year they were not together. The physicality of lust briefly fills the gaps of time and distance.

Initially the couple meets at the end of carnival when attendees burn their costumes "and feign weeping" as Ash Wednesday approaches.[22] The wife's convincing weeping attracts the husband to her, and he believes that "if she could grieve so passionately on demand, he thought, perhaps she could love even more."[23] What the husband perceives as true passion is actually an inherent part of his wife and exists beyond the surface of carnival role play. Accordingly, he soon discovers, when she joins him in New York, that the grief she exhibited so passionately during carnival returns, possibly because of the isolation the wife experiences or because of language barriers and unfamiliarity of surroundings: "He simply wanted to extinguish the carnivals burning in her head."[24] The chapter ends with the couple on a Saturday excursion, that makes the wife happy. He takes her to Prospect Park and reflects: "This immense garden, he told her, was where he came to ponder seasons, lost time, and interminable distances."[25] Entering the park, the couple traverse space and time. In the text, ellipsis follow the quote and signal the gap in time and space that the character describes in the aforementioned quote. As the trees and greenery envelop the couple, the separation between the man-made structure of the city and the lush natural surroundings of the park alludes to the separation of the physical realm and the spiritual realm. The couple exists in a liminal space between the reality of New York City that surrounds the park and the spiritual space the park offers. The serenity of the park is a juxtaposition of the raucousness of carnival; in the park they are exposed like Adam and Eve and in carnival they masquerade as bride and groom. Although the couple's union is tenuous as they enter the Eden-like landscape of the park, they enter it hand and hand. Impersonating Christianity's first divine union, Adam and Eve in the garden of Eden, the couple in "Seven" soon discover the truth of the internal makeup of their union, as it stripped naked and sheds the physical and topical covering, exposing the hidden interior dimensions of the spiritual body. However, juxtaposed to the Christian version of Adam and Eve's fall from heaven, moving from a spiritual place to an earthly place, the couple goes from the physical to the spiritual.

As the chapter's title invokes, "Seven," the couple is met by the Kemetic goddess Seshat.[26] The husband observes that, "she had reached for his hand at 5:11 p.m., he had noted, and had not released it since."[27] The combination of the numbers in the time when the wife reaches for the husband's hand equals seven. Marriage is a symbolic signifier of the sacred union that occurs when two souls become one. It is the embodiment of the most sacred bond between two people. Therefore, the couple depicted in "Seven" represent the spiritual body, the divine union, the marriage of the masculine and feminine and inner and outer persona. The totality of their union underscored and measured out by their interaction with Seshat, reveals, once stretched to capacity, the limitations of their union. When the couple emerges from the thicket, the husband notes that, "it was past seven o'clock" signifying that the time for their union had also passed.[28] They long to go back to the moment in time when they feigned love and performed the traditional carnival ritual where a man and a woman play a bridegroom. They are dressed in traditional wedding clothes, but the joke is that the man is dressed as a bride, and the woman a groom. An unsuspecting reveler, and usually one not enjoying themselves, is chosen and the couple asks if the person will marry them. Yet, for the couple in "Seven" the time for this has passed. The carnival costumes are gone, and the couple is trying to "see" each other as if for the first time. They cannot see each other and cannot complete the "traditional puzzle of bride and groom," and the distance between them is palpable.[29] In other words, their union does not measure up.

The false image of the wedding performance mimics the false persona of the Dew Breaker. Like the couple's juxtaposition to the naturalness of the garden and the masquerade of the carnival scene where they met, the Dew Breaker negotiates the liminal space between his past as a henchman in the Duvalier regime, and his assumed persona of the New York barber and family man. Although he masquerades as a quiet and simple barber, the internal measurement and structure of his spiritual body is incongruent to his physical personification. There is a disconnection between his inner and outer persona. In "Seven," the Dew Breaker begins "The Opening of Mouth" ritual by sculpting his own funerary statue to match his true specifications and measurements. While his performance of the barber may mask his spiritual makeup in the physical realm, the measurements for the funerary statue where his spiritual body will reside proves stunted and underdeveloped like the couple's union. Hidden, the Dew Breaker's spiritual body has not had room to grow and cannot stretch beyond the boundaries of its limitations. Although the ritual is performed by Pharaohs to erect a temple, this chapter builds a funerary statue representative of the Dew Breaker's spiritual body. The combination of the ritual is symbolic of the Dew Breaker's attempt to traverse from his physical reality into the spiritual and is represented by the couple's tenuous union in the chapter. Ultimately, the ritual combination mimics the crossroads. As the "Opening of the Mouth and Eyes" ritual represents the parameters of the Dew Breaker's physical body, the "Stretching of the Cord" ritual represents the parameter of the Dew Breaker's spiritual body. The combination of the ritual representation forms of these two ceremonies serves as a textual temple for the soul and heart.

The chapter "Water Child" signals the novel's shift in focus from the spiritual body to the heart or Ab. As the chapter chronicles the pain and grief of a mother, Nadine, who aborts an unborn fetus, the heart motif is of particular importance. Fittingly, in Ancient Kemet it was theorized that the heart of an unborn child was formed from the mother's blood. Notably, as the heart is the only internal organ left in the body during the mummification process, the heart is believed to represent the totality of an individual and reflect Maat's "seven cardinal virtues . . . truth, justice, propriety, harmony, balance, reciprocity and order."[30] Thus, the weighing of the heart is done with the feather of Maat, and the heart must be equal to the weight of the feather if one is to go into the afterlife. In "Water Child," the overwhelming grief Nadine feels about the loss of her child produces a proverbial heavy heart. Attempting to heal, Nadine performs the Japanese ritual, "Mizuko Jizo," to ease the child's transition into the afterlife and her grief.[31] Similar to the combination of rituals in "Seven," "Water Child" utilizes the Japanese ritual for abortions "Mizuko Jizo" and the Kemetic ritual for entrance into the eternal afterlife "Weighing of the Soul" or heart. Nadine's ability to guide her unborn baby into the eternal afterlife will also determine her ability to move beyond the pain and grief she associates with the abortion.

Outwardly, Nadine masks her inherent pain over the loss of her child with a cool and collective reserve that her coworkers acknowledge and accept and her parents chalk up to Nadine being overworked. However, inwardly Nadine struggles with her choice and even builds and altar where she places mementos from the unborn child's father, Eric—the husband in the preceding chapter "Seven"—and her favorite glass filled with water and a stone. The altar stands as a silent tribute to the unborn child, but also serves as a physical manifestation of the trauma Nadine carries, impregnated, and has yet to birth. Ultimately, Nadine finds the meaning and comfort she needs to face her trauma in an unlikely place and from and unlikely source. The chapter's ritualistic transformation resides in the symbolic act of birth between Nadine and her patient, Ms. Hinds.

In a fit of rage as Ms. Hinds fights the nursing staff, Nadine sees and hears Ms. Hinds through her silence induced by her laryngectomy. Nadine describes Ms. Hinds like a newborn. She is small and hairless "thrashing about" like a newborn baby's traumatic entrance into the world. Nadine instructs the staff to "Leave her alone [and] with her need to struggle suddenly gone, Ms. Hinds curled into a fetal position."[32] Although Ms. Hinds is unable to speak, Nadine inquires of Ms. Hinds's needs. Ms. Hinds is unable to utter the words or sounds she attempts to voice, and Nadine gives her pen and paper. As they begin a written exchange about her inability to speak, Ms. Hinds questions why they would send her home in her state. Nadine tries to provide her with a standard and surface response regarding speech therapists and artificial voice boxes when Ms. Hinds interjects. She scribes: "Feel like a basenji . . . A dog that doesn't bark."[33] Ms. Hinds's description and questioning of her state of being also personifies Nadine's state. Both women are in pain because of their silence. Nadine identifies with Ms. Hinds as both women suffer from a lack of voice. While Ms. Hinds physically cannot speak, Nadine suffers from a spiritual silence. Like Ms. Hinds's surgically induced silence, Nadine's suffers from a traumatically induced silence. However, the two women must cross the barrier of voicelessness to survive. As Ms. Hinds confirms for Nadine that dogs who do not bark really exists, she illuminates the two women's journey to find meaning and existence in the silent landscapes they inhabit.

Ms. Hinds is representative of Nadine's aborted fetus and the transition that the Japanese ritual performs to usher aborted fetuses to the other side of the water. Nadine is like a midwife ushering her from a fetal womb into the physical world. Ms. Hinds's "cerulean-blue hospital gown" is representative of the amniotic fluid that encases a fetus, and missing neck tub is symbolic of the cutting of the umbilical cord. Thus, Nadine's act of helping Ms. Hinds from voicelessness to vocalization through writing transforms and births both women, as Nadine longs for someone to ease her pain and to transfer it to the other side of the water.[34]

As Nadine delivers Ms. Hinds and helps her cross to the other side of the water through the words that inscribe and give her voice, Nadine longs to ease the pain of her own unspoken trauma. Accordingly, that night she calls Eric, with no answer as his number has been changed to one unlisted, and then her parents. In a whisper, she gets through a conversation with her parents but still does not reveal her trauma. Instead, her mother switches from subject to subject, focusing mainly on the birds. As she ends the conversation with her parents, Nadine's mother refers to her as "my heart" and Nadine promises to call again.[35] On the other side of the water, in Haiti, Nadine's mother lends words and meaning to her and gives birth to Nadine's trauma. Nadine's heart is broken.

The following morning, Ms. Hinds emerges to be discharged from the hospital wearing a yellow jogging suit resembling a new baby chick. Nadine wants to give her parting advice but realizes, in the end, like all patients being voiceless is a lifelong and daily trauma that parting words do not have the ability to ease. Nadine's sentiments about parting words for Ms. Hinds, illuminate advice that pertains to her own situation. After saying goodbye and seeing Ms. Hinds off, Nadine stands alone in front of the metal elevator doors acknowledging that "had she carried to full term, her child . . . would have likely been born today."[36] Although Nadine delivers Ms. Hinds, like her unborn child, Nadine must deliver herself. The similarity between the two women forces Nadine to confront her own hurt and trauma, to see herself as a "widened unrecognizable woman staring back at her from the closed elevator doors."[37] Who Nadine presents and who she really conflicts with one another, and as she stands in front of an unrecognizable image of herself the reality is clear. The altar and ritual are supposed to guide her unborn child into the afterlife, to the other side of the water, soothing thirst and suffering with offerings of water. However, Nadine must also guide herself to life on other side of the water.

The heaviness of Nadine's heart and the perceived difficulty of her fetus' journey to the "land of the dead" is indicative of the Dew Breaker's heart and the struggle to cross to the other side. Signaling a failed "weighing of the soul," like Nadine, the Dew Breaker must face his inner truth and trauma that he has carried and hidden during his lifetime. The premature nature of Nadine's abortion further infers the Dew Breaker's underdevelopment and indeterminate status in the afterlife. Regardless, the rituals performed in "Seven" and "Water Child" necessitate movement and transition. The Dew Breaker's body must ascend from a place of physicality and death to a spiritual space, shifting his cosmographic position. After death, the next position on the cosmogram is Musoni. This moment of the sun is characterized as rebirth and represents the soul's journey at midnight. In other words, Musoni is a womb-like position where the soul shifts from physical death into a spiritual rebirth.

The next three chapters in the novel, "The Book of Miracles," "Night Talkers," and "The Bridal Seamstress"—symbolic of the Ka, Ba, and Shadow in the nine affinities—combine to construct the Ancient Kemetic symbol of the Ankh: "Much like the Yoruba orisha Eshu, the deity of the crossroads, the ankh in ancient Egypt, although not a representative of a deity, is a powerful object for social and political transformation."[38] The intertextuality created by the indirect relationship and conversation between these three chapters, and the symbol that they depict, create a textual crossroads for the Dew Breaker's newly formed spiritual body to traverse and connect with his Ka, Ba, and Shadow. Even when he is not directly in the text, a passageway and dialogue exist between the Dew Breaker and the characters, often because of the trauma he once afflicted, within the chapters. The Dew Breaker exists within the pages as a referential shadow-like figure whose presence, even in his physical absence, is felt.

The next phase of Dew Breaker's journey is to form his own double, or Ka. "The Book of Miracles" focuses on a ritual of Christmas Eve mass that the family attends annually and is set in the past and before the Dew Breaker reveals himself to his daughter Ka. The chapter functions as a palimpsest, "turning it into a fragmented collage with as many additions as erasures."[39] "The Book of Miracles" foils and rewrites "The Book of the Dead" from Anne's, the Dew Breaker's wife's, perspective. If one will recall, the novel begins with Ka and her father traveling to and from Florida, and the continuum of time allows a textual double of a space and time where Anne becomes a double of herself. Anne, as the Dew Breaker does, forms her Ka and exists at the intersection of the physical and the spiritual realm, the crossroads. Physically, within mass, Anne invokes the Virgin Mary as she sits next to Ka on the pew. As a physical double, Anne recalls the death of her brother who drowns as she is having an epileptic seizure on the shore. Never reclaiming his body, Anne images the young lost soul of her brother being found and claimed by the Virgin Mary: "Anne hoped that the Virgin would choose her young brother to go up to Heaven and sing with the choir of angels . . . and if he were chosen to go up to Heaven, maybe the Holy Mother would keep him there."[40] Therefore, the Dew Breaker serves as her brother's double, a lost soul who Anne imagines saving from an eternity of limbo or purgatory. Spiritually, Anne functions for the Dew Breaker as an Isis figure resurrecting her husband by piecing together the scattered pieces of his body that his double life creates; he is at once the barber and the Dew Breaker. Anne births Ka, like Isis births Horus to right a wrong, to redeem the Dew Breaker. As an earthly Isis, or Virgin Mary figure as Isis is sometimes depicted, Anne is unable to perform miracles to ensure her brother's rank among the angels or, as Isis does for Osiris, to resurrect her husband and give birth to a "good angel" or a Ka. So, every Christmas Eve Anne quietly hopes and prays her brother, although already dead, and the Dew Breaker, although an adult, would be chosen by the Virgin Mary to enter heaven. Thus, "midnight on Christmas Eve . . . The gates of Paradise were opened [and] The Virgin Mary was choosing among the sleeping children of the world for some to invite to Heaven to serenade her son."[41]

Memory and the movement of time within the chapter resurrects and transforms the narrative space. The text moves between the past and present in various ways. For example, Anne's memory of her brother's death shifts her, and the reader, into a liminal space between the present moment of the mass and the memory of her brother and his death. Likewise, Ka's false identification of the Dew Breaker recalls her father's past and, also, punctuates his confession in the first chapter. This amplifies and underscores the separation between father and daughter after his confession. Although her ignorance of the Dew Breaker's identity still exists in the physical and real time that the chapter represents, Ka believes she recognizes the Dew Breaker, Emmanuel Constant who is wanted for the crimes he committed in Haiti. However, the irony at play here is that during mass she is oblivious of her father's identity, but Ka spiritually recognizes her father's true Ka. To do so, Ka must exist simultaneously in both realms. In the physical realm, Ka rebirths her father's confession. The space the confession creates allows Ka to simultaneously exist in the spiritual realm and to rebirth and replace the prisoner image of the Dew Breaker that she sculpts in the past with the tortuous and criminal figure Ka believes she see during the mass, Emmanuel Constant. Although both men are Dew Breakers, their "offenses were separated by thirty-plus years," a clear reference to Papa Doc and Baby Doc's regimes.[42] Conversely, instead of the Dew Breaker confessing to her like he does in "The Book of the Dead," in "The Book of Miracles" Ka sees his true and natural form and reveals his Ka to him. In the end, the man that Ka identifies is not Emmanuel Constant but an unassuming parishioner, which plays on the double identity of her father. At the end of mass when Ka attempts to grab Constant's hand to get a good look at him, "her father reached over, lowered it, and held it to her side until the man was beyond her reach."[43] A mimesis moment in "The Book of the Dead" when he grabs her wrists as she laughs in anger at his confession creates a doubling, or the Dew Breaker's Ka.

The duality of the chapter is also demonstrated through Anne and Ka's interaction and conversation. Within the present time in the physical realm, Anne maintains the consistent and omissive narrative about Dew Breaker. The openness of the spiritual realm allows Anne a doubling of voice and narrative. Anne wants to confess the Dew Breaker's identity to her daughter and demonstrate that he is not the same man. The chapter's ending recalls, "That was the miracle that Anne wanted to share with her daughter on this Christmas Eve night, the simple miracle of her husband's transformation . . . so instead she told of another kind of miracle."[44] However, in the act of retelling miracles, Anne creates a space to confess the truth of the past with the clarity of the present. Therefore, Anne's memories bring Ka back to the space and place where miracles are performed. As Anne tries to rebirth the Dew Breaker's image, simultaneously Ka rebirths his true Ka. She identifies a man who she believes was a Dew Breaker, giving shape and contour to the likeness of her father she could not sculpt. In mass, as Anne relishes in her "favorite sixty seconds of the year. . . . Her daughter chose that exact moment" to point out Emmanuel Constant.[45] This moment between mother and daughter reinforces the duality of realms and good and evil present within the text; Anne illuminates the good of heaven, and Ka the evils of hell. Anne's image of her innocent brother in heaven reconstructs or reassembles his body within that realm like Isis reclaims Osiris's parts and pieces him back together. Conversely, Ka's recognition and identification, albeit false, of Emmanuel Constant bring into the mass the presence of corruption and evil of a man accused of crimes against his brothers and sisters, like Set. The coexistence of good and evil creates a textual overlap of myth.[46] In the end, Ka explains to Anne that she was not going to hurt the man, she only wants to ask his name. Ka explains: "I wouldn't do anything like that. I don't know what happened. I wasn't there." Anne responds in a silent confession, "but I was."[47] Like her silent confession, Anne's silence about her husband, particularly her lack of discursiveness with Ka, renders her an accomplice to the horrors and atrocities the Dew Breaker commits.

Symbolic of the soul passing from one realm to the next, the chapter "Night Talkers" emphasizes the journey of the soul or Ba.[48] Representative of transcendence, the Ba travels between life and death and illustrates the ancestral interaction between the realms as well. The journey of the Ba illuminates the concept of the cosmogram via the crossroads and demonstrates the journey the soul embarks upon to rebirth itself after judgment. The soul, detached of a physical form to reside within, takes flight carrying with it the essence of the person, and, thus, transforming the death of the physical body into the rebirth of a spiritual one.

Dany, in the "Night Talkers," travels back to a remote village in a Haitian
mountain range to visit his Aunt Estina. Dany and Estina share a particularly
close bond because she raised him after his parents are killed by the Tonton
Macoute in a case of mistaken identity. Estina and Dany, who escape the
family's burning home, survive, but Estina is permanently blinded by the fire.
Dany, who left Haiti for New York ten years previously, returns to his aunt's
home in the mountains, that is surrounded by "the teal ten-place mausoleum
that harbored the bones of many of her forebears."[49] Dany must ascend a
mountain to his aunt's house. A physically arduous journey, Dany's ascent to
Aunt Estina's home symbolizes the land of the ancestors and his soul's journey to understanding the consequences of good and evil, and the path of one's
soul after a decision is waged and weighed like one's heart on Maat's scale.

Accordingly, "Night Talkers," provides the novel with a representation of
the Maatian ritual of the "weighing of souls." Back in New York, Dany finds
himself at a crossroads with the man he identifies as his parent's killer. Living
in his basement for months, Dany is given the chance to avenge his parent's
death and kill the Dew Breaker. His life, unbeknownst to the Dew Breaker,
is in Dany's hand. However, "Night Talkers" underscores the divine decree
associated with the ability to give and to take away life. The consequences
of usurping divine power for one's own benefit overwhelms Dany. Looming
over the Dew Breaker, Dany loses his longing to kill him:

> He was too angry for pity. It was something else, something less measurable. It
> was the dread of being wrong, of harming the wrong man, or making the wrong
> woman a widow and the wrong child an orphan. It was the realization that . . .
> one single person had been given the power to destroy his entire life.[50]

The chapter is steeped in Ancient Kemetic traditions and symbols. However,
the localization of the narrative in Haiti prompts an intermingling with the
crossroads deity Papa Légbá.[51] Climbing over a mountain leading to his Aunt
Estina's home, Dany is struck with severe pain because of the altitude and
finds himself lost and unsure about the path he has taken to her house. He
looks for signposts to reassure him, "there were many paths to his aunt's
house, and seeing the lone saguaro had convinced him that he was on one of
them."[52] However, Dany arrives at a village and encounters a Legba figure
who leads him to his Aunt's house.

Old Zo is "toothless . . . with a grizzly white bread and a face full of folds
and creases that deemed to map out every road he had traveled in his life."[53]
Legba is described as the "gatekeeper who owns all the options or roads.
. . . The messenger between God, the orisha, and mankind."[54] While he maintains his powers in the "New World," in Haiti, Papa Légbá is described as a
mature counter to his Continental image and presence: "They say that he is an

old peasant who has worked his fields hard all his life and is now at the end of his powers." As the crossroads deity, Légbá's presence in the physical and the spiritual realm is required. A symbol of Légbá's reach and grasp in the realms is the "center-post of the peristyle, called the *poteau-Legba.*"[55] Fittingly Old Zo, after greeting Dany, holds firmly onto one of three posts stabilizing his house. After being offered a gourd filled with water and lighting a pipe, Old Zo asks, "where are you going, my son?" When Dany relays that he is there to see his aunt, the old man said, "Come, I'll take you to Estina Estème."[56]

Representative of the return to one's origin, Dany seems to continue to spiritually travel even though he has reached his destination of Estina's home. Although the mountain ranges are barren, Estina's home is thriving with life. Among his ancestors, Dany is taken beyond the physical landscape of his surroundings. The next morning, Dany is sent to bathe in the stream at the end of the waterfall behind his Aunt's house. A daily ritual and representative of a new day, bathing in nature connects back to ancient practices and rituals. In the land of his ancestors, Dany engages this ritual with vigor. Submerging his body in the cold water, Dany says that "he welcomed the sensation of having almost every muscle in his body contract, as if to salute the dawn."[57] Dawn, or Kala on the cosmogram, is the moment of birth when sun is rising and giving form to a soul rebirthed. Dany enters the water, a spiritual watery womb, and emerges to the surface a cleansed and freshened being. Symbolic of his soul's movement on the cosmogram, Dany meets Claude who Estina has sent for and is "one of the boys who was sent back."[58] A doubling of the possibility of Dany's fate, Claude murdered his father in New York, and, after his release from jail, is deported back to Haiti, a country and a people foreign to him. Claude expresses to Dany that the community, and, especially Estina, has been good to him: "She's really taken me under her wing." "Claude flapped his heavily tattooed arms, as if to illustrate the word 'wing.'"[59] Claude's reference to bird wings is symbolic of Maat divine laws and principles. Establishing Estina as a Maatian-like figure, Claude opens the realms for Dany to travel through spiritually. Although physically blind, Estina's spiritual eye knows Dany needs to see the consequences of his actions. Dany, through Claude, is able to weigh his heart on Maat's scale. Thus, Dany's purpose in returning to Haiti is punctuated by Claude's forced return, as one of the ones sent back because his heart was not as light as a feather.

That night, Dany fully reveals his purpose in coming. In a dream state, Dany tells his aunt that he has found the Dew Breaker. Sleeping is the medium that allows Estina and Dany to simultaneously exist in both the physical and the spiritual realms. Their night talking is indicative of the Ba leaving and returning to the body, journeying at night. Dany is awakened by the sound of his own voice and finds Estina awake too. After apologizing for waking her, Estina says that she should have let him tell the whole story of why he returned. Yet, as Dany begins to question her about his parent's death, Estina offers him the last words she will ever utter: "There is a belief that if you kill people, you can take their knowledge, become everything that they were. Maybe they wanted to take all that knowledge for themselves."[60]

Aunt Estina's physical blindness lends her a spiritual inner eye indicative of Maat's virtues and principles. Estina's parting words to Dany provide him with the insight of not only the consequences of killing the Dew Breaker, but also the divine law and judgment as part and parcel of a decision to kill. It is through the words spoken somewhere between consciousness and slumber that Estina meets Dany at the crossroads. Speaking into his consciousness, Estina changes Dany's course of action.[61] In death, Aunt Estina continues guide Dany, and her principles and virtues exists with her in the physical and spiritual realm. As Estina's soul is transitioning from the physical realm to the spiritual realm, her Ba taking flight, her body is dressed in a blue dress representing Maat and the seventh principle of her virtues, reciprocity. In an act to preserve her physical memory, Dany performs a ritual of transformation and symbolizes the transition of a soul from one realm to the next: "He's heard his aunt talk about this ritual, this branding of final cloths, but he had never seen it done before."[62] With the power of Estina's insight, Dany cuts pieces of her burial dress, and "now in his pocket he had three tiny pieces of cloth that had been removed from the lining of his aunt's last dress, and he would carry them forever."[63] In the morning hours of Aunt Estina's burial, Dany sees himself in Claude, and realizes how easily he could have been him. In the end, Dany honors his aunt by living and practicing what she represents. "The only thing Dany could think to do for his aunt now was to keep Claude speaking . . . since Claude was already a member of their tribe . . . a night talker."[64]

The "Bridal Seamstress" chronicles a seemingly trivial interaction between a young reporter, Aline, and a bridal seamstress, Beatrice. Aline is sent to cover what she considers an insignificant story about a locally famous Haitian wedding dress maker's, Beatrice, retirement. However, the story Aline uncovers about Beatrice's life far outweighs her beat assignment. Beatrice recounts to Aline the horror she suffered in Haiti at the hands of the Dew Breaker. Beatrice believes that the Dew Breaker is now a prison guard and follows her as she moves from place to place, living in her neighborhood. When Aline inquires whether Beatrice is sure that it is the same man from all those years ago, she replies that "I would know him anywhere."[65] The image of the Dew Breaker is seared into Beatrice's memory. Representative of the Kemetic notion of the shadow, Beatrice's narrative stiches together, like her wedding dresses, the lasting impact of the trauma she suffers at the hands of the Dew Breaker. Thus, the "Bridal Seamstress" reflects the stories that plague people in the shadows long after a trauma occurs.

Symbolic of the bridal attire she hand-sews, Beatrice wears her trauma like a garment. Beatrice's description of the wedding dresses she makes reveals her complete embodiment with the dresses: "The way I see it, I am that dress. It's like everyone is looking at me."[66] Aline shatters the respectful distance Beatrice shares with her "girls," as she makes the brides-to-be call her "mother," by inquiring if Beatrice has ever been married. Beatrice scolds Aline insisting that young women should not ask older women about their marital status. Beatrice says "I've never wanted to be asked that question. That's why the girls call me Mother."[67] Aline's line of questioning opens the realms of communication, and Beatrice reveals the intimate details of her trauma. When the Dew Breaker, back in Haiti, asks her on a date, Beatrice refuses because she is involved with someone. As a punishment, the Dew Breaker arrests and tortures her: "He tied me to some type of rack in the prison and whipped the bottom of my feet until they bled. Then he made me walk home. Barefoot. On tar roads. In the hot sun. At high noon."[68] Rather than the typical ghostly haunting when an apparition seeks out someone to haunt, Beatrice says that she finds the Dew Breaker wherever she goes or lives. What seems to haunt Beatrice the most is what she has lost, love. Her precision and obsession with wedding dresses underscores the loss of her possibility of marriage, and ultimately love. This loss continues to conjure with each of the dresses she sews, quietly lurking in the crevices of her mind and spirit. Aptly, when Aline conveys to her that the house where Beatrice says the Dew Breaker lives is, in fact, empty, Beatrice explains: "That's where he hides out these days, in empty houses."[69] While his physical presence is not manifest, the Dew Breaker's spirit, or in this case shadow, exists on the periphery. For Beatrice, the Dew Breaker is present in each of the girls she dresses, plaguing happy unions like her own.

The joining of the Ka, Ba, and shadow in the chapters "The Book of Miracles," "Night Talkers," and "The Bridal Mistress" form the ultimate Kemetic symbol, the Ankh. Signifying life, the ankh aligns all forces in the universe into a "creation of new life."[70] Tracing the movement of one's soul on the cosmogram, the ankh connects with the moment of the sun, Kala or birth: "Symbolically, the oval represents the womb, the vertical shaft depicts the phallus and the horizontal bar expresses the coming into existence of a new life."[71] Moreover, the ankh's ideographic similarity to the Christian cross forms an image of the crossroads signaling movement from one realm to the next. Utilizing the repetition of myth and song, the chapters "Monkey Tails" and "The Funeral Singer" give birth to a new spirit and form beyond the Dew Breaker's spiritual construction thus far.

Encased between the past and the future, "Monkey Tails" constructs a new spiritual container for the sons of Haiti to exist within. Utilizing modernized forms of communication, the chapter imbeds, through the act of storytelling, a contemporary encapsulation of myth. In modern epistolary form, Michel records his story on cassettes for his soon to be born son.[72] "Monkey Tails" reiterates the story of two friends, Michel and Romain, who spend their young lives searching for fathers that they find at the end of the Duvalier regime's rule; the chapter begins the day the elder Duvalier's son and political successor, Jean Claude, also known as Baby Doc, flees Haiti for France in exile. Even though Michel and Romain's fathers are in plain sight most of their lives, neither will not claim the boys, and their mother's provide mythical versions of their fathers to them. However, both boys know the truth about their fathers. Michel is a product of an affair between his mother and Monsieur Christophe, a local owner of a water station; Romain's father, Regulus, is a member of the reviled Tonton Macoute and rejected Romain as an infant. The narrative takes a turn when, at the height of civil celebration and disruption caused by the younger Duvalier's exile. Romain leaves Haiti in search of his father who he believes has fled the country, and Romain tells Michel: "Know thyself and you will know the world of the gods."[73] Even though Romain tells him that he must leave the country, Michel knows that Romain seeks his father. The friends never see or hear from each other again.

While both of their fathers never acknowledge them, creating a "generation of mostly fatherless boys," it is upon Michel's shoulders to live the proverbial tale of monkeys: "Some tree Monkeys have tails that are longer than their bodies tails that they use to swing from tree to tree."[74] Michel escapes the grips of his past and lays a foundation for the future, laying to rest the narrative body or myths told to them by their mothers about their fathers. "Monkey Tails" finds the space between the two friends, a brotherhood, that transcends time and space and creates a new narrative about what it means to be a friend and a father:

> I tell and retell the myth that my mother so carefully crafted and guarded for me, that my father perished before I was born. . . . As for you, my son, your myth is this . . . if you're born today, on this the anniversary of the day that everything changed for me, on the day that I became a man, your name will be Romain, after my first true friend.[75]

As a tribute to his friend, Romain, Michel tells his yet-to-be born son the origin of his name, Romain. Employing the myth of his father, Michel disassociates from the reality and truth of his fatherlessness at the hands of an absentee father, and takes on a new narrative, albeit mythical, legacy, and tradition for his son. By doing so, Michel constructs a narrative story congruent with the person who taught him how to be a man, Romain, and to provide his son with a name and patriarchal lineage. Haiti, as a nation, is on the precipice of birthing a new national identity and spirit with the fleeing of Duvalier and his regime, the new terrain symbolizes the sons of Haiti, like Michel's son, are no longer ruled by an absentee father, and can find a lineage in freedom.

The results of the Duvalier regimes can be felt throughout this novel, but the migratory pattern of those effected is exemplified in "The Funeral Singer," which chronicles the lives of three Haitian women who meet at a secretarial school and form a friendship during the fourteen-week course. The course is supposed to help the women find gainful employment to recreate lives in the United States. Two of the women have been exiled from Haiti. However, all three have suffered trauma at the hands of the Duvalier regime. Mariselle left Haiti because husband was killed as a result of an unbecoming picture he painted of the president. Reiza, who owns the Haitian restaurant where the women gather after class, and the only one passing the practice tests at school, was raped as a girl by one of the Tonton Macoute. Freda was asked to leave by her mother after she refuses to sing at the national palace. Each of the women are trying to come to terms with their identity and form a new life in the nebulous space of limbo. Their transnational, especially as a result of forced migration, existence requires a negotiation of a new place that is now home and an old home that is now a place. Punctuated by the impending exam that two of the women seem likely to fail, "The Funeral Singer" utilizes the repetition of song to explore the implication of exile, forced or self-imposed, on lives of these three women.

Through the evolution of her most beloved funeral song, "Brother Timonie," Freda forms her identity. The song begins and ends her narrative, following her progression throughout the story. In class, she wishes she could sing the song as her introduction so that "everyone would be listening too hard to look at me."[76] Professional mourners or funeral singers were also commonplace in Kemet and are recorded in funerary scenes and texts like "The Book of the Dead." In ancient times, the singers sang songs to the dead. Freda always sings Brother Timonie, her "father's fishing song," at funerals and says that "sometimes I improvise my own, right there, next to the coffin."[77] As Freda recounts the song to Mariselle and Reiza, the women join in and sing in triplicate. Thus, the song takes place in the past, present, and the future. Memorializing her father and the dead, Freda also extemporizes her own song. Through the repetition of funerary rites, the song takes on a new form.

"The Funeral Singer" emphasizes the fate of the three women by utilizing the triplicate nature the song takes on in the text. Freda says: "My mother used to say that we'll all have three deaths: the one when our breath leaves our bodies to rejoin the air, the one when we are put back in the earth, and the one that will erase us completely and no one will remember us at all."[78] Each one of the deaths correlate to the women and represents their past, present, and future. Mariselle acquires a job in a gallery and will sell some of her husband's paintings. Reiza, who already has a restaurant, and is steeped to pass the course's exam, is a transplant whose has found a new home to establish roots. However, Freda, who is one of the last remaining "professional funeral singers of my generation," has an ambiguous fate.[79] When asked by Mariselle and Reiza what she plans to do at the end of the course, Freda says that she will join a militia and go back to Haiti and fight. Telling Freda that her fate is death, Reiza asks who will sing Freda's funeral song. As it is clear no one will sing Freda's funeral song, the women ask her to sing it for them now. Reiza adds: "We'll help you."[80] In what Freda deems her "final performance," she sings "Brother Timonie" and, "Reiza and Mariselle catch on quickly and join in. We sing until our voices grow hoarse, sometimes making Brother Timonie a sister."[81] Freda's tenuous fate seems destined for death, lending power and significance to her song. The addition of the other women's voices allows Freda's presence and her song to exists within the physical and spiritual realm. The women will carry the memory of Freda and her song, so regardless of where Freda exists, her song exists in memorial on both sides of the water, Haiti and America.

While the long-lasting effects of the trauma that he inflicts upon his fellow citizen will follow him into the ever-after, in the end, the true name of the Dew Breaker is never revealed. The question of whether he is able to transform is, ultimately, up to the great scale in the Hall of Maat. However, what lingers on is the story of his atrocities in the lives of his fellow brothers and sisters of Haiti. And, if the novel's title is any indication, who he was before he was a Dew Breaker has been long since forgotten and his name and identity are simultaneously "The Dew Breaker." Overarchingly, the last chapter retells the myth of Osiris and the closing of funerary ritual and the spiritual transformation of the Dew Breaker.

The last chapter, "The Dew Breaker," is the ultimate act of transformation and catapults the titular character into his own realm of being, forming the full narrative body of his existence before he leaves Haiti. Told in thirteen parts, the chapter recounts the trauma that brings the Dew Breaker and Anne together, piecing together the past like Isis reconstructs Osiris's body. The entirety of his story is divulged and everyone and everything is named except the Dew Breaker. Kemetic tradition dictates that "if the name of a man is destroyed, then they would be erased."[82] Although his role within the Duvalier regime is named, the Dew Breaker's true identity is never revealed. This glaring omission seems to indicate that his deeds in Haiti outweigh any of his deeds thereafter, and, perhaps, his name like his identity are eternally erased. Traversing from the past to the present, the chapter shows the devolution of the Dew Breaker and the evolution of the father we meet at the beginning of the novel, and, as the previously discussed chapters, this writes anew the family's history. "The Dew Breaker" transcribes a new form through the retelling of his past. On the surface, the transformation the omniscient narrator describes seems to be the Dew Breaker's, but the reader's knowledge of the past crosses time and space and transmutes the narrative into a crossroads where myth cannot only be revised but rewritten. Thus, the chapter's focus is transformation and higher consciousness.

"The Dew Breaker" recounts the murder of Anne's brother and Ka's uncle, the "Famous Preacher" in jail because of his truth-telling radio show and Sunday sermons. Because of the handling of the arrest, the Dew Breaker is told to release the preacher. He tells the preacher that "all I want to tell you is that you must stop what you've been doing."[83] The Dew Breaker tries to convince the preacher that he will be free if he stops espousing rhetoric that is damaging to the image of the government and men of "law." Moving closer to the preacher, the Dew Breaker attempts to help the preacher out of his chair and release him. The chair collapses and shatters into multiple pieces, like Osiris scattered body pieces, as the preacher tries to move away from the Dew Breaker and his extended hand. The preacher believing that he is going to be killed, "grabbed the piece of wood and aimed . . . to strike the fat man's eye, but instead the spiked stub ended up in the man's right cheek and sank in an inch or so."[84] The fat man, or the Dew Breaker, shoots the preacher to death, and brother kills brother.

Symbolic of the scattered pieces of Osiris, the Dew Breaker is unable to restore or mend back together the broken bits because he is complicit in the evil acts, like Set murdering his brother Osiris. Thus, the myth must be rewritten and recreated. Here the preacher is representative of a father and brother (Osiris) and, in death, the son of God/Haiti (Horus). In addition, the concept of goodness (light) embodies a crossroads and provides the narrative opening to shift the myth in form and structure. As Horus avenges his father's death, Set, his uncle, stabs his eye. The Preacher and uncle miss the Dew Breaker's eye but scars his face. Instead of the Dew Breaker transforming into the "all seeing" spiritual symbol Horus's eye depicts, he is left with a physical blemish he must explain each time he is asked, reliving and recalling all the trauma he inflicted as a Dew Breaker. The preacher recounts: "Every time people asked what happened to his face, he would have to tell a lie, a lie that would further remind him of the truth."[85] The singular act of lying, cements his identity as the Dew Breaker and is the method he must use to conceal his identity. While he may present himself as a good person, the truth of the scar defines the evils he has committed.

The role of good and evil are inverted because of the positionality of the uncle in this revamped mythical expression. "Cosmologically, Set (Satan) represents the setting sun (sunset), which brings on darkness (evil, fear and ignorance). Horus personifies the forces of life and his symbol (the rising sun) banishes the night and overpowers the forces of evil."[86] However, unlike the myth Anne, or Isis, and the Dew Breaker's paths have not intersected. So, the uncle takes on his role as Anne's brother and the Set like figure transposes to the Dew Breaker. The incident scars the Dew Breaker physically, as his scarred face becomes not only a part of his outward physical identity, but also his spiritual presence. Even when he physically loses weight on the other side of the water, he is not transformed. The Dew Breaker does nothing to change spiritually, in fact, he conceals his true self from everyone except Anne. Ironically, through his death, it is the Preacher who is transformed into the symbol. What is left is the sign of evil, like the mark of the beast that the Dew Breaker must wear as a badge for the rest of his life, so his only choice is to flee, shedding his former life like a snake sheds skin.

The story echoes the action of Ka's father when he destroys the statue in the beginning of the text. The preacher sees his brothers being destroyed in jail and refuses to succumb to the same fate: "They were being destroyed piece by piece, day by day, disappearing like the flesh from their bones."[87] The statue of the prisoner, "Naked, kneeling . . . his back arched . . . his downcast eyes," is finally given a true likeness of the preacher who is, ironically, Anne's brother, the Dew Breaker's brother-in-law, and Ka's uncle.[88] Danticat utilizes the concept of the other side of the water to link the narratives, and it is as if the statue was thrown into the primordial waters of Nun to be transformed throughout the novel. Through the retelling, Ka's creation transforms identity and forms the person she tries so desperately to recreate, giving a name and definition to the prey, her uncle the preacher.

The Dew Breaker's defiant act of killing the preacher, despite being told otherwise, disrupts his narrative and forces him to leave. Although he eventually wants to leave Haiti, he envisions quietly slipping away and disappearing on his own terms. Killing the preacher forces the Dew Breaker, whether he is ready or not, to change the course, and, thus, the narrative, of his life. The mythical shift of the narrative positions him at the crossroads. "At first he was alone out there near the gates."[89] The other guards form a circle around him and watch him vomit the entire content of his stomach. Empty, "Rosalie signaled for the gatekeeper, whom the wardens had nicknamed Legba, to open the gates to let him out. . . . He walked through the front gate thinking that he was going to shot in the back, either by one of his colleagues or by Legba, the gatekeeper."[90] Crossing the threshold of the gate, leaving one realm, and moving to the next, the Dew Breaker and Anne physically collide. Anne is there to inquire of her brother, the preacher. They both utter pleas to each other. The Dew Breaker desires Anne's pity and healing, while Anne wants to gain entry to the prison to find her brother. Knowing that Anne could not enter the prison without becoming a prisoner or that he could not reenter without succumbing to the same of fate of death as his last victim, the Dew Breaker rushes Anne away from the prison and back to his house.

The next morning, Anne traverses her own crossroads before fleeing with the Dew Breaker to the United States. Before she leaves his room in the wee hours of the morning to get something to aide in healing the side of his face, Anne watches "an early-morning funeral procession on its way to the cemetery."[91] The marketplace, a representative marker of Legba and the crossroads, Anne gathers items from a vendor. Not having any money, the vendors asks if she is "Buying these for a sick person."[92] He allows her to take the items at no cost. When Anne returns, she asks: "What did they do to *you*? This was the most forgiving question he'd ever been asked."[93] She assumes, as the Dew Breaker will assume as his persona and identity in the "new world" of New York to which they flee, that he is not the "the hunter and not the prey" he later confesses to be to Ka.[94] With the help of Anne, his Isis, the Dew Breaker flees embodied and emblazoned in his new identity and persona. Newly constructed, the Dew Breaker's narrative body is replete and spiritual container is complete.

By becoming the container of the spirit of the Haitian People's mythical narrative, *The Dew Breaker* is transformed into a divine funerary text. Danticat transports her readers back to the diasporically-centered narrative that utilizes the cosmological and ontological underpinnings of Ancient Kemet to create alternative space to reimagine and revise historical traumas plaguing diasporic people. Through myth, Danticat weaves a spiritual narrative capable of redeeming and transforming history into a living and breathing entity rather than a fixture of the past. Instead, she breaks the mold of traditional Western historiography and writes anew a narrative body that relays the narrative of the people through the voice of the people.

NOTES

1. The harsh dictatorship of both Papa Doc, Francois Duvalier, and his son, Jean Claude Duvalier or Baby Doc, are well documented.

2. Edwidge Danticat. *The Dew Breaker* (New York: Vintage Books, 2005), 20.

3. Although there are various versions of Osiris' myth, this chapter utilizes E. A. Wallis Budge. trans. *The Book of the Dead: The Papyrus of Ani in the British Museum.* (New York: Dover Publications, 1967).

4. Ibid., 14.

5. *The Book of Coming Forth by Day*, erroneously titled *The Book of the Dead* as articulated by Maulana Karenga in *Maat: The Moral Ideal in Ancient Egypt*, "refers to a process which involves breaking the bonds of death and grave and coming forth to bask in sunlight in a spiritual sense. It is both a vision and aspiration to overcome death, to go and come freely in heaven and earth, and assume any form in any place one's spirit wishes to be" Karenga, Maulana. *Maat, the Moral Ideal in Ancient Egypt:*

A Study in Classical African Ethics (Los Angeles: University of Sankore Press, 2006), 131–132.

6."Because Osiris represents eternal life, the nb'nkh [sarcophagus] is designed to protect the body for eternity, ensure the well-being of the deceased in the afterlife, and provide a house for the ka." Molefi K. Asante and Ama Mazama. *Encyclopedia of African Religion* (Thousand Oaks: Sage, 2009), 595.

7. Ibid., 137.

8. Ibid., 14.

9. Ritual elements work on multiple levels. While they ritualize a physical space, they also provide an opening between the physical and spiritual realm. Although not a comprehensive list, Somé includes the imperative elements in the structure of ritual, which include Invocation, Dialog, Repetition, and Opening and Closure. Of note, Abu Shardow Abarry, author of "Mpai: Libation Oratory," in his discussion of ritual, lists Invocation, Introduction, Supplication, and Conclusion as elements of ritual structure Kariamu Welsh-Asante. *The African Aesthetic: Keeper of the Traditions* (Westport: Greenwood Press, 1993), 93.

10. Accordingly, "*The Book of the Dead* is a compilation of about 200 chants or spells [and . . . allude to the internal makeup of man and his struggles within himself as reflected in the nine inseparable affinities of man." The eponymously titled chapter, "The Book of the Dead," acts as the text's invocation and inscribes the meaning of the text that ensues, as chapter one forms the container for the Dew Breaker's funerary text that will succeed the "continuation of the soul's journey," Asante, *Encyclopedia*, 137.

11. Danticat, *Dew Breaker*, 3.

12. Ibid., 6.

13. Ibid., 6.

14. Ibid., 6.

15. Ibid., 18.

16. In Kemet, nature represents divine nature: "it was understood and believed that the most solid and authentic grounding of natural reality was Maat because it made the stars shine, the sun gives life, the river overflow, and the king the great representative of the divine on Earth." Asante, *Encyclopedia*, 399.

17. Danticat, *Dew Breaker*, 20.

18. Accordingly, "within *The Book of the Dead* the people were able to see the elaboration of the battle between good and evil, such as the story of Horus and Set." Asante, *Encyclopedia*, 137.

19. Danticat, *Dew Breaker*, 20.

20. "One could not imagine that the Ka would enter an unritualized statue, and the only way for the deceased to be assured of eternal life was for the Ka to live. Thus, the ceremony had to be performed." Asante, *Encyclopedia*, 494.

21. Suitably, "the ritual illustrates a concept of sculpture as birth. This concept finds expression in the Egyptian language, in its vocabulary for sculpture: The fashioning of the image is 'giving birth.'" In the "'Opening of the Mouth,'" the special ritual implements for consecration may derive from blades used in childbirth." Ann Macy

Roth. "Fingers, Stars, and the 'Opening of the Mouth': The Nature and Function of the Ntrwj-Blades." *The Journal of Egyptian Archaeology* 79 (1993): 57–79.

22. Danticat, *Dew Breaker*, 48.

23. Ibid., 49.

24. Ibid., 49.

25. Ibid., 51.

26. Accordingly, Seshat represents the number seven and her symbol is a flower with seven petals. Seshat is often depicted with a palm frond atop her head symbolizing the passage of time. She is most noted for a ritual of time and measurement called the "Stretching of the Cord," which Pharaoh's used to outline the specification and measurements for a temple: "The idea of Seshat assisting the king in the ritual of 'stretching the cord' for proportional measurement . . . can be advanced to explain the inspiration . . . to achieve *Maat* (i.e., balance, harmony, and straightness)." Seshat's union with Djhuity is also significant. Seshat who is the ruler of books, even referred to as a librarian, and Djhuity who is the scribe of the afterlife, in combination, comprise the book of the afterlife, or the Book of the Dead. The union of these divine scribes forms a complete and divine text. Moreover, Seshat's representative number seven is often conceptualized as a divine number representing completion just as a union should encompass. Asante, *Encyclopedia*, 609.

27. Danticat, *Dew Breaker*, 51.

28. Ibid., 51.

29. Ibid., 52.

30. Anthony T. Browder. *Nile Valley Contributions to Civilization: Study Guide.* Exploding the Myths, Vol. 1 (Washington, DC: Institute of Karmic Guidance, 1994), 82.

31. The ritual, "'Mizuko Jizo' literally means Bodhisattva, or potential Buddha, of the water-babies." The ritual's performance is meant to help aborted fetuses get to the "land of the dead." Although the ritual originated for both miscarriages and abortions, contemporarily the ritual is more commonly performed for abortions. Sheryl WuDunn. "In Japan, a Ritual of Mourning for Abortions." *New York Times* (1996): 145.

32. Danticat, *Dew Breaker*, 60.

33. Ibid., 62.

34. Ibid., 60–61.

35. Ibid., 62.

36. Ibid., 68.

37. Danticat, *Dew Breaker*, 68.

38. Asante, *Encyclopedia*, 61.

39. Danticat, *Dew Breaker*, 79.

40. Ibid., 77.

41. Ibid., 77.

42. Ibid., 80.

43. Ibid., 83.

44. Ibid., 72–73.

45. Ibid., 77–78.

46. "Within *The Book of the Dead*, the people were able to see the elaboration of the battle between good and evil, such as the story of Horus and Set." Asante, *Encyclopedia*, 137.

47. Danticat, *Dew Breaker*, 86.

48. In Ancient Kemet, "the Ba was represented by the bearded head of a man on the body of a hawk. . . . The bird's body represented the soul's ability to move between heaven and Earth." Browder, *Nile Valley Contributions to Civilization*, 91.

49. Danticat, *Dew Breaker*, 93.

50. Ibid., 107.

51. "Legba . . . is himself the destined answer to the riddle of the Sphinx: he was once the new-born infant son, lived through the fertile prime of his noon, and is now the old sun, walking with a cane—the third leg." As the quotes suggests, Legba grows out of the ancient tradition, practices, and beliefs of Ancient Kemet. His status at the crossroads is the answer to the riddle of the Sphinx and, thus, crosses time and space. Gary Edwards and John Mason. *Black Gods—Òrìṣà Studies in the New World*. Rev. 4th (Brooklyn, NY: Yorùbá Theological Archministry, 1998), 98–99.

52. Danticat, *Dew Breaker*, 109.

53. Ibid., 91.

54. Edwards, *Black Gods*, 11–12.

55. Maya Deren. *Divine Horsemen: Voodoo Gods of Haiti* (New York: Chelsea House, 1970), 97.

56. Danticat, *Dew Breaker*, 91–93.

57. Ibid., 99.

58. Ibid., 100.

59. Ibid., 101.

60. Ibid., 109.

61. It is argued that "Nommo is remarkably present in powerful utterances that are based in Maatic principles." Asante, *Encyclopedia*, 455.

62. Danticat, *Dew Breaker*, 113.

63. Ibid., 113.

64. Ibid., 120.

65. Ibid., 132.

66. Ibid., 127.

67. Ibid., 127.

68. Ibid., 132.

69. Ibid., 137.

70. Asante, *Encyclopedia*, 67.

71. Asante, *Encyclopedia*, 67

72. "When the Egyptian wrote a letter or a treatise, one of the most appropriate endings was to wish for the recipient all life, or eternal life, *ankh neheh.*" Asante, *Encyclopedia*, 59.

73. Danticat, *Dew Breaker*, 153.

74. Ibid., 163.

75. Ibid., 164.

76. Ibid., 166.

77. Ibid., 175.
78. Ibid., 177.
79. Ibid., 177.
80. Ibid., 177.
81. Ibid., 181.
82. Asante, *Encyclopedia*, 137.
83. Danticat, *Dew Breaker*, 224.
84. Ibid., 226.
85. Ibid., 228.
86. Asante, *Encyclopedia*, 97.
87. Ibid., 225.
88. Ibid., 6.
89. Ibid., 230.
90. Ibid., 230.
91. Ibid., 233.
92. Ibid., 235.
93. Ibid., 237.
94. Ibid., 20.

Chapter 3

Lót Bót Dlo (The Other Side of the Water)

Examining the Cosmogram in *Danticat's* The Farming of Bones

The Farming of Bones is a novel that explores the brutal 1937 massacre of Haitians living and working in the border towns between Haiti and the Dominican Republic.[1] Orchestrated by Generalissimo Rafael Trujillo and executed by his soldiers, these massacres—often referred to as "The Parsley Massacres," "El Corte," "The Cutting," "Kout Kouto," and "The Stabbing"— create the textual landscape and backdrop the novel uses to navigate the interior lives of the massacre victims.[2] Narrated by the main protagonist Amabelle Désir, *The Farming of Bones* functions as a testimonial that bears witness to the untold stories and history of the massacre.[3] Paralleled with the death of Joël, an itinerant sugarcane cutter, the novel begins and ends at the site of the narrative's trauma, on the banks of the Dajabón River, where Amabelle must confront the life-altering tragedy of her parent's death and later traverse to save her own life. Her parents' death leads to a traumatic exile from home, Haiti, and her bloodline. Forced to build a new life or die, Amabelle creates a home and a family with other Haitian workers "stuck" in a place where belonging is always in question. Joël's death, which foreshadows the advent of the great massacre, is the catalyst that begins to reveal the answer to the fundamental question, for the Haitian domestic workers living and working on the Dominican Republic side of Hispaniola, of whether to remain or to go home. Each of the novel's main characters—Amabelle, Sebastien, Joël, Kongo, Yves, and Father Romain—must negotiate the line between life and death. The crossroads for Amabelle and Sebastien is love, for Kongo and Joël it is a place to call home, for Yves it is the freedom to live life, and, Father Romain, it is cultural and spiritual continuity. Ultimately, *The Farming of*

Bones is a novel about endurance through pain, struggle, and trauma. And like all souls at the crossroads, each of these characters must return to the site of new beginnings the Kalunga, the primordial waters, via Amabelle, to heal and transform life. As water gestures toward the great beyond, a liquid passageway that leads to both the beginning and end simultaneously, water also provides a metaphor for the reflective relationship between the spiritual and physical realms.

As a central perspective of this chapter, the paralleling of the spiritual and physical realms is an imperative structural element of Danticat's *Farming*. The novel employs water as a conduit and utilizes its ebb and flow to bridge the narrative passageways that allow characters to move through realms of the cosmogram. In particular, Amabelle moves through realms defining major points in her life along the way. The novel's epigraph points to water as the essential motif and theme, as Amabelle submits the story, and ultimately herself, to the "Mother of the River." Replicating the primordial waters of the other side, Amabelle is the novel's physical midwife who ushers in life and death, like her earthly mother and her spiritual mother, Yemoja.[4] Hence, Amabelle's position for the majority of the novel is in the Dominican Republic while her memory and spiritual connections reside in Haiti. Water is the entity that separates the two locales as it also separates Amabelle's physical reality from her spiritual memorial manifestations. The novel's conclusion converges the two realms as her final crossing and submersion into the river indicate. However, beyond her positionality within the novel, the textual mechanism of parallelism which enables Amabelle's voice and her ability to carry the narratives of her community to the other side of the water is also a fundamental and imperative structural element to consider.

The textual format that *Farming* employs inscribes the structural element of paralleling realms. The oscillating font in various chapters separates the spiritual realm from the physical realm within the narrative space; however, the paralleling of realms functions through the unifying voice of Amabelle and the cyclical movement of her narrative. In fact, it is the interchanging font that indicates Amabelle's movement through realms. The bolded font corresponds to Amabelle's spiritual and memorial movement, while the standard font represents her life's physical movement and the novel's plot. For example, in Chapter 1 as Amabelle introduces Sebastien and recalls an intimate moment between them the font is bold: "**His name is Sebastien Onius.**"[5] Comparatively, Chapter 2's discussion of Amabelle's role as Señora Valencia's midwife is cast in typical typeface: "I never thought I would help at a birth myself until the screams rang through the valley that morning."[6] The doubling of the font also permits the doubling of voice. As such, Amabelle is the agent in the reconstruction and retelling of her narrative, history, and trauma both in oral and written form. Ultimately, because Amabelle functions within two realms, she is also bequeathed the duty to speak into existence the truth of her people. Amabelle's act of testimonial functions as a paralleling feature within the novel. On the one hand, the stories in the novel that Amabelle's narration reveals are a fictional recounting of a true and traumatic piece of history. On the other hand, Amabelle's narration fills in the historical gaps, narratives, and evidence that Trujillo and his regime attempted to erase.

Historically, Amabelle's character plays an integral role in the reconstruction of this particular period in Haiti's history and the narration of the great trauma and tragedy of this massacre. *The Farming of Bones* operates in the shadows and empty monuments dedicated to the great heroes and great history of Haiti's venerated past but also exposes the narrative of Haiti's hidden trauma. The doubling of visible historical memorials of the past alongside the invisible historical trauma of the massacre creates an opening of narrative space within the historical record to dispel preconceived notions of Haiti and Haitians by exposing truths. In his forward to Gina Athena Ulysee's text *Why Haiti Needs New Narratives,* Robin D. G. Kelly argues that "both narratives treat Haiti as a symbol, a metaphor, rather than see Haitians as subjects and agents, as complex human beings with desires, imaginations, fears, frustrations, and ideas about justice, democracy, family, community, the land, and what it means to live a good life."[7] These intersecting identities, as one not bound in heroic nationalistic identity or victimology, create space for a revision of Haiti's representation. Although a creative endeavor, *The Farming of Bones* constructs a realistic narrative of Haiti and Haitians by piecing together a history that functions not as a still-life snapshot stuck in time, but as a moving and ever dynamic narrative that represents and communicates the interior lives of the people—an ideograph.

To construct the interiority of a people and a culture, however, an extrapolation of cultural and historical roots is necessary. Envisioning who a people were and where they came from informs who and how they became their modern iteration. Danticat utilizes the Haitian myths and legends that permeate scared texts to recreate a people and offer alternative spaces for the characters within the novel to define their subjectivity and create autonomous selves, regardless of their present reality. The paralleling Danticat employs as a structural element in *The Farming of Bones*, from motif to textual inscription, extends the boundaries of the novel's pagination and creates liminal spaces for cultural signs and signposts to exist. Mirroring the alternating font that allows Amabelle to exists in both the physical and spiritual realm, the Kongo cosmogram functions as the cosmological and philosophical underpinnings ensconced within *Farming*.[8] The novel employs this cruciform to form textual spaces that bridge and parallel the physical and spiritual realms extant in the lives of the characters. Representative and reflective of the characters in the novel, the cosmogram creates liminal space that traverses the boundary of the page, etching within and beyond the parameter of the novel, offering characters a duality of existence and consciousness whereby to contemplate their fates within the mundane and spiritual spheres. As the novel provides space for the characters' duality within the realms, the Kongo cosmogram provides the cultural and religious container of the realms the characters traverse. As sign and signpost, the cosmogram reifies communal ideals, consciousness, and practices. The cosmogram's spatial augmentation also functions within the historical context by further extending the spatiality of realms to offer a reconstruction of a particular place in time from an emergent and new perspective. In essence, the simultaneous nature of the realms within the cosmogram lends itself to duplicity of time. Symbolic of ritual and the entry point of the cosmogram, the crossroads is an important sign and signpost because the lines of the cruciform delineate the four points of the cosmogram and provides a visual representation of the cosmological and philosophical framework of the cosmogram.[9] Additionally, at this juncture, it is important to note that Robert Farris Thompson deems Haiti "Africa in the West Indies,"[10] which directly relates to enslaved West Africans, namely Dahomean and Yoruba peoples forcibly transported to Haiti, carrying with them cosmological and ontological frameworks to rebuild and recreate themselves in the "New World." Perhaps the most important and influential religious concept, the symbol of the crossroads maintains its relevance in traditional West African religion and has transfigured in the "New World" syncretic religions such as Haitian Vodun, a fusion of Bakongo cosmology into Catholic religious structure. A symbol imbued with a cosmological and ontological framework, the crossroads provides an essential function as a major structural component in religious occurrences, and in particular ritual. Every time the crossroads, symbolized by the cross, is manifest the merging of two worlds, two realms, is replete. Hence, the import of the crossroads from a cosmological perspective remains paramount in the religious philosophy and actions like ritual. In fact, in order for ritual to occur, the physical and the spiritual realms must intersect or meet at the crossroads. The center of the roads, represented by the peristyle in Vodun, is where great change, decisions, and destiny occur.[11] Thus, everyone must negotiate this divine intersection. At the water's edge, the great Kalunga, is where the divine intersection exists. Grey Gundaker, in her discussion of the cultural implication of the cosmogram posits: "For the BaKongo, the ocean Kalunga separates the land of the living from Mpemda, and in crossing Kalunga's waters, one travels to the other world. Kalunga not only separates the worlds but also subsequently links the two."[12] Imperative to the discussion of the division of the realms is their convergence. The crossroads as representative of the cosmogram embodies the distinct positions or moments of the sun the cosmogram represents.

To textually construct and inscribe the cosmological symbol of the Kongo cosmogram and crossroads, Danticat reframes the parallel dimensions of the cosmogram on the page by separate punctuations of the four moments of the sun, as it refers to the four points of cosmogram, and the converging realms the crossroads represents. Much like the water in the novel is emblematic of the crossroads, and Danticat's structural choice of Amabelle's double-voiced narrative creates parallel realms, the cosmogram's narrative inscription in *Farming* works similarly to Grey Gundaker's description of the cosmogram's graphic system in "The Kongo Cosmogram in Historical Archaeology and the Moral Compass of Dave the Potter":

> Like African and diasporic twinning, doubling graphic systems implies the existence of a third presence, an implicit "and" born from and reframing the two stated "boths," obviating their duality. . . . Such doubling expands the communicative range of a message, ensures wider readership, capitalizes on how two systems never quite say the same thing, shows mastery of both schooled and ancestral codes, and foregrounds the inscriber's command of practical (alphabetic) and deep (dikenga/old-time) knowledge.[13]

Gundaker's theory of graphic systems expands the notion of doubling by exposing the implied third space produced by the combination of the double. The space for third presence exposes a potential spatial augmentation that the novel form provides. This combination of the spiritual, physical, and novel space creates a fourth space—the ritual and liminal dwelling of the cosmogram. Indeed, the meeting of the spiritual and the physical realms in a diasporic context signifies the necessity and potentiality for ritual. Ritual functions as the interconnector between realms and also creates, like the common ritualistic element of water, a passageway to transcend spatial reality. Moreover, ritual as a fourth space recreates a complete replicated image of the cosmogram in ideographic form.

Hence, this chapter argues that Danticat's *The Farming of Bones* textualizes the symbolic ideograph and principles of the Kongo cosmogram through the conceptual framework of the crossroads. Expanding the notion of twinning and doubling by doubling the double, Danticat creates mirror images of the physical and spiritual realms, and thus, the novel constructs a quadruple graphic that textually follows the cosmogram's directional force and form and reflects the four stages that lead anyone at the crossroads to the highest point or full consciousness on the cosmogram.[14] The four points of the cosmogram are Tukula—supreme consciousness or high noon; LuVemba—Death or the setting sun; Musoni—rebirth or midnight; and, Kala—birth or the sunrise.[15] These evolving and emergent realities and realms develop a textual ideograph of the cosmogram whereby the written word is inscribed with the principles of the cosmogram. As the words are so imbued, meaning is able to transcend mere pagination. The textual inscription creates a mimesis of the path and passageways through the quadrants of the cosmogram. Beginning with death, the textual cosmographic movement and form shapes the trajectory of Danticat's novels and follows the patterns of the cosmogram spanning textual ideograph, textual inscription, and textual apotheosis, respectively.

LUVEMBA

A textual ideograph refers to the transmission that the representation of an emblem communicates. LuVemba, as a textual ideograph, contextualizes two realms, death and rebirth, of the cosmogram by emphasizing the movement between them. Life gives way to death, and death gives way to the rebirth of life. As the cosmogram moves in a counterclockwise motion, death, or LuVemba's position, is a significant point of entry. Ritual is initiated to transform an issue or problem and move a participant from one space to another. LuVemba, represents this point as the death of one thing and the rebirth of another. Thus, death precipitates rebirth, communicating the movement from one point of the cosmogram to the next. The rituals that occur as a result of death provide a poignant example of a textual ideograph.

Death alters the course of life and necessitates ritual to restore balance in the universe. Death requires life as sunset requires sunrise. Between the two is rebirth, the liminal womb where life is recreated after death. Rituals of death dictate and transmit the ancient methods of cosmology to a modern people. It passes tradition, belief, and knowledge from one generation to the next. For example, in *Farming*, Joël's death functions as the catalyst that changes the directional course for all the characters and sets in motion the natural movement and balance of the cosmogram. Thus, Joël is the crossroads. His death inscribes the cruciform within the narrative spaces of the novel and functions as a cultural roadmap leading to the other side of the water where departed souls go, the road that leads the soul from the physical into the spiritual. The other side of the water also signals the origins and cultural practices the community engages and signifies as cultural roots. After Joël's death, Kongo says that Don Ignacio "wanted to make a cross and write my boy's name on it . . . to put the cross on my son's grave. I told him no more crosses on my boy's back."[16] Kongo makes an important distinction. Although the cosmogram in form makes a cross, it is not the cross to which Don Ignacio refers. Kongo is unwilling to allow Joël, even in death, to bear the burden of his demise like a sacrificial lamb that the Christian cross represents. Instead, Kongo buries Joël on the road where he died. Joël's body, then, physically becomes embedded in the organic composition of the road and land. While Joël exists in the communal and cultural memory, spiritually he resides in the hereafter. Because Joël's body is an indelible part of the physical and spiritual land- scape, his death functions as convergence of realms, a crossroads, and opens communication between the realms.

Kongo, alone, buries his son. Physically carrying Joël on his back, Kongo returns his son's body to the earth. Kongo bears the weight of Joël's physi- cal body with the spiritual burden of being unable to return him back home. Kongo recounts to Amabelle: "I wanted to bury him in our own land where he was born . . . but he was too heavy to carry so far. . . . It wasn't ceremonious the way I buried him, I know. No clothes, no coffin, nothing between him and the dry ground."[17] Kongo, unable to physically return Joël, and symbolically his people, to the "other side of the water," inters him in the earth naked, the way he came into the world, creating an earthen womb-like coffin for Joël's body to reside. As he physically moves his son from above the ground to underground, Kongo symbolically parallels the cosmological shift of the cosmogram. Kongo's mention of the burial not being ceremony gestures toward ritual, a symbolic sign operating in a state of limbo, transnationally and diasporically, while also exposing the physical constraints and limitations of returning "home." However, Joël's burial offers possibilities for rebirth in a new land as his earthen burial and grave signify implantation of organic material for later spiritual harvest. Hence, it is Joël's death that precipitates the meeting of the physical and the spiritual realms necessary for ritual to occur, and, thus, moves the text, characters, and audience through another dimension of the cosmogram.

Kongo's positionality in the novel is neither fixed nor static, and he func- tions as manifestation of the inherent parallel of the realms. Thus, Kongo resides at the crossroads—in between life and death, Haiti (location) and Africa (origin), spirit and humanity—connecting and bridging together paral- lel spaces. Kongo is emblematic of the cosmological concept of the other side of the water, as his name suggests, and symbolizes the cultural and physical origin of this particular group of diasporic people, and holistically the origin of all of humankind. A textual and symbolic father, Kongo bears a name that gestures to the land from which the waterways carried the enslaved from their homeland to the newfoundland, which for Haitians became an exten- sion of Africa through their gained independence and cultural retentions. The character Kongo represents the spiritual realm lingering beyond the horizon and the physical realm where he is a constant reality. As such, the character Kongo functions as the locator of his people's history, traditions, and origins. Veritably in *Farming*, Kongo personifies Babalúaiyé: "Father, Lord of the World . . . He is depicted as a human being . . . forced to endure the earth's anger and is the symbol of what happens when the earth turns against you."[18] A patriarchal fixture, Kongo's loss of bloodline, through Joël's murder, and inevitably his existence because of the massacre, harkens the image of Babalú. The total eradication of what it means to physically exist in the world positions Kongo in the spiritual realm and signals movement between the points. "Babalú, like Elégbá, is an orisa of the road."[19] Even though Kongo will not travel beyond the borders and boundaries of his physical space to the other side of the water, his role remains imperative to the text and characters. Kongo prepares others for the journey to the other side, imparting spiritual and communal knowledge and traditions for the travelers to take. In particular, as will be discussed in detail later, Kongo bequeaths Amabelle with the responsibility of carrying him and Joël back to Haiti, or to the other side, after blessing her journey. Representative of the textual crossroads, Kongo's spiritual symbolism is woven into the physical and proceeding occurrences of the plot.

MUSONI

Textual inscription relates to the form and function of interweaving a people's cosmological perspective, through myths, fables, and folktales, into their everyday physical lives and narratives. The mythical and the mundane create two narrative spheres interdependent in the creation of the textual life narrative of a people. The combinatory relationship between mythical and mundane and spiritual and physical realms of existence, again, etches the quadruple graphic of the cosmogram and reflects the philosophical and cosmological underpinnings of an ancient and modern community of people by retelling and reinscribing the ancient into the modern. While the ideograph of the cosmogram is symbolic, its function, nevertheless, remains visible through the concept of the crossroads inherent in the social order and ritual practices. The implicit nature of the cosmogram is explicitly inscribed into the textual form of *The Farming of Bones*. As the directionality of the cosmogram moves the text through the four points—death, rebirth, birth, and consciousness—it reproduces the symbolic meaning of and a people's relationship to the points. Ultimately, the movement provides a method to "read" communal and spiritual consciousness in *Farming*.

Myths, fables, and folktales prepare the consciousness of a people by establishing a matrix for communal being. Community exists through the interconnection between the spiritual realm and physical realm and between people and ancestors. The relationship between the community and ancestors reinforces not only the realms of the cosmogram, but also the philosophical framework of the cosmogram. In *Farming*, Amabelle's movement through the plot creates cosmographic direction for the characters in the novel while her subconscious movement, doubling of inner and outer voice, re-members the narrative of the characters, including her own, to the cultural consciousness and fabric of the community.[20] Akin to the doubling or paralleling Danticat utilizes as structural elements within the novel, storytelling creates a bridge between spaces, real and liminal, and allows the characters to exist in both spheres simultaneously. The connection between space and place also creates a connection between people. Amabelle recalls:

> Father Romain always made much of our being from the same place. . . . Most people here did. . . . It was their way of returning home, with you as a witness or as someone to bring them back to the present, either with a yawn, a plea to be excused, or the skillful intrusion of your own tale.[21]

The notion of communal recollection also recalls the past and the present adjoining liminal space for a person to insert themselves into a community that is at once here and there. Although on the Dominican side of the Dajabón River, the notion of existing, even if not at present, on the Haitian side of the water, converges the two sides, like the physical and spiritual realms, allowing a parallel existence. Through the communal consciousness of the people, one can "travel" through realms and exist in both the present state of reality and the spiritual space and memory of home. The ability to double the self and exist within two realms simultaneously is imperative to the preservation of a people's identity, collectivity, and ideology. Regardless of locale, the maintenance of cultural norms and practices through recollection reifies the importance of community to one's subjectivity and existence. Amabelle says: "This was how people left imprints of themselves in each other's memory so that if you left first and went back to the common village, you could carry, if not a letter, a piece of treasured clothing, some message to their loved ones that their place was still among the living."[22] While the act of recollection in the novel is oral in form, its manifestation on the written page firmly entrenches the recollection in cosmographical spaces that extend beyond the form or mode utilized to recall the memory. The connective tissue of the narrative inscription of the cosmogram ensures the survival of individuals and the community immemorial. If one is intertwined into the narrative fabric of the community, then one can never be extracted from it. Or as Amabelle recounts: "In his sermons to the Haitian congregants of the valley, [Father Romain] often reminded everyone of common ties: language, foods, history, carnival, songs, tales, and prayers. His creed was one of memory, how remembering—though sometimes painful—can make you strong."[23] The cosmographic inscription of memory is, as Father Romain comports, the strength of a people. The conscious act of memory as a ritualistic component reinforces the philosophical and cosmological underpinnings of a community.

Remembering craves out the liminal space essential for ritual and the healing transformation necessary after trauma.

The trauma of Joël's death necessitates ritual to occur. Kongo's lone burial of his son, as a result, removes the community's immediate response and action. However, in order for Joël's death to become and to remain a part of communal memory and commemoration, ritual must occur. Central to any ritual is the presence and veneration of the ancestors and òrishas, whose presence intertwines the past and the present, the spiritual and physical, and the mythical and mundane. *Farming* illustrates the role of ancestors and òrishas in the everyday life and routine of the community and, in particular, through the community's response to Joël's death. As the community bathes in the river, a normal daily practice, the simple act transforms into a performance of ritual. The paralleling of the occurrence of bathing and ritual mimics the paralleling of the physical and spiritual realms. In addition, the convergence of the realms within the novel's textual spheres signals the presence of the divine within the ritual experience. The textual inscription of the òrishas via ritual also doubles with the characters' movement through this portion of the plot and creates intertextuality between the people's narrative and the myth and lore of the divine. The physical motions of ritual teach and reinforce ritual practices to adherents, while also tapping into divine knowledge and understanding the òrishas provide. The community's response in the river to Joël's death and impromptu death ritual illustrates this point.

With the exception of Amabelle's observation of the bathing scene, no words are spoken to initiate a ritual for Joël. However, communal knowledge and understanding occasion the transformation of a daily routine into a performative spiritual act. Amabelle recalls that, in a stream with "women . . . who were ancient enough to be our great-grandmothers . . . helping a few of the orphaned girls to wash themselves," the community gathers to usher, communally and ritually, Joël into the next realm. In this moment, the significance and meaning of the water and cleansing is not to be lost. Preparing a body for burial requires the cleansing of the deceased's flesh. Amabelle recounts that, "we used pési, perejil, parsley . . . to wash . . . a corpse's remains one final time."[24] Although void of Joël's physical body, the corporality of bathing instructs the young adherents in the ritualistic process, as the scene demonstrates, and spiritually cleanses Joël. Without a body to bury, the cleansing of the communal and corporeal body in the river signifies and prepares both the members of the community, and by extension Joël, to commune with the spiritual realm. The elders help the younger ones with the ritual practices and imprint them by way of demonstrative and performative acts. The act both teaches and ensures continuity among the community. Once those who help to prepare the young adherents pass into the next realm, the adherents will possess the knowledge and understanding the performative acts, like bathing, represent and communicate. Through the practice of ritual people learn how the mythical and mundane coexist and interact. For example, Gundaker, in discussing diasporic burial rituals posits that " . . . Community members incorporated cosmographic motion into burial ritual . . . reminding us that cosmograms are performed and that gestures are thresholds to understanding. [Cosmograms,] . . . Commemorate the dead, instruct the living, assert rights in place, and proclaim stature in the community in the face of oppressors."[25] Moreover, through the physical motions of bathing, the community taps into the spiritual realm and ritual occurs. Here again, water functions as a conduit for the crossroads, and exemplifies the two realms or the contrasting sides of the water. Kongo's solitary act of burying his son negates the role of ceremony, often embedded in funeral practices, and confirms the requirement of ritual. Accordingly, Amabelle recalls, "Void of ceremony, this was a silent farewell to Joël, a quiet wake at dawn." Ironically the novel juxtaposes the ceremonial and elaborate mass of "Doña Eva. . . for the anniversary of her birth."[26] The contrasting scenes of life and death demonstrate the directional movement of the cosmogram and foreshadow the impending massacre of many of the same people in the river.

Furthering the irony of life and death is the symbolic doubling of the ritual burial of Joël and what can be read as divine warning of the massacre. Of note, is the novel's constant tension between the Haitians living on the Dominican Republic side of Hispaniola and the "citizens" of the Dominican Republic, like the juxtaposition of Joël's silent farewell in the river and Doña Eva's elaborate mass to celebrate the anniversary of her birth. Life and death, in the novel, seemingly underscore the sense of belonging that the massacre represents. The bathing in the river scene, previously discussed, illustrates this line of argument. Ominously Kongo, "the most respected elder," cleanses his body with parsley as the community spiritually cleanses Joël's body to ensure him a safe passage from one realm to the next.[27] Kongo remains separate from the community, even as they ritualize Joël's death and spherical transition. Kongo's previous burial of Joël evokes ritual practice, as he interns him back into the earth naked and signals a previous occurrence of the ritualistic bathing of the corpse. Kongo's intermediate position between the realms, as previously discussed, highlights his performative acts at the river and distinguishes his acts from the community's. As the community focuses on the immediacy of Joël's transition, Kongo foresees and engages something greater—the impending fate of the community. Amabelle observes:

> He moved slowly to . . . allow the parsley to brush over the map of scars on his muscular back, all the while staring at the water's surface, as though he could see more than his reflection there. Kongo dropped the used parsley in the stream

and raised his machete from the water. Holding his work tool up to the sun, he stroked the edge of his blade as though it were made of flesh.[28]

Forming a separate sphere, a liminal space, a crossroads, amid the community, Kongo bathes. The interaction of Kongo and the water functions on a quadruple level that mimics the cosmogram. First, Kongo's bathing in the river with the community simulates his presence and delineates the physical realm. Moreover, his use of parsley symbolizes his engagement in the ritualistic cleansing. The parsley replaces Kongo's machete in the water and shifts of position of these objects and shifts their role and significance within the respective realms. Amabelle's mention of Kongo's insight into something beyond his reflection in the river illustrates his engagement with something deeper, something on the other side of the water. Kongo's blade moving from the above-head and high-noon sun position to the edge of the water signifies the movement from high consciousness, Tukala, to rebirth, Musoni, its direct opposite in positionality. The movement both indicates Kongo's position of high consciousness, the reader of signs, and foreshadows the community's impending cosmographic position, as the death from the massacre leads to spiritual rebirth of the community. In addition, the blade slicing through the water reenacts the method of death the massacre will employ and symbolically slices through the agent of ritualistic and ethnic cleansing—parsley. The Spanish word for parsley, Perejil, was used as an indicator of whether one was Dominican or Haitian and its mispronunciation warranted death, often by machete: "El General has found his word: perejil./Who says it, lives."[29] Thus parsley, which becomes the agent of death and ethnic cleansing Trujillo and his regime utilize in their massacre of Haitians, is ironically the same agent of cleansing for the Haitian community. Amid realms, Kongo is the receptor of the vision and knowledge of the fate of his people. Kongo understands that most of the people in the river will not survive the massacre, and it is time for those who will survive to return to the other side of the river, Haiti.

As the impending massacre looms in the periphery, the community's focus on Joël's death and burial centers Amabelle's thoughts on Haiti and home, as is represented by her reengagement with her greatest trauma, her parent's death. She begins to conceptualize the idea of returning to a home and "a life that would be fully mine . . . hoping for a voice to call to me from across the river, someone to arrive saying 'I have come for you to bring you back.'"[30] However, Amabelle's vision of a peaceful crossing lead by a spiritual force is in direct conflict with the reality of her eventual crossing and the memory of her parent's attempt to safely cross the river. On the one hand, her parent's death determines Amabelle's positionality on the Dominican side of Hispaniola and stands as a barrier between Amabelle's return to Haiti. On the other hand, Joël's death as symbolic of the impending massacre, opens the roads home reengaging Amabelle with the other side of the water, by renegotiating her positionality and sense of belonging. Joël's death signifies the apex of this tension, and the novel's resolution, as Joël's death prompts Amabelle to re-member the turbulent moments leading to her parent's death. In Chapter 9, and shortly after the death of Joël, Amabelle recalls the story of her parents at the river: "It is a Friday, market day. My mother, my father, and me, we cross into Dajabón, the first Dominican town across the river. My mother wants to buy cooking pots."[31] The threat of rain hurries their crossing back onto Haitian soil, and Amabelle's father's attempts to gauge the safety of crossing the swelling river.

Amabelle's recollection of parent's imminent death moves the occurrence from mere tragedy to a cosmographic shifting of positions. In particular, the reference to pots and the river moves the narrative beyond the page, utilizing the liminal space of the cosmogram. Emily Clark contends: "the cosmogram suggests that the bowls possessed [pots in *Farming*] religious and ritual properties. . . . Their presence in rivers connects directly to the symbolism of the cosmogram itself."[32] And while the pots are not marked with the cosmogram as the quotation indicates, because the characters are at a literal crossing and the crossroads is textually inscribed, the cosmogram is implied. Given the intermingling of the divine and the mundane worlds, Amabelle's parents' death requires ritual, like Joël's death mandates: "The cosmogram would properly consecrate the space and prepare it for religious ritual by establishing a connection between the space . . . and the world of the spirits."[33] At the center of the crossroads, Amabelle pays heeds Papa Légbá's warning by choosing life, and ritualizes her parents' transition from the physical to the spiritual by throwing the pots to the other side of the water.[34] Inevitably, Amabelle must return to the crossroads to complete her journey home. As the initial site of trauma and death, the river functions as a mirror reflecting and doubling what she has and must endure to survive the journey home. The contrast between this attempt to return home and the death of her parents in the first attempt is the use of ritual and understanding her providential role.

The textual inscription of the family's crossing constructs a cruciform and symbolically connotes the crossroads and the presence of the crossroads deity, Papa Légbá. Her mother professes: "Hold the pots . . . Papa will come back for you soon," and Amabelle observes, "a few river rats, young boys . . . are afraid to cross."[35] The spherical opening of this passage augments the textual possibilities and references. Amabelle assumes, as may the reader, that her mother is referring to her biological Papa. However, further examination of the signs and signposts the text offers in the moment suggest otherwise. For example, the reference to the rats at the textual site of the crossroads points to the reference of Papa to mean Papa Légbá. Rats commonly symbolize the presence of Papa Légbá and like the rat and the young orphan boys on the bank, Légbá "is a homeless wandering spirit who inhabits the marketplace, the crossroads."[36] Further, Amabelle's parents do not pay particular attention to the physical manifestations of Papa Légbá as the river rats and, instead, give homage and reverence to other órishas and other religions. In ritual, Papa Légbá, who sits at the crossroads and intervenes between the realms, must be given reverence first. Papa Légbá is the divine interpreter or intermediary that translates messages between the realms. This is imperative because the opening of the crossroads, or the point of convergence between the realms, is what initiates and necessitates ritual. Moreover, proper homage ensures open communication and interpretation between the realms. Amabelle recounts; "My father . . . sprinkles his face with water, as if to salute the spirit of the river and request her permission to enter. My mother crosses herself three times and looks up at the sky."[37] However, West African reverence to Papa Légbá as the purveyor of crossings retains continuity. As a result, the river swallows Amabelle's parents, and she is left holding the pots. She says: "I walk to the sands to throw the pots into the water and then myself [. . .] two of the river boys grab me and drag me by the armpits away from the river. . . . Unless you want to die, one of them says, you will never see those people again."[38] Although her parent's death is sealed, Papa Légbá intervenes in Amabelle's case. At the crossroads Papa Légbá gives Amabelle a choice between life and death, and her mother's omen proves true. The river rats representing Papa Légbá come back for her. The pots that Amabelle throws back into the river return to the spiritual "mother of the rivers" she submits her narrative to in the beginning. Accordingly, Yemoja symbolizes "a pot of river water . . . [and is] the matriarch who resides over the bloodstreams of the world."[39] This also fulfills her father's request to enter the river. Joël's death prompts the retelling of her parents' tragic end and reinscribes Amabelle's own obligation to bear witness and carry forth ancestral, communal, and spiritual lines of her people. In order to do so, Amabelle must again negotiate the intersections of life and death, the crossroads.

As the reality of the massacre's occurrence becomes more difficult to deny, Amabelle, along with Sébastien, Yves, and Mimi, prepare to return to Haiti via the Dajabón River. Representative of the crossroads, the crossing of the river invokes ritual yet again. Understanding the limitation of his own physical existence, Kongo prepares the way by invoking Papa Légbá to ensure safe passage for those traveling. He creates a vévé "a large letter V on the floor."[40] Thompson explains a vévé as "ritual ground paintings . . . traced by priests or priestesses in powdered substances (normally cornmeal) on the earth about the central column of the vodun dancing court."[41] Just as a cosmogram is a visual inscription that communicates and functions as a representation of the connection between the spiritual and the physical realm, "the vévé represent[s] the physical crossroads connection between the worlds."[42] In a

Vodun ritual, openings and closings are traditionally performed by a priest or priestess, a person highly trained in proper practices to ensure the success of a ritual and the transformation of adherents. Suggesting a long line of priests, Kongo explains to Amabelle, Yves, and Sebastien that "this is something my old grandfather used to do before I went on a journey."[43] A further indication of his role as a priest are the clothes he wears, ironically Joël's burial clothes: "He was wearing a yellow shirt and black pants that Sebastien had given him to dress his son for burial."[44] As the color black traditionally symbolizes death, " . . . in Yorubaland members of [Elégbá's] priesthood wear yellow to commemorate his close association with Orunmila (deity of divination)."[45] Therefore, Kongo prepares the travelers, and in particular Amabelle, for the journey back to Haiti. Kongo tells them, "I make this mark for you. . . . Your trail of rivers and mountains, and on your journey you will require protection."[46] At the conclusion of the ritual, as Amabelle, Sebastien, and Yves prepare to leave, Kongo's eyes are fixed on the vévé etched into the ground, seemingly reading the inscription and interpreting the events to come for the trio.

Significant to the textual inscription of the cosmogram is Kongo's reference to "Saint Christophe," whose African counterpart is Aganju: "Aganju is also said to be the ferryman and the custodian of the river . . . Aganju carries people across great obstacles."[47] The reference is particularly important in the ritual space created by the vévé because as the text suggests, this would likely be the last time any of the three would see Kongo alive. Amabelle laments: "I would never hear about it when Kongo dies."[48] Kongo knows that he must pass on the traditions and customs of his people to someone. But with his son dead, Kongo ordains Amabelle, the holder of Joël's death mask, to become the priestess who will carry with her the memory of her people back to their land. Gary Edwards and John Mason posit that "Aganju is important to the growth of civilization because he . . . opens uncharted geographic and psychological frontiers, and stimulates cosmopolitanism."[49] Without someone to carry the memory of the community, the community would cease to exist. Who better to navigate the river than one who can ferry the community back to existence? Although the community will not survive the massacre on the Dominican side of the island, their narratives, memories, and traditions cross with Amabelle. Like the act of bringing back word of someone to assert their existence, Amabelle's possession and proof of their existence asserts the community's subjectivity within a narrative meant to erase them. The continuation of her journey indicates the rebirth of a divine being whose story of love through trauma serves as a witness and testimony to all those at a crossroads.

This is also evident when Kongo makes the mask of Joël's face: "It was the death face of his son." Kongo relays: "I've made many, for all those who, even when I'm gone, will keep my son in mind. If I could, I would carry them all around my neck . . . like some men wear their amulets."[50] No one sees him after his death, but his death is the catalyst for change and move-ment, like Oya who is often associated and referenced as change. Fittingly, Oya represents the wind, an entity that comes from all directions and whose strength and force does not diminish but is intensified with the addition of other elements. Edwards and Mason contend: "Oya is the idea of something that is felt more often than seen. For this reason, one of her major symbols is the mask. Her true face is always concealed and no one can see what she truly looks like."[51] Underscoring Joël's catalytic function as the crossroads in the novel, Kongo chooses Amabelle to carry on the memory of her son, his bloodline, by retaining the image of his death when Kongo is no longer able. Signaling toward Amabelle's reversed Maafa back to Haiti, Kongo says: "I give this one to you because you have a safe place to preserve it."[52] Further, Kongo entrusts Amabelle as the keeper and carrier of tradition when in the same visit he stands in for Sebastien's parents to ask for Amabelle's hand in marriage, for this is what " . . . the old customs demand."[53] Beyond the scope of his son's memory, Kongo passes on "old traditions" to Amabelle. Kongo as spiritual receptor knows that Amabelle will survive the crossing and, ulti-mately, the massacre. As such, Kongo imparts cultural traditions that ensure the longevity of the community to Amabelle. Amabelle passes Joël's mask on to Felice, his lover, as to deify his story like Sebastien's. Ostensibly, both of the women remain after the massacre and their remembrance of their lovers, Sebastien and Joël, is what endures after the men's physical elimination.

Love elevates and personalizes the retention of communal narratives by giving specific name and spiritual space within the community. As such, Amabelle not only submits her narrative to the mother of the river but also identifies Sebastien and begins her narrative intertwined with his. The inter-weaving of narratives inscribes into the text the ideological beliefs a com-munity shares and passes on to future generations. In a diasporic context, the retention of ideological beliefs garnered through symbols, stories and practices connect both the continuity and community back to its origins. Syncretism and other cultural influences may add to the evolution of an ideol-ogy but does not detract from the connection to the origin. Gundaker, discuss-ing the symbolic implication of the cosmogram, adds: "It stands to reason that people have used mnemonic signs to help them continually remake a recognizable world."[54] The massacre's occurrence relocates Amabelle and the community from one side of the water to the other, and the cosmogram via the great crossroads aids them in re-envisioning.

KALA

At the heart of this novel is the all-encompassing love story of Amabelle and Sebastien. After the massacre, Amabelle returns to the Dominican side of the Dajabón and attempts to find Sebastien at the site representative of their love, the waterfall leading to a cave. As the first place the two sexually commune, the waterfall and cave function as yet another intersection between the physical and spiritual planes, and Amabelle and Sebastien cross from their physical reality and into the spiritual womb of the cave. However, she fails to find him or the cave, and their love remains in the spiritual space the womb-like cave represents. Akin to the way Oya deifies Sango after his death, Amabelle narratively speaks the stories of the dead and effectively, as Teresa Washington proclaims: "Unleashed the winds of change and propelled . . . [them] to immediate ancestral transmigration and Orisa status."[55]After bestowing her narrative to "Metrès Dlo, Mother of the Rivers," Amabelle begins her account with a memory of Sebastien. Amabelle's dialogue that she submits, written in bold font, **"His name is Sebastien Onius,"** indicates the spiritual realm.[56] Although Sebastien does not cross the river physically, spiritually his narrative is inscribed within Amabelle's memory and on her flesh. Amabelle, as the narrative witness to and keeper of communal knowledge and history, especially of the dead, proclaims: "Now my flesh was simply . . . a marred testament."[57] By telling the story of the massacre and those lost to this tragedy, *Farming* becomes the material site for the monuments that, historically, were not erected in honor of those who perished. While the Haitian government establishes a process to "hear" testimonies of the massacre's survivors and offer recompense, most stories are never heard. Moreover, the stories that are heard only live within the heart and cultural beat of the people. Amabelle's words build shrines to honor the dead and the survivors of the massacre and birth a narrative replete with what was hidden.

Living in plain sight with the injuries of the massacre impeding her every move, Amabelle attempts to settle into everyday life. However, once she completes her life's work of carrying the stories of the dead back home, Amabelle's purpose and role in the novel becomes less and less imperative. She searches for meaning and purpose in mundane tasks like sewing but finds no life for herself among the living. In the greatest act of the novel, Amabelle does for herself what no one else can: she submits her life to the "Mother of the Rivers." Slipping into the river, an act and shift in realm, Amabelle searches within the depths of the river for her path and destiny. Amabelle ends the novel with the words "he, like me, was looking for the dawn."[58] Kongo's priesthood legacy that he bestows to Amabelle is replanted and rebirthed in Haiti. Like Aganju, Amabelle's submission, "allows . . . new realities and is associated with the rising sun and the dawn of a new day."[59] Her words, just like the words of the dead, point to the motion of Amabelle moving toward the highest point of consciousness. Amabelle experiences everything she needs in the physical realm, and now her journey will continue in the spiritual realm. The continuation of her journey indicates the rebirth of a divine being whose story of love through trauma serves as a witness and testimony to all those at a crossroads.

TUKULA

The brilliance of Danticat and, in essence, of *The Farming of Bones*, is that all along the reader believes that it is Amabelle's, and the novel's, burden alone to carry the stories of her people back home. However, by the end of the novel the reader realizes that they have become a witness, participant, and receptor too. High consciousness, the Tukula position on the cosmogram, extends beyond the borders and the boundaries of the textual pagination and creates a liminal space for the reader to engage the characters and the text. As the characters engage the crossroads, so does the reader. The material manifestation of the cosmogram, the reader, must journey through the trauma with the characters and, thus, participate in the narrative movement through the cosmogram and ritual practices. As ritual transforms all who participate, it heals as the collective speaks or "reads" the words of trauma that open the crossroads and ask the divine for healing balm. Danticat's text is a living narrative, an embodied text, a breathing text that functions within the liminal spaces of the physical and the spiritual realm waiting for a willing participant take on the journey.

The cosmographic and spherical space of *Farming* creates a space for the hidden narrative of this 1937 massacre to exist, and, through the usage of the cruciform, transform a community, meant for evisceration, to survive. Although the characters and stories are often read tragic, with the use of the crossroads, there is triumph in the possibility of a "new dawn," a new day, a new life the novel's end gestures toward—the creation of "Quisqueya," an idyllic place where diasporic people can exist without any preconceived notion of self and being, or as Danticat opines, our "Precolumbian selves."[60] A place where the Black body is not a site of exploration and discovery at the hands of an oppressor, but, rather, is a site of agency that engenders self-definition and personhood. *The Farming of Bones* creates a spiritual text and guide for this deliverance and insistently gestures to the crossroads.

NOTES

1. This chapter is reprinted from Joyce White, "*Lòt Bò Dlo*, The Other Side of the Water: Examining the Kongo Cosmogram in Edwidge Danticat's *The Farming of Bones*." In *Narrating History, Home, and Dyaspora: Critical Essays on Edwidge Danticat*, eds. Maia L. Butler, Joanna Davis-McElligatt, and Megan Feifer (Jackson: University Press of Mississippi, 2022).

2. Celeste Headlee, "Dominicans, Haitians Remember Parsley Massacre": Julia Alvarez and Edwidge Danticat. dir. (2012). *Tell Me More.* NPR News.

3. For further information of the concept of testimonials see George Yudice, 1991. "*Testimonio* and Postmodernism." *Latin American Perspectives* 18, no. 3 (Summer, 1991): 18–19.

4. For further discussion of Yemoja see Gary Edwards and John Mason, *Black Gods–Òrìṣà Studies in the New World*. Rev. 4th (Brooklyn, NY: Yorùbá Theological Archministry, 1998).

5. Edwidge Danticat, *The Farming of Bones* (New York: Soho Press, 1998), 2.

6. Ibid., 5.

7. Gina A. Ulysse, and Robin D. G. Kelley, *Why Haiti Needs New Narratives: A Post-Quake Chronicle*. Translated by Ménard Nadève and Trouillot Évelyne (Middletown: Wesleyan University Press, 2015), xiii.

8. See the Introduction for an overview of the Cosmogram.

9. Thompson's *Flash of the Spirit* illustrates the concept of the crossroads within the framework of the cosmogram and through cultural roots of the Bakongo people brought to Haiti. While further elaboration of the cosmogram and crossroads can be found in the introduction, see Robert Farris Thompson, *Flash of the Spirit: African and Afro-American Art and Philosophy* (First Vintage Books. New York: Vintage Books, 1984), 164.

10. Ibid., 164.

11. "Peristyle" refers to the center post of a ritual structure and demarcates the center of the crossroads and the convergence of the physical and spiritual realm. For a more complete explanation and discussion of the concept see Thompson's *Flash of the Spirit*, 164.

12. Grey Gundaker, "The Kongo Cosmogram in Historical Archaeology and the Moral Compass of Dave the Potter." *Historical Archaeology* 45, no. 2 (2011): 159.

13. Ibid., 179.

14. For further discussion of the Marassa as it relates to twinning and doubling, see, Maya Deren, *Divine Horsemen: Voodoo Gods of Haiti* (New York: Chelsea House, 1970), 41.

15. See Thompson's *Flash of the Spirit* for a cosmogram graphic.

16. Danticat, *The Farming of Bones*, 144.

17. Ibid., 108.

18. Edwards and Mason, *Black Gods*, 70.

19. Ibid., 72.

20. For further explanation of the concept of "rememory," see Toni Morrison, *Beloved: A Novel* (First Vintage International. New York: Vintage International, 2004), 35–36.

21. Danticat, *The Farming of Bones*, 73.

22. Ibid., 73.

23. Ibid., 73.

24. Ibid., 62.

25. Gundaker, "The Kongo Cosmogram," 177–178.

26. Danticat, *The Farming of Bones*, 60–63.

27. Ibid., 62.

28. Ibid., 62.

29. Rita Dove, "Parsley." *The Norton Anthology of African American Literature*, edited by Henry Louis Gates and Valerie A. Smith (W.W. Norton & Company, 2014), 1360.

30. Ibid., 80.

31. Ibid., 50.

32. Emily Clark, "Cosmogram." In *World of a Slave: Encyclopedia of the Material Life of Slaves in the United States*, edited by Martha B. Katz-Hyman and Kym S. Rice. Vol. 1: A - I (Santa Barbara: Greenwood, 2011), 160.

33. Ibid., 160.

34. Elégbá is used to refer to the West African iteration of the orisha, while Papa Légbá refers to the Haitian and new world iteration.

35. Danticat, *The Farming of Bones*, 51.

36. Edwards and Mason, *Black Gods*, 18.

37. Danticat, *The Farming of Bones*, 51.

38. Ibid., 52.

39. Clark, "Cosmogram," 160.

40. Danticat, *The Farming of Bones*, 146.

41. Thompson, *Flash of the Spirit*, 188.

42. Clark, "Cosmogram," 160.

43. Danticat, *The Farming of Bones*, 146.

44. Ibid., 146.

45. Edwards and Mason, *Black Gods*, 119.

46. Danticat, *The Farming of Bones*, 146.

47. Edwards and Mason, *Black Gods*, 50.

48. Danticat, *The Farming of Bones*, 147.

49. Edwards and Mason, *Black Gods*, 51.

50. Danticat, *The Farming of Bones*, 120–123.

51. Edwards and Mason, *Black Gods*, 92.

52. Danticat, *The Farming of Bones*, 123.

53. Ibid., 123.

54. Gundaker, "The Kongo Cosmogram," 176.

55. Teresa Washington, *Our Mothers, Our Powers, Our Texts: Manifestations of Àjé in Africana Literature* (Bloomington: Indiana University Press, 2005).

56. Danticat, *The Farming of Bones*, 1.

57. Ibid., 227.

58. Ibid., 310.

59. Edwards and Mason, *Black Gods*, 50.

60. Ginetta E. B. Candelario, Edwidge Danticat, Loida Maritza Perez, Myriam J. A Chancy, and Nelly Rosario. "Voices from Hispaniola: A Meridians Roundtable with Edwidge Danticat, Loida Maritza Perez, Myriam J. A. Chancy, and Nelly Rosario." *Meridians: Feminism, Race, Transnationalism* 5, no. 1 (2004): 72.

Chapter 4

A Seat at The Table

Constructing Identity in Danticat's Claire of the Sea Light

Edwidge Danticat in "Daughters of Memory," a chapter in *Create Dangerously: The Immigrant Artist at Work*, discusses the memory and legacy of Haitian women writers who—a space Danticat and her writing find a familial belonging—explore the notion of suffering asking if "suffering [is] truly equal when we live in a society that would never allow the people who are suffering to be considered equal?"[1] In her widely acclaimed novel, *Claire of the Sea Light*, Danticat seems to begin her interrogation of this question, meandering through the lanes and streets of the novel's fictional sea town, Ville Rose, in search of the answer and the core of her question. Thus, *Claire of the Sea Light* is a novel that explores the demarcated delineations of belonging and acceptance that all human beings must negotiate in order to be considered a part of society. However, Danticat interrogates what happens when a society is deemed inferior, as is the case with designations and perceptions of the "Third World" prescribed to places such as Haiti and people such as Haitians. How does one exist in a hierarchy that privileges the same constructs that the larger world employs to deem a place and/or a people inferior? How does this double intersection, an intersection within an intersection, trouble the notion of intrinsic humanity? Said differently, how does one construct and possess an identity outside of the prescribed and imposed identity by one's society and conflated by the greater world? Ultimately, the streets of Ville Rose create a textual double intersection where intersectionalities, communal and worldly, converge—class, sex, race, age, location, gender, identity, and naming—and are examined on a microcosmic level through the existence, lives, and destiny of the town's denizens. Hence, *Claire of the Sea Light* is a novel that examines the complexities and vicissitudes of identity construction in places where the ability to develop and construct one's own identity is confined to minute spaces outside of the Occidental gaze.

Claire of the Sea Light is a novel that renegotiates the notions of identity and belonging by craving out pockets of liminal textual topography within the defined parameters of hegemonic discourse. The creation of space and place, through the extension of perceived boundaries, engenders a formation of identity and belonging within a landscape fertile for such a project. The dominant discourse of European subjectivity creates an illusion of a universal human experience to preserve an ostensibly inherent superiority. Often employed as a literary trope, the universality of human experience constructs a hegemonic terrain that asks its subjects to accept ideological assumptions that assert who they are and what they feel is created by a system of free will and free choice, landscapes where ontological contemplations occur in equal, tangent, and parallel ecological systems for everyone.[2] While nature is universal, the universality of human nature, though, is predicated on the false assumptions of an open and free system that operates in a closed system, which prohibits alternative narratives of ontology to exist within the same landscape. Alternative narratives are "otherized" and cast as aberrant and unnatural, counter to "nature."[3] However, diasporic women writers, like Danticat, signify upon the notion of nature by connecting acts of self-definition and self-expression with textual spaces and ground to create a world within a world. Jasmine Farah Griffin, in "Textual Healing," explores the necessity of these textual landscapes as a response to canonical and historical iterations of human nature. Griffin asserts:

> These discourses help to justify the litany of torture and dismemberment, also familiar by now: lynched bodies, broken necks, mutilated genitals, severed hands and feet. In addition to these historical acts of physical torture, Black peoples also have been subjected to ideals and standards . . . that are created in opposition to them.[4]

As Griffin suggests, the narrative inscribed to Black bodies carries with it a historicized devaluation, incompleteness, and brokenness characterized in the legacy of white supremacist thought in Americas. Hegemonic discourse utilizes universal binaries as a mechanism in maintaining and perpetuating "natural" divisions in nature, and in particular natural racialized spaces within nature. But if, as Griffin ruminates,

> The idea of the black body as despised, diseased, and ugly is an historical idea, it is an idea that can be revised in ways that allow for alternative descriptions. . . . This process of reimagining black women's bodies moves from focusing on a body that is constructed in history and that carries that history within and on it, to a body capable of being remade.[5]

Nature becomes sign and signpost of the construction of new ground, where the body politic is reimagined and rewritten by diasporic women. Of particular import is the apparatus diasporic women, like Danticat, utilize in order to create liminal spaces with the ability to transform and re-create the nature of Black women.

In *Claire of the Sea Light*, Edwidge Danticat utilizes ritual to create liminal spaces outside of the borders and boundaries of intersectionality that seek to define Claire—class, race, age, location, gender, identity, and naming—to engender self-creative possibilities for the titular character. Through the creation of liminal space, Danticat disrupts the hegemonic impetus for universalization by creating a character that at once embodies the fullness of intersectionality, and also challenges prescribed mores assigned to those intersectionalities; Claire is a seven-year-old, poor Black girl from Ville Rose, Haiti. Claire's embodiment of these lived intersectionalities renders her identity and, simultaneously, primes the textual landscape for the insertion of subjectivity and expression on her own terms and turf. Yet, the challenges to the definitions assigned to her intersectionalities force Claire to exist in a liminal space where questions of existence are contemplated and resolved. The intersection of these two points creates a symbolic crossroads, where the space of the novel is utilized to renegotiate given and predetermined spaces. Akin to E. Patrick Johnson's "theories in the flesh," the crossroads where Claire exists is the liminal space created where both the embodied intersectionalities and the definitions assigned to them exist simultaneously. Johnson posits that "This politics of resistance is manifest in vernacular tradition such as performance, folklore, literature, and verbal arts."[6] Thus, Claire's crossroads mandates new ground where the nature of her existence can be examined without the Occidental gaze that seeks to negate her humanity or being. Through the text Danticat creates the ultimate double intersection, the crossroads, for Claire to contemplate her destiny and fate outside of the realms of hetero and hegemonic normativity. Thus, this inquiry argues that *Claire of the Sea Light* transcends the intersectionalities inherent in identity construction through a series of rituals whereby Claire is ultimately given the opportunity to construct an identity of her own making. Utilizing the four positions of the crossroads as points of entry, the crossroad deities in *Claire of the Sea Light* open ritualized spaces to offer Claire protection and places to contemplate her fate.[7] The four points on the cosmogram are Tukula, LuVemba, Musoni, and Kala, and each of the points corresponds to a definitive position of the sun.[8] Employing a ritual of death, *Dessounin*, and the rites of reclamation, Claire is able to shed the identity prescribed by society and to take on her true and divine identity.[9]

The novel revolves around the disappearance and appearance of the titular character and prompts the retelling of Claire's life. Just as the eight phases of the moon is a process of waxing and waning, appearance and disappearance,

Claire's story, through the novel's eight chapters and eight phases of the moon, unfolds and evolves through her appearance and disappearance within the narratives of the other characters. Beginning with Claire's seventh birthday and the death of the fisherman, Caleb, the novel follows a descending annual trajectory of Claire's existence and weaves her narrative into the storied cyclical and interwoven fabric and terrain of the Ville Rose community. At its culmination, the novel ends precisely where it begins, on the precipice of life and death that mark the anniversary of Claire's birth. Claire's disappearance and reappearance in the novel creates alternative places for one to exist, spaces within the liminal creating new terrain, fertile ground, where the seeds of identity have room to grow. This is the country within a country, land within a land, spiritual within the physical. Thus, Claire's character in the novel functions as a bridge between spaces seen and unseen and creates the liminal spaces of ritual. Claire's disappearance and appearance also undergirds her function and state of existence within the text. Claire presence, or lack thereof, extends and defines the borders and boundaries of the novel. Although she exists, Claire can be seen and unseen, signaling her physical and worldly reality and her spiritual and other worldly existence. Because both exist within the text simultaneously, as does Claire, it creates the crossroads the novel utilizes to extend the boundaries of the page and narrative and delineates the liminal space of Claire's existence.

Utilizing the most vulnerable of society, and arguably the world, a poor Black girl in a "Third World" country, Danticat forces readers to consider the choices the characters have in developing an identity and what it means when agency, because of position and lot in life, is challenged by the very nature of one's existence. In a 2011 interview with *Democracy Now*, Edwidge Danticat posits that "Haitian people are very resilient. But it doesn't mean that they can suffer more than other people."[10] Claire faces the ultimate challenge in the novel as her father's, Nozias Faustin, yearly attempt to give her away to the town's wealthy fabric vendor, Gaëlle, comes to fruition. Claire Limyé Lanmé Faustin's, or Claire of the Sea Light, vanishes, running away, upon learning the news and only lingers in the words of the novel. Claire reappears at the novel's close with a new name, Claire de Lune, signaling vast possibilities on the horizon for her life. Within the eroding Mountainside of Mon Initil, a space that residents are afraid of because of the belief it is haunted by the souls of marooned ancestors, exists among the untamed and spiritually possessed nature of the mountain the community's greatest asset. As Claire seemingly contemplates her fate as a maroon or as Gaëlle's daughter, the novel illuminates the essential and existential question of human existence, to be or not to be.[11]

The crossroads perform a significant role in the novel's construction of ritualized spaces for Claire's subjectivity to be considered and revised. The points and intersections of the crossroads produce liminal spaces outside of the real time and real space creating a world within a world, or a mirror image of the cosmic and terrestrial landscapes. In describing the crossroads, Maya Deren extends the understanding and import of this ritualistic symbol to Haiti and Haitians in her text *Divine Horsemen: The Living Gods of Haiti*. Deren describes the concept of the crossroads as,

> The metaphor for the mirror's depth is the cross/roads: the symbol of the cross. . . . It is above all, a figure for the intersection of the horizontal plane, which is this mortal world, by the vertical place, the metaphysical axis, which plunges into the mirror. The crossroads, then, is the point of access of the world of les Invisibles, which is the soul of the cosmos, the source of life force, the cosmic memory, and the cosmic wisdom.[12]

The notion of the crossroads is of particular import for the novel, and Claire, specifically, because it provides and allows subjective considerations outside of the Occidental gaze. The point where the physical world meets the divine, the crossroads creates the liminal space diasporic novels utilize to insert voice and subjectivity to challenge preconceived notions of identity. A symbol of the convergence of realms, and as a result of ritual, the crossroads invites the notion of revision as each of the points or moments of the sun on the cosmogram leads to one another, illustrating the soul's progression and transition through a life cycle. Thus, the crossroads in *Claire of the Sea Light* cosmologically reimagines a world where one's destiny is in the hands of the divine. Signifying upon Vilokan, the "Cosmic mirror" and place of resident of the loas, Danticat creates the reflective world or a world within a world: "The mirror is the metaphor for the cosmography of Haitian myth. The loas are addressed as minor images and summoned by references to a mirrored surface."[13] By incorporating the physical and spiritual realms as reflective spaces in the novel, the cosmic mirror or world within a world is manifest. This also merges the divine with the mundane and encounters of human and spiritual natures also take place. For example, in *Claire* the citizens of Ville Rose often come in direct contact with loas. Textually, some of the characters double as loas. Most pertinent, on every birthday Claire encounters a deity who intervenes on her behalf. However, on her seventh birthday, the representative number of completion, Claire recognizes that she is at her own crossroads and travels the intersections seemingly alone. With her destiny securely in her hands, Claire transforms the course of her life. Deren adds: "For this reason, the cross-roads is the most important of all ritual figures. . . . The foot of this vertical plane rests in the waters of the abyss, the source of all life . . . Guinée, Africa."[14] The crossroads creates and signals liminal space where the divine and mundane converge. When and where these two spherical spaces interact, the ensuing communication is a ritual meant to transform those at the crossroads.

Claire's birth is punctuated by the death of her mother. Claire's delivery and her mother's subsequent death shocks the community, as she was healthy up to the day of the delivery: "When a mother died and the child survived and the mother had shown no sign of sickness before, people assumed that a battle had taken place and the one with the stronger will had won."[15] From the moment of her existence in the physical world, Claire's communal designation and identity is assigned and decided for her. The community labels Claire a revenan, or "a child who had entered the world just as her mother was leaving."[16] Overwhelmingly, the concern is that Claire will try to rejoin her mother, follow her back into the spiritual realm and into the land of the unliving where departed souls reside. However, "Nozias liked to think of it, though, as a kind of loving surrender. Only one of them was meant to survive, and the mother had surrendered her place."[17] In this context, Claire and her mother represent the Marassa, two halves of the same soul divided by the realms, or a "metaphysical reflection" of one another.[18] Claire's mother resides in the spiritual realm following her death and Claire lives in the physical world, as indicative of her birth.

As the Marassa, mother and daughter form a literal crossroads and represent the convergence and the distinction of the two realms, physical and spiritual. As such, Deren contends that "The worship of the Marassa, the Divine Twins, is a celebration of man's twinned nature: half matter, half metaphysical; half mortal, half immortal; half human, half divine."[19] Naming also demonstrates the mother daughter duo's reflection as the Marassa. Both mother and daughter share the same first name, Claire. The distinguishing factor between them is a naming descriptor following their first name, as the additional names Narcis and Limyè Lanmè differentiate mother from daughter. More importantly, the meaning of the descriptors designates their position within the realms: "The Marassa, as the first cosmic totality, may also be thought of as intersected on the vertical axis as well as the horizontal one."[20] For example, Limyè Lanmè refers to the physical entity of the sea's light. The meaning of Narcis is derived from the flower the name represents, the daffodil. Narcissus is another name the daffodil is commonly called. The flower is associated with renewal and rebirth because it blooms in early spring.[21] Musoni, the position of rebirth, reflects Narcis' position in the spiritual realm. Prior to Claire's birth, her mother tells Nozias, her father, the name of their unborn daughter: "Limyè Lanmè. Sea Light . . . Claire like me. Then Limyè Lanmè. Claire of the Sea Light."[22] Claire Narcis calls up Claire's spirit, naming her as a physical being in the land of the living. Representing the light, Claire Limyè Lanmè, embodies the position of Kala on the cosmogram and her birth physically aligns with the position of Kala, the sunrise. Claire as the sea's light mirrors the representative image of the Kala light rising and birthing light within the physical realm. The connection between life and death, and the bond of the novel's mother and daughter relationship, extends beyond the familial and represents the cosmic bonds between humanity and the divine.

As various interactions with deities and humanity exist within the novel and will be discussed in latter parts of this inquiry, Mami Wata plays an integral role in the formation, preservation, and protection of Claire of the Sea Light. In fact, Mami Wata appears when Claire is named. Symbolic of the crossroads, Mami Wata connects the physical and the spiritual realm through her division above and below the water. Often described as a mermaid, half human and half fish, Mami Wata is a deity living at the intersection of the realms. Mami Wata as a deity is

> reestablished, revisualized, and revitalized in [the] diaspora, Mami Wata emerged in new communities and under different guises, among them Lasirèn, Yemanja, Santa Marta la Dominadora, and Oxum. African-based faiths continue to flourish in communities throughout the Americas, Haiti, Brazil, the Dominican Republic, and elsewhere.[23]

Represented in the novel, Mami Wata shows up the night that Claire's mother names Claire, and the same night Nozias learns that his wife is pregnant. As the couple ventures out to fish at night, Nozias reflects: "That night, the wind seemed to be circling them, and he found himself going around and around the same small area before his sloop stalled as if it had reached a wall."[24] Other worldly in nature, the wind and water work to position Nozias and Claire at the crossroads:

> Water connects—world with otherworld, life with afterlife—for many African and African Atlantic peoples—Yoruba, Kongo, Fon, and others. And among Africans dispersed across vast oceans, those waters are emblematic of the ultimate journey back home to all those distant yet living ancestors. In Haiti, it is the journey home to Guinee, across the rippling Kalanga boundary of existence, imagined as a vast expanse of water, between life and afterlife. This is the abode of Mami Wata, Simbi, Olokun, Yemoja, La Baleine, La Sirene, Watramama, Maman d'Eau, River Maids, and all the water divinities of Africa and the African Atlantic.[25]

Claire jumps into the water half submerged and swims away from Nozias, mimicking the intersection of Mami Wata's half submerged body as the point of the realms' intersection. Of significance is the inversion of mother and daughter positionality in regard to the realms. Furthering the Marassa trope, Claire and her mother mirror the split spherical designations of the Marassa, one in the physical realm and one in the spiritual realm. Claire, in utero, is submerged in the water representing her existence in the spiritual realm and the womb-like atmosphere of the water, while her mother is above in the physical realm. Drewel in "Mami Wata: Arts for Water Spirits in Africa and Its Diasporas," examines various rituals for initiates of Mami Wata. Specifically, Drewel asserts: "Young Sande/Bondo girls are said to 'go under water' during the first part of their initiation."[26] As he rows to where Claire is, Nozias sees that "surrounding her was a dazzling glow. It was as though her patch of the sea were being lit from below."[27] Claire's submergence in the ocean initiates an interaction with Mami Wata. Signaling the physical world of the sea intermingling with the spiritual realm and representative of the depths and darkness of the ocean's bottom of Vilokan, a supernatural occurrence commences. The ambiguity of name and the use of only pronouns blurs the lines of identity and seemingly spooks Nozias. Fearing a shark attack or some eminent danger, Nozias urges Claire to return to the boat. In fear he clearly calls her by name. Thus, Nozias's fear is an indication of his intuition about the fate of his wife and unborn child because, "in that moment she was his Lasirèn, his long-haired, long-bodied brown goddess of the sea . . . Like most fishermen he knew, Nozias . . . kept a burlap sack in which he has a mirror, a comb, and conch shell, an amulet to attract Lasirèn's protection."[28] A clear invocation to Mami Wata, Claire surfaces and heads back to the boat, swimming quickly, reminiscent of a mermaid, in a sea Nozias describes as ominous. Like many of those associated with the Mami Wata figure, "her devotees might take on an other worldly appearance and behave strangely."[29] In the midst of the sea lit by the moon and illumination from silver fish, Claire Narcis names her daughter. Even though her sex is not determined, it is clear to Claire that it is a girl. Claire naming her daughter is also a clear indication of her other worldly fate. Thus, Claire of the Sea Light is not only called forth to the physical realm, but also blessed by Mami Wata.

Claire's naming, and also the protection she is given by Mami Wata before her birth, extends to her after her birth and further reiterates the Marassa trope in the novel. As her mother, Claire Narcis invokes the mother of mothers, Mami Wata, when she names her daughter, and the deity returns after Claire's birth to protect her from death. Dying during childbirth, Claire Narcis crosses the great Kalanga and switches realms with her daughter, and a supernatural mother daughter inversion also occurs. The midwife leaves to find food for Claire but does not return, and Nozias is forced to fend for the newborn. He wraps her in a yellow blanket and heads toward town seeking food. Walking through the town, a mimesis of the mother/daughter shift of realm positionality transpires. Mami Wata's daughter Oya, represented by the seventh hour of the day, seven being her number, and through the supernatural act of a windstorm, opens the intersection of the realms and ensures young Claire's survival. Like the wind, "Oya is the idea of something that is felt more often than seen."[30] Signaling change, the winds of Oya remove death from the newborn. The winds force people to seek shelter leaving Nozias and Claire practically alone. Passing the church, Nozias wonders if "given the way that she was born and given what some people thought about children like her, he wondered if he should stop and have Claire blessed. Just at that moment Pè Marignan . . . raised his hand and hastily blessed them from a distance."[31] The priest's physical manifestation of the cross opens the realms and symbolizes the convergence of life and death. While Mami Wata gives life, Oya represents death "and that the spirits of the dead are her subjects."[32] Mami Wata in this context functions as the supernatural womb that sends forth and births the unborn into the living, while Oya's presence ensures Claire Narcis' transitions into the spiritual realm. Both mothers, Mami Wata and Claire Narcis, represent the invisible or the spiritual realm, while the daughters are both present in the physical realm.

Following the path past the church, Nozias spots the fabric vendor, Gaëlle, on "Chez Lavaud," the crossroads between the church and her shop. Standing at the intersection between life and death, Gaëlle's "three-year-old daughter [Rose] was tugging at her skirt. Claire began to cry."[33] As Oya's winds represent a shift and change in direction, Gaëlle turns away from Rose to find the source of the crying. Nozias calls out to her and recalls the rumor that the fabric vendor still nurses her daughter, Rose, despite her age. She gestures for father and daughter to enter the fabric store. Aware that Claire's mother died giving birth, Gaëlle opens her blouse like the intersections of the crossroads and feeds Claire her first meal in the physical realm, confirming Claire's place among the living. Filling in as her surrogate mother, "Claire . . . emptied both the fabric vendor's breast while Rose looked on awestruck and brokenhearted, as though she had not been aware until that moment that this was something her mother could do for anyone but her."[34] As Gaëlle nurses Claire, Rose is rendered invisible. The mother's attention is on Claire's health and vitality and not her own blood child's needs. Hence, Rose is sacrificed for Claire's survival. As Claire literally takes her mother's milk away from Rose, Nozias reflects that, "he was thinking that his child and hers were now milk sisters."[35] The sharing of a mother's milk maternally links the two girls. Representative of sisterhood, Claire and Rose form another example of the Marassa trope. Claire's gaining of sustenance firmly places her into the physical realm, while Rose's exclusion and erasure from the physical action of feeding extends the boundary of her existence into the spiritual realm. While the two girls are linked because of the sharing of Gaëlle's milk, they are also spherically separated by the milk Gaëlle has to offer.

Although void of blood relation or age proximity, Claire and Rose still represent the divine twins. Cosmically placed, Gaëlle functions as the intersection between the two "milk sisters."[36] Made invisible by her mother's act of sacrificing her milk for Claire, Rose can be read as the spiritual side of the Divine Twins' positionality. If one recalls, it is Rose's tugging on her mother's hem that prompts Gaëlle to turn towards Claire. Symbolic of the crossroads, the fabric vendor stands as an axis point between the two girls. Once in the fabric shop, Gaëlle, Nozias, and Claire sit on the bench, while Rose is not mentioned among the trio. Essentially, Rose is another space, or for the purposes of this reading of the novel, realm. As such, Claire ingestion of Gaëlle's milk turns an untenable existence into one that is tenable, and her physical nourishment guarantees her existence in the physical realm.

In addition to the textual rendition of Claire and Rose as symbolic Marassa is Danticat's use of the myth of Sister Rose and St. Clare, which reinforces the twinning of the girls. Joan Dayan, in *Haiti, History, and Gods,* recounts Haitian writer Marie Vieux-Chauvet's use of Claire and Rose in her serial novel trilogy *Amour, Colère et Folie,* or *Love, Anger, and Madness*, to discuss the historicized use of color and women's bodies as forms and images of land and domination enacted upon by dictatorial state powers. Both of the women in the myths are defined and subjugated based on their color. For Claire, her status as a mulatta is sullied by her visibly darker skin. Claire's family has historically whitewashed their bloodline, however Claire embraces the African strain within her. Dayan's discussion of the myths stresses the color descriptor inherent in the name of the women and the myth. She posits: "Claire (the French word used in Haiti for those with light skin also evokes St. Clare, the virgin founder of the Poor Ladies of San Damiano)."[37] On the other hand, Dayan explains that "Recall the legend of Sister Rose, the black ancestress who must be ravished in order for the color composite that is Haiti to be born."[38] Rose sullies her body and, thus, her image, which is represented by her color and the societal status that the color represents, by willingly engaging in sex with a solider, an obvious representation of Duvalier's henchmen called "the gorilla." Chauvet's rendition of Rose in *Colère* shows how the voluntarily act of giving herself to male domination in an effort to save the family's "lands" reduces her status and dirties her image.[39] The insertion of blackness by the solider further solidifies the idea. Instead of Rose being rape by white domination to whitewash Haiti as the myth recounts, Rose is blackened by the sacrificial offering of her white body to the Black solider. As mythical milk sisters, the two women represent dualistic and distinct inverted positions within the same realm, which in this case is a male dominated landscape and population. Rose disembodies the identity that her skin's lightness bestows, while Claire disembodies the inherent identity markers the darkness her color skin gives to her, as "Claire (the dark Sycorax or old hag) and Rose (the fallen lady) both give off 'an odor of death, of clotted blood and rottenness.'"[40] Rose becomes dark and Claire becomes light. In a twist of mythical fate, the two images of these twins, the Marassa, show up in Danticat's *Claire of the Sea Light*.

Maya Deren argues that "since the twins are, essentially, one, that which affects one part affects the other and whatever disease or accident may beset one twin is understood to threaten the other; and their violent separation may lead to disaster."[41] As a major influence in Danticat's works, Chauvet's expression of these two figures finds a home among what Danticat refers to as "my self-created folklore—my fake lore—my hybrid."[42] Rose's darkness in Chauvet's novel is symbolized in *Claire of the Sea Light* not through the caste of skin color, Rose is described as being light skinned, but through the positionality of realms. Rose's invisibility while Gaëlle is breastfeeding Claire symbolizes a death of bond between mother and daughter. Rose's erasure from the intimate act emphasizes her transition from one point to the next, as it memorializes what once had been and now is over; Rose's time for breast milk has passed. Rose is confused and hurt by the action, and Rose's pending death on Claire's fourth birthday also reifies her position in the spiritual realm, or the dark womb-like representation of Musoni, rebirth. As in Chauvet's version, Danticat's Rose is described as a fallen body. Nozias recalls on the day of her death that, "Rose's body ascended . . . actually flying . . . an angel."[43] Further, even the name Rose represents death. The rose is "a symbol of death . . . it takes its colour from the first blood spilled on Earth. . . . The mysterious flower came to be dedicated to the Virgin Mary and *Rosa mystica* became Mary herself. Red Roses symbolized Mary's suffering . . . and virgins devoted to God were given the name Rose."[44]

In contrast, Claire's lightness, represented by her name sea light, firmly places her in the physical realm. The divine interaction with Mami Wata in the sea prior to her birth represents Claire's journey from the land of the unborn to the land of the living, illuminating the divine womb and securing her role in the physical world. The divine intervention in Claire's birth and first hours on the earth also signify her place among the living. The winds leading Nozias to the fabric vendor's shop signal the change from death to life for Claire and remove the typical revenan designation given to a child of her birth and circumstance. Gaëlle's life-giving sustenance reinforces Claire's physical existence as she literally ingests life. The death that is to follow Claire, as Claire's mother dies giving her life, befalls her milk sister, as Rose symbolically dies giving Claire life becoming the left behind and sacrificial fallen body of Chauvet's Rose. As children, and not women, Claire and Rose in Danticat's text escape the sexual landscapes that Chauvet's Claire and Rose must navigate. Also, their status as children squarely places the two girls in the Marassa realm. Moreover, Danticat's use of the light and dark color caste of Chauvet's Claire and Rose, transposes the idea of the two women surviving a male dominated and dictatorial narrative about Haiti that uses women as the site and source of regeneration to birth a nation and instead gives the regenerative power of life back to women. It is the mothers, as inversions of each other, who will watch over the girls in their respective realms.

Gaëlle makes it clear to Nozias that her milk is only intended for Rose, and she will not breastfeed Claire again. Instead, the fabric vendor inquiries about other potential caretakers for Claire. Since Nozias does not have sisters, Gaëlle suggests his in-laws as a solution: "If you don't have a sister, you should send them to your woman's people."[45] Removing Claire, from the place where her mother dies, is the beginning of Claire's revenan distinction being removed. The novel posits that "the only way to save them [revenan] is to immediately sever them from the place where they were born, even for a short while."[46] After Claire's fate is discussed, Gaëlle also offers a part of her family's cemetery plot for Nozias to bury his dead wife and Claire's dead mother. Here the mothers of the milk sisters also exist as sisters. In the spiritual realm Claire will look after Rose, and in the physical realm Gaëlle will look after Claire. As Nozias leaves the fabric vendor's shop, he notices that "the wind had subsided."[47] Claire's fate is sealed, and the winds of change cease to blow. Nozias returns to his fishing shack and is greeted by the midwife who has procured food and goods for Claire. The fabric vendor sends blankets and other goods to Nozias the next day, and Nozias is able to send Claire to his wife's people with clothes and money.

Claire's designation as a revenan ostensibly leaves an indelible mark of death upon her life. However, as the cessation of winds indicate, Claire's fate not only changes but is also sealed. Provisions to sustain Claire's life outside of Ville Rose are made and enable Nozias to send a two-day-old Claire to live with his wife's people. By giving up his daughter, Nozias performs the ultimate lifesaving and sustaining act for Claire. Her erasure from the landscape of Ville Rose enables a spiritual rebirthing of Claire into the physical realm, distancing her from the moniker of revenan her birth assigns. Nozias entrusts the first three years of Claire's life to his wife's people who live in the mountains. Claire's relatives wash and dress the dead and are professional mourners, like her mother prior to death. Their occupation plays a significant role in Claire receding physically from the text and Ville Rose. As people who prepare the dead for burial, Claire's relatives wash death from her body and remove its defining nomenclature from her being. Claire's ascension into the mountains marks her movement from one place to another. Her ascension removes her from a space and place of death and delivers into a liminal space, a womb-like space between the death she leaves and her living return to Ville Rose. Claire's three-year tenure in the mountains shifts her from the position of death that defines her to a space of limbo where her rebirth can occur. Moreover, since she physically exists and provisions have been made to sustain her existence, it is the spiritual existence within the space of death that needs addressing. Claire's physical disappearance into the mountains is symbolic of the Musoni position on the cosmogram, the dark spiritual womb of rebirth, and signals the preparation of spiritual rebirth. Although Claire physically disappears, she remains textually in a spiritual periphery. Claire's essence remains in Ville Rose through the memory and thoughts her father has of her, especially when at sea. In addition, Nozias keeps the dress his wife made for Claire to wear on her first birthday and recalls that "often he'd lay it across his chest at night, as he might have done with the child if she were with him."[48] The imitation of her physical presence, initiated by Nozias, gives Claire form in the physical realm despite being invisible. Creating a form of Claire out of her birthday dress allows her to exist in the physical realm and the act creates the spiritual realm of her memory. Nozias recreates Claire's physical existence through her mother's creation and thus, keeping alive the image of her mother, rebirths Claire. As Claire follows the path of the crossroads, beginning again at death, this time death for Claire is spiritual as demonstrated through her physical disappearance and symbolic of the work of her family in the mountains. In a divine effort to redefine her personhood and identity, living in the mountains, Claire reenters a maternal and spiritual womb and reenters the world through a symbolic and spiritual birth.

The anniversary of Claire's day of birth illustrates the intersections of life in death, or the crossroads, in *Claire of the Sea Light*. In the novel, Claire reappears at the age of three and on her actual third birthday. Returning from a three-year tenure in the mountain, Claire's reformation is replete and the moniker of revenan no longer remains. Birthed out of the womb-like surroundings of the mountains, Nozias observes upon her return that Claire is "a smaller version of her mother."[49] She reappears in Ville Rose primed to firmly join the physical realm. Symbolic of rebirth, Claire's return and third birthday recall the memory her physical birth and textually recreates Claire's tenuous existence between life and death, the crossroads. Nozias materializes and memorializes her return by having a new dress sewn for her. Pointedly, the dress is recreated every year matching and mimicking Claire's growth. The resemblance to her mother, especially after being raised by her family in seclusion, gestures toward the notion of Claire of the Sea Light being physically rebirthed in her mother's, Claire Narcis, physical image. Claire's embodiment of her mother's physical image, and not the death designation assigned at birth, personifies Claire as living entity. Mirroring her mother's spiritual presence in a physical space, Claire's reappearance is a convergence of realms. Claire's third birthday and return ritualizes birth and life in the physical realm and deemphasizes the cloud of death that surrounds her birth. Existing on the line of the great Kalanga, in essence, Claire rebirths Claire, and, through the ritual of birth, Claire is reborn.

Claire's reposition into the physical world provides another angle to view the implications her physical return has in other areas, and, in particular, the status she shares with Rose living in Ville Rose as milk sisters. Demonstrating the Marassa again, Claire and Rose exist within the same spherical space and the positionality of life and death is in limbo. The milk sisters Rose and Claire never technically exist for any given duration in one space until Claire returns to Ville Rose at the age of three. Their dual existence within one realm seemingly disrupts the novel's Marassa trope as previously discussed. However, Claire's fourth birthday firmly entrenches the two into a permeant state of Marassa. Claire's fourth birthday symbolizes the spheres of life and death on the cosmogram, as the two girls' position within realms etches the divide. Thus, Rose dies a year after Claire's return, on her fourth birthday, and cements the positionality of the girls within the physical and spiritual realms. Claire's birthday representing life and Rose's death representing death converge and develop a textual crossroads. However, in order for each of the girls to remain in their perspective realms, a ritual must occur. Maya Deren, in her discussion of the rituals of death, notes: "A specific person, composed of a body, a gros/bon/ange, understood as the spiritual double of the body, and the ti/bon/ange or spirit. The rituals of death are designed to restore each successfully to its proper province."[50] Mimicking the rites of death, *Dessounin,* Rose seemingly separates from her physical body to join the spiritual realm. Rose, the "town's namesake," riding on the back of a moto taxi with her caretaker is struck by a car. As the town's namesake, Rose's obvious province should be Ville Rose and as an extension the physical realm. However, when Rose is struck, it is her spiritual double that witnesses see: "Those who like Nozias witnessed the accident swore that . . . she seemed to actually be flying out of her primary-school uniform, an angel in a navy pleated skirt and white blouse, raising both her hands and flapping them like wings, before she hit the ground."[51] Like an angel, Rose ascends to the spiritual realm from the taxi leaving her flesh behind to hit the ground. Although tragic, Rose's death restores the cosmic balance of the realms and restores Rose to the proper realm.

The stories surrounding Claire and Rose's existence in their mother's wombs reinforces their positionality within realms. As they enter into the land of the living, both are given clear designations. Claire's divine experience with Mami Wata is in stark contrast to the description of Rose's experience with a dead frog. From conception, Rose's death looms. Gaëlle's doctor and husband urge her to abort Rose, but she wants to see the pregnancy to term. The doctor warns, that even if she does make it to term, the likelihood of survival is slim because of a growth on Rose's spine. Thus, Rose is marked by death in utero. While pregnant with Rose, dying frogs bombard the town, dying in the extreme heat like the biblical plague. Daily, Gaëlle seeks and gathers the dead frogs and buries them in shallow graves near a brook, mimicking small scale funerals for her own child that seems doomed to die. That is until the day Gaëlle finds a dead baby frog. Ant infested, Gaëlle wipes the dead frog clean, letting the ants bit her, and forces herself to swallow the dead amphibian. Literally ingesting death, Gaëlle consumes the fate of her daughter within the womb-like waters of the Musoni position. The coexistence of death represented by the frog and Rose in utero symbolizes Rose's final position within the realms of life and death. Instead of life, Rose's birth represents death. Deren describes the return of souls upon dying and posits: "Here is Guinée . . . the Island Below the Sea. . . . To it the souls of the dead return, taking, Marine or insect forms until their reclamation into the world, their rebirth."[52] Gaëlle actions reinforces Rose's natural course, and Rose cannot sustain the expectations of her mother or the life given to her, and, thus, she is doomed from conception. Ominously, Claire Narcis before the birth of Rose and the conception of Claire, continually brings baby clothes to Gaëlle even after she is urged not to because of the surplus. She says to Gaëlle that "we must look after each other."[53] Gaëlle assumes her to mean woman to woman. However, Claire's words foreshadow the fate of the two girls and their respective realms. Claire Narcis watches over Rose in the spiritual realm, and Gaëlle watches over Claire in the physical realm. Ironically, perhaps, some of the clothes that Claire sews for Rose, Gaëlle gives to Nozias for Claire when she is born.

As Claire's birthdays are punctuated with death, the year anniversary of Rose's death holds a special significance in Claire's life. On her fifth birthday, Claire finds herself in the midst of the crossroads, as she makes her annual visit to her mother's grave. Mirroring the path Nozias took the night Claire was born and her mother dies, the duo makes their way to the cemetery. In slight a contrast, however, the pair pass a Catholic church and a Vodun temple and Nozias points out Ezili Freda saying "your mother liked her."[54] The sword that perpetually pierces Ezili's heart also is "the cosmic cross-roads where man ascends and the gods descend."[55] Rather than the priest blessing Claire from afar, making the cruciform in the air as Nozias and infant Claire pass, the etching of the crossroads intersection in the text can be read by Ezili's presence. Passing through the town's center, Claire recalls that it is "a Wednesday, Market Day."[56] Mirroring the day of her birth, the deity Oya is also present. Indicative of Wednesday, her day, Oya is also "the patroness of marketplace."[57] Accordingly, as previously mentioned, she is representative of the cemetery and "it is said that her house is built in the cemetery and the dead are her subjects."[58] As Oya's wind signals change, transformation seems to be on the horizon for Claire. Taking a detour, Nozias and Claire avoid the main road in favor of obscure and unpaved side roads. They encounter an old man with a cane-burdened mule who asks if they were "paying a visit to the dead, Msye Nozias and Manzé Claire?"[59] Significantly Oya, known for masking herself and obscuring her identity, is ostensibly masked as a Papa Lègba figure and a representative symbol of the crossroads.[60] Ezili's presence opens the crossroads, and Oya creates the atmosphere conducive for a shift and transformation in Claire's life.

As Nozias cleans Claire Narcis' graveside cross with his white shirt, Claire of the Sea Light, for the first time, is able to read the name: "Claire could only this year read the letter of her mother's name."[61] Ironically, Claire has never seen a picture of her mother, nor could she readily pick out her cross. However, as mother and daughter share the same name, her identity is bound with her mother in name. Admiring Rose's mausoleum from her mother's cross, "this was one of the many times that Claire wished she knew how to read and write more than her own name . . . to tell her who the child was who had been left such a pretty child's wreath and white flowers."[62] Searching for her own identity, Claire picks Rose's grave to admire, but, because of limitation, Claire cannot read her name. Neither can her father who she does not seek out for answer regarding Rose's identity. Leaving the cemetery, Nozias and Claire bump into Gaëlle. In an attempt to convince Gaëlle to take Claire, Nozias asks if she remembers her. But, Gaëlle rebuffs Nozias asking him to let her remember her own daughter, Rose. Poignantly, this is also one year after the death of Rose and the white roses on her tomb, like the white govis used in the "Rite of Reclamation" ritual, reinforce the permanency of Rose's position.[63] The two girls, again, form the intersections of life and death. Claire reads herself into existence of the physical realm, while Rose's place in the spiritual, or invisible realm, is reified by Claire's inability to read her name.

Claire's sixth birthday coincides with the mayoral election of the town's undertaker Albert Vincent: "Albert Vincent's victory rally was held at the town's center—the ovule of the rose—across from the Sainte Rose de Cathedral, which had been repainted a deeper lilac for the inauguration."[64] Another year and another intersection finds Claire in the middle of a crossroads with a representative deity interceding on her behalf. Claire's mother worked for Albert Vincent washing the dead, and he always provides, in turn, Claire a proper education. As both the mayor and undertaker, Albert Vincent is often to butt of jokes in Ville Rose. However, Albert's position in Ville Rose mirrors his symbolic role within the novel as a Ghede figure, a ruler or head of the underworld. A counterpart to Oya, Ghede "is the keeper of the cemetery, guardian of the past, of the history and heritage of the race . . . so whoever would seek ancestral counsel or support must first address Ghede."[65] Ghede also watches over and protects the Marassa, the divine twins, symbolic of his crossroads identity. Like Lègba, Ghede represents the crossroads and, as such, he is representative of the cross. Lègba and Ghede also represent the division of realms. As Lègba exists in the land of the living, Ghede exists in the land of the unliving. Their mirrored existence also creates a crossroads. Albert Vincent's inauguration at the church begins to provide the context for Ghede's presence. Fittingly, Ghede is "the King and Clown," which is how the undertaker becoming a mayor is perceived in Ville Rose.[66] Albert's physical description and dress also convey his manifestation of Ghede. Always dressed in a suit, Albert also always dons a "black fedora few had ever seen on his head."[67] His unsteady and shaky hands are symbolic of him being out of place in the land of the living. Although Ghede is typically depicted as wearing sunglasses, Vincent's lavender eyes, in this context, and the purple hue are formed by cataracts that shield his eyes. Of note, purple is a color associated with Ghede.[68]

As Albert Vincent delivers his inauguration speech about the history of the town in front of the purple-colored church, Claire, hoisted upon her father's shoulders, is among the crowd. In particular, Claire and Nozias are standing next to Gaëlle. Every year of Claire's life Nozias positions himself near Gaëlle trying to give his daughter to the fabric vendor. Echoing the exchange had the previous year in the cemetery, Nozias whispers his sentiments about Gaëlle taking his daughter just out of Claire's earshot. Ghede, in the form of Albert Vincent, is in cahoots with Oya the winds change. As Gaëlle, after the inauguration of Albert Vincent, comes to visit Claire and Nozias at their seaside shack. Claire thinks that she will be sent to a neighbor's house so that her father and Gaëlle can be alone, but, to her surprise, this is not the case. Nozias and Gaëlle begin discussing the terms of Claire going to live with Gaëlle. At first, Claire does not understand who they are referring to, but soon Claire understands "Who this her was that they were talking about, and that her father was trying to give her away."[69] The previous year Claire was only able to recognize her name, but "from where she was standing, Claire could see her own stretched-out shadow moving along with the others over the fading words."[70] Although Gaëlle decides not to take Claire, it is important to note that the year before Claire names herself into existence, but this year Claire envisions herself into existence. Claire recognizes her identity and feels the weight of her existence. Intermingling with the words her mother had pasted on the wall, Claire comprehends that life as she had known it could end, as her newly formed identity is fading like the words her mother pasted on the wall. Her identity, like the shadow on the wall, is not yet something she fully embodies and is a fleeting entity. In the past, time and space expand as a result of Claire's interaction with the crossroads deities. However, Claire's knowledge and understanding of her own subjectivity provides her with the opportunity to participate in the creation of time and space to contemplate her subjectivity.

To set the stage for Claire's complete transformation the structure of the novel creates liminal spaces for ritual to occur on her seventh birthday.

Vilokan or *Guinée* is the world within a world structure previously referenced. On the surface, the novel seems to begin and end with chronicling of
a day in the life of Ville Rose. Although a tragic day because of the death of
one of the town's fishermen, Caleb, the events read as typical and mundane.
However, centered on the precipice of life and death, Claire's birthday is
anything but typical. Creating a textual crossroads, Caleb's death invokes
a merging of the realms. Caleb is offered to Légbá as a ritual offering, and
opens the realm where Claire's fate and destiny are considered. Légbá dwells
in the realm of fate, in fact, his seat at the crossroads positions him squarely
in the middle of fate, representative of the *poteau-mitan*.[71] The center post in
a ritual, the *poteau-mitan* represents the crossroads. The entry point of the
divine, the *poteau-mitan* is the convergence of the divine and the physical.
Deren in a description of ritual offerings made to Légba suggests that "common offerings to the god include the temper-soothing palm oil and blood of
animals such a dog, pig, or he-goat."[72] Caleb in Hebrew means dog in reference to a dog's loyalty and, thus, Caleb's loyalty to god. On the one hand,
Caleb can be read as a sacrificial offering to Légbá, and, on the other hand, he
can be read as a soul taken by Ghede: "Ghede is that eternal figure in black,
posted at the timeless cross-roads at which all men and even the sun one day
arrives."[73] Either way, Caleb functions as a symbolic figure moving between
realms. The possibilities inherent in how Caleb's death is read also mimics
the duality of deistic counterparts, life and death, of the crossroads. Lègba and
Ghede form a mirror-image of one another, a world within a world where life
and death coexist. Resembling the movement of a soul on the cosmogram,
Légba and Ghede define and separate the realms of the cosmogram and the
points represented within the realms. With a stance in the two worlds, Caleb
must make the full transformation of a soul. The "Rites of Reclamation" is
a ritual that typically occurs a year after the death of a loved one. However,
with the lack of a physical body, the "Rites of Reclamation" occurs the night
of Caleb's death.

   At dusk, after the search for Caleb's body yields no results, "as Josephine,
Caleb's wife, silently wept, Nozias and the other fishermen sat on the warm
sand next to her, drank kleren, and played cards, just as they would at an official wake."[74] Two priests and a group of women, all dressed in white, arrive to
offer their condolences and pray for and with Josephine. In the ritual Rites of
Reclamation, "it is known that the prayers include those addressed to Légbá,
loa of the cross-roads, and Baron Samedi, or Ghede, loa of the dead."[75] With
the convergence of life and death the crossroads opens and souls are led to a
point on the cosmogram. When the prayers conclude, fittingly, Albert Vincent
shows up and chats with Josephine. The novel recounts: "Albert Vincent was
looking around him, as if searching not just for a corpse, but for a ghost."[76]

This particular ritual symbolizes the third birth of man and represents the soul passing from the physical realm to the spiritual realm, or a rebirthing of the soul. As the community mourns, Albert is looking for the dead, and in particular Caleb. The presence of Albert also clearly aligns Caleb's destination of the land of the dead. Hence, Caleb's soul must move to the proper position. Deren adds: "The houngan [or priest], functioning as midwife, assists the third birth, the rebirth of the soul from the abysmal waters."[77] Thus, Caleb dying on Claire's seventh birthday, a number symbolic of completion, signifies Claire's third and final birth in terms of identity.

The merging of the crossroads illuminated by Caleb's death coincides with Claire's seventh birthday. In fact, her birthday, and annual fixture on the precipice of life and death, begins and ends the novel. Claire's birth finds her on the brink of death and some divine intervention, while her seventh birthday, in particular, finds her on the brink of a new life. As the wake and ritual for Caleb occurs, Claire's life transforms. In a complete twist of fate, Gaëlle finally agrees to take Claire. For Claire, there is no denying the intention of Nozias and Gaëlle this time, and Claire removes herself from their imagined plan expressing her desire to gather her things in preparation for her departure. Instead, Claire escapes to the mountains to contemplate her fate. It is clear that Claire's existence is about to change, that she will become Gaëlle's daughter. However, Claire does not understand the implications of this parental transfer on her life. She flees, creating time and space, to contemplate her destiny. It is not until she makes her decision that Claire is seen again.

In the final chapter, aptly titled "Claire De Lune" or Claire of the Moonlight, Claire reimagines her birth on her seventh birthday. Claire transitioning from the spiritual realm into the physical realm symbolizes her third and final birth. The midwife Claire imagines is an Oya figure who uses a broom to "sweep her out" of her mother's womb.[78] Brooms are often linked to Oya, "symbolic of the wind and sweeping changes."[79] As Claire imagines, the midwife ushers in life mediating between two worlds, as Claire comes into the physical realm and her mother goes into the spiritual. In a baptismal and funerary scene, Claire pictures that "the midwife would wash her body, plunging her into a pot of blood-warm water, then the midwife would use the same water to wash her mother."[80] As a contrast to the physical reimagining of her birth, Claire reenacts being inside her mother's womb. With her body half submerged in the sea, Claire conceives of the warm sea water as her mother's womb. Between worlds, the lapping waves mimics her mother's heartbeat "and the sunlight the tunnel that guided her out the day her mother died."[81] Claire spiritually and physically delivers herself in this last chapter, birthing her own image and realizing the power to define her identity is in her hands. Rebirthing her own image, Claire, in essence, creates her own creation story; Claire of the Sea Light becomes Claire of the Moonlight.

Claire ascends to the mountains to receive clarity about whether or not she will become Gaëlle's daughter. Despite the plans Nozias and Gaëlle concoct, Claire seeks to contemplate her own fate. Physically extracting herself from the community and it structures, looking down upon it from the mountains, Claire embarks upon a spiritual journey to find herself. Reminiscent of her physical absence from Ville Rose until the age of three, Claire returns to the mountain to live among her ancestors. Using nature as her lens, Claire becomes clairvoyant, as the moon represents, seeing beyond the physical landscape and the cornered position her life has taken, seemingly offering no way out. In the mountain under the moonlight, the novel underscores the Haitian myth "Mother of the Waters," recomposing Claire's creation story.[82] "Mother of the Waters" is a Haitian myth, that irregular to form, chronicles how a young girl's disobedience leads her to a destiny beyond her prescribed role as a servant. Myth opens up liminal spaces within the text that create a place for rituals and transformation to occur. These spaces invite revision and transformation, which is at the heart of the Haitian myth "Mother of the Waters."

The myth recalls a young servant girl who loses a silver spoon belonging to her mistress, as she washes the utensils in the river. She is told not to come back until she finds the spoon. Searching all day, she finds herself without the spoon, out of options, and on the verge of life and death. Approached by an old sea hag, the young girl despite her own predicament performs a kind act for the sea hag and washes her sore ridden and thorny back. The sea hag takes the girl to her home in the mountains. The following day, the old hag teaches the girl how to make a robust meal out of scant ingredients. After they share a meal, the hag, on her way out, warns the young girl that a cat will come begging for food, but she is not to feed it. When the cat shows up skinny and malnourished, the young girl's heart is torn and, in an act of defiance, she feeds the cat. When the hag returns, she is pleased and the young girl stays with her for months, always having plenty of food to eat. One day the old hag tells the girl it is time for her to return to her mistress. Knowing she cannot return without the silver spoon, the old woman directs the girl to a crossroads. A set of instructions are given, and, this time, the girl obeys. She is to deny the larger eggs on her path that call out to her and, instead, choose the small egg. Obeying what the old woman tells her, the girl finds the key to her destiny. At the crossroads the young girl receives a box filled with silver utensils and is able to return "home."[83]

Claire also finds herself at a crossroads on the mountain, not sure whether she should return home or remain on the mountaintop. Claire's act of disobedience, her disappearance, like the young girl in the myth provides Claire with the space and time to contemplate her fate outside of the purview of those who would define her based on their own assumptions of worth and value, like the orphan girl's reward because of her actions. Although the myth chronicles the young girl receiving material wealth, like Claire's experience with the crossroads deities, the young orphan gains value through the spiritual exchange she has with the old sea hag.

Similar to the silver utensils that grant the young girl passage home, Claire is brought back into the physical realm by lights forming a circle "like the sun" illuminating Gaëlle and her father, along with a gathering crowd of people, trying to save a man who was pulled out of the sea.[84] Claire's favorite song to play while performing a wonn with the other girl's in the community was a fisherman's song. The song expresses that those or things lost at sea, like the young girl loses the silver spoon in the ocean, will never be found again. However, the community forming in a circle, similar to the wonn Claire played earlier, around the washed up Ardin Max Jr., reminds Claire that sometimes things do return. Claire, herself, embodies the idea of return, each year on the precipice of life and death standing firmly in the land of the living regardless of her birth's designation. Claire realizes in this moment that her destiny will not only transform her life, but all of those who surround her; those lost can, in fact be found. Claire, feeling a shift and change within herself begins to make her way down the mountain, leaving her sandals behind as she made her way down. Shedding the old and embracing the new, Claire runs uninhibited returning home for the last time before birthing herself as Gaëlle's daughter, Claire of the moonlight.

NOTES

1. Edwidge Danticat, *Create Dangerously: The Immigrant Artist at Work* (Princeton: Princeton University Press, 2010), 67.

2. Here I am referencing the ruminations of bell hooks, Toni Morrison, and Cornel West regarding the censure and erasure of universalist ideation in canonical studies and discourse.

3. For a broader discussion of hegemonic ideology see, Kwame Nkrumah, *Consciencism; Philosophy and Ideology for Decolonization and Development with Particular Reference to the African Revolution.* New York: Monthly Review Press (1964): 57.

4. Jasmine Farah Griffin, "Textual Healing: Claiming Black Women's Bodies, the Erotic Resistance in Contemporary Novels of Slavery." *Callaloo* 19, no. 2 (1996): 520.

5. Ibid., 525.

6. E. Patrick Johnson, and Mae Henderson. *Black Queer Studies: A Critical Anthology* (Durham: Duke University Press, 2005), 127.

7. Of note, I will refer to deities that are on the precipice of life and death, like Oya as crossroads deities. Here I am merely asserting a positionality between, or

intertwined within, realms. I am not asserting that these deities are like Esú Légbá, or Papa Légbá, who is the orisha of the crossroads.

8. See introduction for description of each of the four positions of the cosmogram.

9. For a more in-depth explanation and discussion of the concept of *Dessounin* see Maya Deren, *Divine Horsemen: Voodoo Gods of Haiti* (New York: Chelsea House, 1970), 41.

10. Amy Goodman, Interview with Edwidge Danticat. *Novelist Edwidge Danticat: "Haitians are Very Resilient, But it Does Not Mean They Can Suffer More Than Other People."* Democracy Now! (Organization), dir. 2011. *Democracy Now!* Democracy Now!

11. This is a reference to Shakespeare's *Hamlet*.

12. Deren, *Divine Horsemen*, 35.

13. Of note, loas are the Haitian equivalent of West African orishas, in that they both refer to deities. Deren, *Divine Horsemen*, 34.

14. Ibid., 35–36.

15. Edwidge Danticat, *Claire of the Sea Light* (New York: Alfred A. Knopf, 2013),16.

16. Ibid., 16.

17. Ibid., 17.

18. For more in-depth explanation and discussion of the concept of the Marassa see Deren, *Divine Horsemen*, 40.

19. Ibid., 38.

20. Ibid., 39.

21. Mandy Kirby, *The Language of Flowers: A Miscellany* (London: Macmillan, 2011), 23.

22. Danticat, *Claire of the Sea Light*, 35.

23. Henry John Drewal, Marilyn Houlberg, and Fowler Museum at UCLA, *Mami Wata: Arts for Water Spirits in Africa and Its Diasporas* (Los Angeles: Fowler Museum at UCLA, 2008) 61.

24. Danticat, *Claire of the Sea Light*, 32.

25. Drewal, *Mami Wata*, 78.

26. Ibid., 64.

27. Danticat, *Claire of the Sea Light*, 33.

28. Ibid., 34.

29. Drewal, *Mami Wata*, 76.

30. Gary Edwards, and John Mason, *Black Gods—Òrìṣà Studies in the New World*. Rev. 4th (Brooklyn, NY: Yorùbá Theological Archministry, 1998), 92.

31. Danticat, *Claire of the Sea Light*, 21.

32. Edwards and Mason, *Black Gods*, 94.

33. Danticat, *Claire of the Sea Light*, 22.

34. Ibid., 23.

35. Ibid., 23.

36. Ibid., 23.

37. Joan Dayan, *Haiti, History, and the Gods* (Berkeley: University of California Press, 1998), 91.

38. Ibid., 92.

39. Ibid., 93.

40. Ibid., 93.

41. Deren, *Divine Horsemen,* 39.

42. Danticat, *Create Dangerously,* 68.

43. Danticat, *Claire of the Sea Light,* 14.

44. Kirby, *The Language of Flowers,* 74.

45. Danticat, *Claire of the Sea Light,* 24.

46. Ibid., 16.

47. Ibid., 24.

48. Ibid., 26.

49. Ibid., 25.

50. Deren, *Divine Horsemen,* 41.

51. Danticat, *Claire of the Sea Light,* 14.

52. Deren, *Divine Horsemen,* 36.

53. Danticat, *Claire of the Sea Light,* 54.

54. Ibid., 11.

55. Deren, *Divine Horsemen,* 145.

56. Danticat, *Claire of the Sea Light,* 10.

57. Edwards and Mason, *Black Gods,* 92.

58. Ibid., 94.

59. Danticat, *Claire of the Sea Light,* 12.

60. Elégbá is used to refer to the West African iteration of the órisha, while Papa Légbá refers to the Haitian and new world iteration. "They say that he is an old peasant who has worked his fields hard all his life and is now at the end of his powers." See Deren or Edwards and Mason for further explanations.

61. Danticat, *Claire of the Sea Light,* 12.

62. Ibid., 13.

63. For more discussion of the "Rites of Reclamation" see Deren, *Divine Horsemen,* 49.

64. Danticat, *Claire of the Sea Light,* 5.

65. Deren, *Divine Horsemen,* 103.

66. Ibid., 102.

67. Danticat, *Claire of the Sea Light,* 5.

68. Deren, *Divine Horsemen,* 102.

69. Danticat, *Claire of the Sea Light,* 7.

70. Ibid., 7.

71. See Deren, *Divine Horsemen,* 146–147.

72. Ibid., 247.

73. Ibid., 102.

74. Danticat, *Claire of the Sea Light,* 28.

75. Deren, *Divine Horsemen,* 49.

76. Danticat, *Claire of the Sea Light,* 29.

77. Deren, *Divine Horsemen,* 49.

78. Danticat, *Claire of the Sea Light,* 211.

79. Deren, *Divine Horsemen,* 94.

80. Danticat, *Claire of the Sea Light*, 211.

81. Ibid., 215.

82. Diane Wolkstein, and Elsa Henriquez, *The Magic Orange Tree: And Other Haitian Folktales* (New York: A. A. Knopf, 1978), 151–156.

83. Ibid., 151–156.

84. Danticat, *Claire of the Sea Light*, 236.

Chapter 5

"May These Words Bring Wings to Your Feet"

Re-membering Ancestral Healing in Breath, Eyes, Memory

Chapter 2 utilizes the myth of Osiris as a recurring tale that reconstructs the narrative body of the titular character, the Dew Breaker. Osiris's myth provides the frame and structure of a body ready and able to pass from one realm to the next, as the myth represents the principles of the cosmogram—Osiris dies, is resurrected or rebirthed, impregnates Isis who births Horus, and the myth and principles of righteousness form the narrative of eternal life within communal consciousness. However, central to this story is Isis and her role in the re-membering of Osiris's body and the birth of his salvation (Horus).[1] Without the love, will, and determination of Isis, Osiris, the afterlife, and the principles he represents would have died and remained dismembered. While Isis is given reverence, her role and narrative is often lost or overshadowed by Osiris and Horus. The historical muting, silencing, and/or erasing of women's narratives and roles is one of familiarity but not one that warrants further discussion here. However, like Isis, in combination with race, the gender/sex dynamic complicates the lives of Black women, and they find themselves doubly bound, existing within the narrative and outside of the narrative simultaneously. At the virtual crossroads of existence, in between life and death, Black women find themselves residing within a liminal space. Hortense Spillers argues, in her article "Interstices: A Small Drama of Words," that, "Black women are the beached whales of the sexual universe, unvoiced, misseen, not doing, awaiting *their* verb."[2] To Spillers's point, the question arises: If Black women are "awaiting *their* verb" in a world that relegates them to a place of inaction, then what is it that Black women *do* within their own liminality, this historically familiar space? Sojourner Truth famously

115

argues in "Ar'n't I a Woman," that Black women are doing their work, which is the work of the most divine. Speaking from within and without of her cultural axis and liminal existence simultaneously, Truth positions women as birthing salvation through Christ without the help or aid of a man. What is significant here, is that as a Black woman, and the interrogative refrain and rhetorical question of Ar'n't I a woman, Truth places herself in the central role of Mary too. She asks: "Whar did your Christ come from? From God and a woman. Man had nothing to do with him."[3] Mary is the later Christian version of Kemet's Isis who gives birth to the savior but also re-members in order to rebirth a God, Osiris. Although Mary exists within the living memory of today because of the pervasive nature of Christianity, Isis predates Mary by, in some estimations, 5000 years. This is significant to the earlier point of Black women's double erasure and silencing, which leads to an existence somewhere between here and there. Sharon Holland describes this phenomenon of Black women's existence in her work *Raising the Dead Readings of Death and (Black) Subjectivity*: "Speaking from a site of familiarity, a place reserved for the dead . . . [creates] a plethora of tensions *within* and *without* existing cultures. Embracing the subjectivity of death allows marginalized peoples to speak about the unspoken—to name the places *within* and *without* their cultural milieu where . . . they have slopped between the cracks of language" much like, for example, the Dahomey Amazonian Warriors whose stories are often subsumed by the modern imagination in the form of Greek warriors or Wonder Woman's lineage.[4] Amid their liminality, Black women stand at the crossroads of myth and reality, life and death, heaven and earth.

Breath, Eyes, Memory, Edwidge Danticat's 1994 debut novel, situates the Caco women, and the matrilineal line they represent, at the center of a crossroads and within a space of liminality. Lead by Grandma Ifé, the matriarch, the novel follows the trajectory of Grandma Ifé, Tante Atie, Martine, and Sophie to examine the ways each of the women utilize liminality to traverse the crossroads. In the center of the crossroads of their trauma, the Caco women give "verb" to their very existence. Thus, *Breath, Eyes, Memory* is a story about how the Caco women, through Sophie, re-member in order to rebirth.[5] Echoing one the of oldest creation stories, Isis and Osiris, *Breath, Eyes, Memory* utilizes the scattered members of the Caco matrilineal line to construct a narrative body. Entrenched in a past marred in sexual violence and trauma, the Caco women journey throughout the pages of the novel in search of the pieces of themselves necessary to re-member what was lost and forgotten, subjectivity. Striving to become both the subject and verb of their narratives, each of the women embark on a journey and traverse the four points of the cosmogram. Like Isis conceives and gives birth to Horus, salvation in the flesh, Danticat empowers the women in her narrative to conceive of and birth their own narratives. It is from this perspective this chapter seeks to explore how Edwidge Danticat in *Breath, Eyes, Memory* utilizes the birth and beginning of the new generation of Caco women, Brigitte Ifé, as the fleshly reincarnation of the ancestral realm that bridges past and present, ancestor and progeny, spiritual and worldly, Guinea and Haiti. Brigitte's birth re-members a new spiritual body on which the creation or origin narrative of the Caco women and family can be rewritten. As an intersectional site between the living dead and living, Brigitte's birth embodies a return to the origin of origins that provide the Caco women a chance to revise or rewrite a historicized narrative of trauma, silence, and erasure. Although Brigitte's conception and birth may be one associated with pain, and a historicized pain at that, her birth is the announcement of the death of trauma and pronouncement of the healing joy of rebirth, birth, and higher consciousness, which represents the movement through the four points of the cosmogram: Grandma Ifé prepares for the afterlife as an ancestor; Atie finds her own narrative in the love of a woman; Martine contemplates a new narrative and pregnancy; and, Sophie creates a pathway to birth a new generation to heal past traumas.

Through representations of African deities and spirits, Edwidge Danticat in *Breath, Eyes, Memory* utilizes femininity as a conduit to the liminal space between the past and present, place and space, and spiritual and secular. Specifically, the characters Tante Atie, Grandma Ifé, and Brigitte act as living embodiments of órishas, ancestral spirits, and the African past that Sophie, a motherless child, requires for spiritual nourishment and healing. Given by her absentee mother, Martine, to be raised by Tante Atie in her formative years, Sophie is on a journey to re-member what is forgotten and lost. The dismemberment of the mother and daughter bond leads Sophie on a journey of self-recovery and healing. In the process, Sophie learns, firsthand, about the trauma her mother, Martine, dreams every night, which leads both women to new sites of trauma inflicted, in some ways, by their own hands. Sophie births Brigitte, a new and old soul who can provide a new textual body and space to rewrite the wrongs of the past, creating an origin story that should be passed on.[6]

As ancestral surrogate mothers, Tante Atie and Grandma Ifé function and harken to Danticat's overarching point. For a people whose cultural compass points to the path back "home," the órishas and ancestors remain a constant part of present living life. As guides who provide the nourishment and healing necessary to survive the harsh reality of Black diasporic life, one must always seek the presence of the spirit. Thus, *Breath, Eyes, Memory* is fraught with allusions and references to Mother Africa which function as the collective consciousness for the Black Diaspora. A textual focus and the cultural center of a diasporic people, women maintain the community's epic memory of Africa. Symbolic of nature's fecundity, women provide a communal womb integral to the cultural existence and preservation of African ancestry. Venetria Patton discusses the importance of the ancestors for their progeny in her text *The Grasp that Reaches Beyond the Grave*. Patton posits:

> The maturation of the younger generation seems in jeopardy without the intervention of elder mothers. . . . These elders take on the role of culture bearers by ensuring that the younger generation maintains some connection with their ancestral roots because they realize that ancestors are a source of strength. . . . In other words, elders serve as conduits of ancestral wisdom through their role as culture bearers because they pass down the wisdom of the ancestors.[7]

Birthing generations of people who embody their African past, the Caco women deliver the vital link between the living and ancestral spiritual realm—the re-membering of the cultural self that is centered within a matrilineal line in the form of Brigitte Ifé. However, in order to remember and deliver, Danticat must first construct the parameters of space and place on a clean page, a tableau rasa, within the novel.

In *Breath, Eyes, Memory*, Danticat constructs space and place through various characters and their manifestations of the órishas and ancestors. *Breath, Eyes, Memory* weaves into its narrative body myths and legends, thus creating a spiritual landscape and text. Haiti becomes a place of origin. Harkening back to the idea of Black women's liminality, Danticat utilizes Grandma Ifé as a sacred space and place for the Caco clan. Signifying on the word Ifé, the novel creates a double meaning, and lexical crossroads with two intersecting sites and meanings. Traditionally, Ifé refers to the city of origin for the Yoruba people. Ifé, a Nigerian city, is also noted as the birthplace of creation and humanity. Still a thriving modern-day city, Ifé is described and, "Regarded as the city where God made the world come into being. It is a sacred place, the mighty spiritual center of all Yoruba because the creation of the world is recognized as starting at this place."[8] Through the naming and reinscription of the word in the naming of the character Grandma Ifé, the land and city of Ifé find a container of existence within the living body of the Caco's matriarch. As a site of intersection and interaction between the divine and physical world, the act of creation maintains centrality in the myth and legend of this city and the narrative body of the novel. Accordingly, this same idea applies to the site of Grandma's Ifé's body as a crossroads. As the mother of mothers, Grandma Ifé embodies the place of Africa, namely Ifé, within the space of Haiti. In other words, Grandma Ifé, by extension, becomes the mother and land and, in essence, the motherland, embodying the dichotomy of the liminality she represents. As a cultural bearer, as Venetria Patton defines, Grandma Ifé also functions as a container for the myths, history, and modality of ancient Africa, namely Ifé's oral tradition. Hence, in the novel, Grandma Ifé does not physically exist outside of the boundaries of her home or homeland, Haiti. Her character is centered within the inner belly and domestic space of home and within the practices and traditions of the homeland, Haiti. Thus, it is Grandma Ifé who provides the cultural nourishment and sustenance, through food and story, the Caco women require daily for survival. The women's relationship and connection to Grandma Ifé mimics that of the diaspora to Mother Africa. Home becomes a place and space for the diaspora to travel back to or to continually be in relationship with. This juxtaposition of space and place also serves to define the spaces outside of Haiti and the old world of Africa. For example, if Haiti, by extension of Africa, becomes a place of origin, the place where myth is born, then New York, where Martine lives and Sophie leaves to go for example, stands as a beacon of the new world, uncharted territory whose only descriptors come from those who explore it boundaries. Martine's tapes provide the connection between here and there, placing her in both the physical and spiritual realm simultaneously. In addition, Haiti as the place of origin functions within the space of the spiritual realm and positions New York, or the new world, within the physical realm. So, no matter where the Caco women reside, even if outside of Ifé, Haiti delineates and specifies which realm they are within.

Central to any people and land are the principles, practices, and philosophies that develop the tenets and systems relating to cosmology and ontology. Notably, Ifé is also home to the Yoruba belief system and practice of Ifá. Vital to any of African-derived religion, balance, order, and virtue constitute major ideologies within the divination system of Ifá. Thus, Ifá is an all-encompassing spiritual, ethical, and religious practice, and "as an oracle, it plays a practical and significant role in Yoruba traditional religion by offering answers and solutions to existential problems in forms of ritual offerings and sacrifices to the appropriate deities."[9] In essence, Ifá is a problem to solution framework of spiritual order. Ifá is made up of a corpus of stories and parables that teach a lesson and relate the proper payment to restore balance in both the physical and spiritual realm. Consultors ask for the guidance of a Babalawo, or Ifá priest, when experiencing issues or problems in their daily lives, as one of the goals in Ifá is living a good life, which, in turn, creates goodness in the world. The role of the Babaowo is of an intercessor, or one who consults with the spiritual realm and reads the signs for the proper recompense in the form of rituals and sacrifices to resolve what ill exists in the life of the consultor. The Babalawo utilizes a diviner's dish and Kola or palm nuts to receive answers that come in the form of Odu Ese—chapter and verse respectively. The ritual consists of the priest striking the diviner's dish, marking four points that mirror those of the cosmogram, thus invoking communication between the realms. The Babalawo receives insight and answers to the consultor's dilemma, and in an iconographic narrative and resolution instructions are provided. The imbalance or disorder that prevents one from performing goodness to others and the earth, or the dis-ease, is what requires correction and typically correction occurs. However, one must ask, what happens when the proper payment and ritual are offered to correct dis-ease, imbalance, or disorder in the physical realm, but the issues or problems continue to persist?[10]

Ayo Opefeyitimi, in "Ayajo as Ifá in Mythical and Sacred Contexts," discusses the result and solution to a consultor's dilemma if a given sacrifice does not resolve a problem or issue. Opefyitimi utilizes an Ifá concept of Ayajo, "Myth-incantation," offering:

> After the performance of the sacrifice, the diviner and inquirer assume that all will be well as far as the treated case is concerned. Meanwhile, if the inquirer keeps complaining about the same or a similar issue, the diviner arranges to tackle the problem the Ayajo way. Here, the diviner arranges with the inquirer to invoke the mythological events as contained in the original odù, since it contains the initial sacrifice performed. In other words, the process of borrowing (yiya) the events of a (primordial) day (Ojo) for use (lo)—that is, yiya + ojo + lo = ayajo (lo)—begins. This is premised upon the belief that any problem facing an individual in contemporary times has an equivalent in the past life of our ancestors, as read by Òrunmílà, who was the first literary expert on earth in the Odù of Ifá.[11]

As in the earlier context of Black women utilizing liminality as a space of creation, the Ayajo intertwining narrative of Ifá utilizes the same liminality as a space or a site of creation. The recreation of creation myth allows the revising of past errs. Andrew Apter, in "Recasting Ifá Historicity and Recursive Recollection in Ifá Divination Texts," further discusses and provides a deeper context of the process by which the idea of Ayajo occurs. Apter posits:

> If the client is concerned with pressing problems of the present, it is only by recourse to a hidden past that his or her situation can be accurately diagnosed and resolved with an appropriate sacrifice. . . . In this basic sense, then, every casting of Ifá contains within itself a prior, originary casting, one that occurred in the past and that returns to illuminate the present situation. Every casting is always a recasting. Every divination contains within itself the original divination—and its associated sacrifice—which it recursively instantiates, presumably tracing back to láílái (time immemorial).[12]

Ayajo is the reading of an ancient divine or sacred narrative within a modern context, which translates into the diviner, and by proxy the client, existing in the past and the present simultaneously. Time, space, place, and name all intersect creating a crossroads of crossroads to the past and present, here and there, named and unnamed.

The incorporation of myths and legends prove imperative and integral to the form and function of the novel because the legacy of sexual violence and trauma hinders the progress and healing of the Caco women and renders their narrative incomplete. In addition, the silence that surrounds sexual violence, trauma, and loss does not lend to a space for words, narratives, or voices that can counter, contest, or challenge the fixed narrative of sexual trauma. The interconnection between the origin of human creation and divination, Ifé and Ifá, intersects within the novel and creates a narrative within a narrative or an Ayajo crossroads. Opefeyitimi utilizes Barbara Babcock's "The Story within the Story: Metanarration in Folk Narrative," to discuss the performative, symbolic, and intersectional quality of Ayajo in Ifá divination. Opefeyitimi recalls: "Babcock suggests that, "we use the term metanarration to refer specifically to narrative performance and discourse and to those devices which comment upon the narrator, the narrating, and the narrative both as message and code."[13] In relation to Ifá the metanarrative, or the story within the story, reinscribes the origin to the present day odu ese, "specifically, the case of Ayajo as Ifá in 'sacred' contexts concerns the use of symbols—verbal symbols and objects or materials—in the performance of the genre."[14] For the Caco matrilineal line, going back to the origin of origins enables textual spaces to revise their narratives and, ultimately, heal. Similarly, bell hooks, in *Sisters of the Yam*, discusses the act of healing within her support group and describes the women as possessing "a space within and without, where [one] can sustain the will to be well and create affirmative habits of being."[15] However, unlike hooks who grieves for the younger generation of women who find themselves outside of this healing circle of elders, Danticat constructs a circle within the circle, or a narrative within a narrative, for the Caco women to liminally exist within and heal all generations.

Danticat utilizes the concept of Ayajo by incorporating myths and legends into the narrative body of *Breath, Eyes, Memory*. Casting a textual Kola nut, Danticat augments the novel's textual space by extending time and place, which affords both characters and readers spaces of contemplation and healing through Ayajo. Replicating the act and form of Ifá divination, the novel both poses questions and attempts to resolve issues and problems the characters experience within their daily lives. However, as Ayajo entails, resolution of a character's ills and woes are tenuous at best and require an interrogation of ancient texts for a complete resolution to occur. Within the novel, for example, this directly applies to the legacy of sexual violence the Caco women are both victim and perpetrator of in their lives. The act of "testing"—an intrusive and violent act where a mother ensures a daughter's hymen is intact and she is still a virgin by inserting a finger into her vagina—that each of the Caco women are subject and object to, generation after generation, continues a legacy of patriarchal control of women's bodies and virtue. Invoking a call and response pattern, Danticat weaves a myth into the narrative and conversation about testing that Sophie attempts to have with Grandma Ifé, the matriarch and symbol of the motherland. In the myth, "The story goes that there was once an extremely wealthy man who married a poor black girl . . . because she was untouched."[16] However, on their wedding night when the young girl does not bleed as he expects, as a matter of honor, the husband stabs her between the legs: "The blood kept flowing like water out of the girl. . . . Finally, drained all of her blood, the girl died."[17] Sexual purity and virtue become a matter of life and death and shows the price young girls and women, in particular, have to pay to keep their virtue intact in service of a patriarchally contrived narrative of female subjectivity. While death is the girl's legacy in this myth, the husband's legacy becomes the consumption of the essence of her virtue, "a drop of her hymen blood to drink."[18] Further expanding the textual topography, Sophie re-members her experience of testing at the hands of her mother, Martine, thus doubling the narrative space as she "had learned to *double* while being *tested*."[19] Danticat further develops and expands this notion with the juxtaposition of Martine's rape by a faceless man, and Martine's own violation of Sophie through testing. Sophie's testing leads her to violently, but in a liberatory act of emancipation, break her own hymen attempting to stop the cycle, narrative, and imperative of testing.

Completing the loop of call and response, Sophie and Grandma Ifé function as consultor and diviner, respectively, and construct and perform the act of Ifá divination. Sophie probes Grandma Ifé for answers to the question of why Grandma Ifé performed testing, knowing how much Martine and Atie, and even Ifé as a young woman, despised the act. Grandma Ifé answers: "I had to keep them clean until they had husbands."[20] While Martine and Atie lack husbands, as Sophie notes, Grandma Ifé's response reinforces the idea that a woman's development of her own subjectivity is at constant odds with the prescribed hegemony of patriarchy and bodily control. As Sophie bears witness to the residual and long-lasting effects of testing to Grandma Ifé, the matriarch, in turn, hands Sophie a statue of Erzulie and imparts: "You cannot always carry the pain. You must liberate yourself. . . . My heart, it weeps like a river for the pain we have caused you."[21] Harkening back to the notion of call and response, Danticat creates a textual refrain functioning in both the past and present, divine and mundane, and myth and reality which constructs the liminality of the crossroads for the characters, and Sophie in this particular case, to exist within. While Grandma Ifé cannot heal Sophie directly, what she can offer is a connection to Ayajo healing through the intertwining of the physical and mythical realms, as "Ifá must be understood both as a method and a deity of divination."[22] An understanding of Erzulie is imperative to one's understanding of this context, as the novel mythically appropriates Erzulie's spirit: "The loa of things as they *could* be, not as they are or even as they normally should be."[23] Here Grandma Ifé, as Babalowa, not only imparts to Sophie wisdom, but also offers her the healing that even Erzulie, herself, does not possess: "The wound of Erzulie is perpetual: she is the dream impaled eternally upon the cosmic cross-roads where the world of men and the world divinity meet, and it is through her pierced heart that 'man ascends to and the gods descend."[24] Spiritually calling forth the essence of Erzulie into the physical realm, Grandma Ifé creates an Ayajo crossroads and provides Sophie with the liminal space to take ownership of her own narrative. The mythical trauma of Erzulie becomes the physical trauma of testing that Sophie suffers, and the doubling of realms offers Sophie a passageway to the origin of origins to heal a wound of mythic and corporal proportion.

To fully examine Ifé and Ifá within the context the novel, one must return, then, to the creation myth of Ifé. As myth and legend play a significant role in the structure of *Breath, Eyes, Memory*, the myths and legends of Ifé also must take center stage in the structure of Ifá divination and communal consciousness. One of the most significant myths of any civilization, and especially of Ifé, is the myth of creation. As a way to order humanity's formation and place and space within the world, creation myths reinscribe the beliefs that a people value and hold in high regard. In Ifé, the creation myth discusses Olodumare's edict to the órishas to create humanity, with the aim of inscribing the underlying value system for humanity and communal consciousness within the landscape of Ifé. Told in the form of a spiritual lesson that the Most Divine delivers to the órishas, the creation myth of Ifé acts a parable for humanity in the present and functions in the novel in a similar way to Ayajo in Ifá divination. In the myth, Olodumare tasks the órishas with forming humanity within Ifé, or the physical realm. Out of the 17 órishas, 16 masculine órishas attempt and fail to form humanity. The erasure of Oshun's voice within the narrative of creation forces the other órishas to return to the most divine and recount their failure. Olodumare asks a central question of them. Regarded as the Oshun question, Olodumare asks: "Are women present and given due respect, that is, in position, participation, and treatment?" This principle, modern Ifá ethics asserts, is morally compelling, especially in all things of importance and for common good.""[25] Oshun's inclusion results in the successful creation of humanity and balance within the physical realm. Thus, as Ifé's creation myth dictates, all must be present and have a role for there to be common good, and at the heart of creation in Ifé, as is at the heart of *Breath, Eyes, Memory*, is the importance and role of Black women in creation. Although this question, because the órishas are masculine, seems to be directed at men, the idea of ethics extends to both men and women. This is of particular importance to the understanding of *Breath, Eyes, Memory*, and this question is also central to the structure of the novel as it provides the Caco women and the audience with a corrective lens to focus on a spiritual and textual crossroads, a new template, to work within. Attempting to correct the sexual violence and trauma that plagues the matrilineal line of the Caco, the women in the novel must return to the site of creation and the Oshun question to restore their matrilineal line and, thus, humanity. Rhetorically refraining through the novel, like Truth's rhetorical question about womanhood, is the ultimate question for the Caco women, and in particular Sophie: are you free? But the question is not what is it that the women need to be free of, but who will free them? Answering the call of the novel's central rhetorical question and aim, the Oshun question finds centrality within the text.

Through the character Sophie, Oshun is visibly present and exists within the novel. Oshun is "the youngest of the òrìsà. She is like the baby in that the last consequence of nature was civilization."[26] Humanity owes to Oshun its formation and existence, as the Caco owe Sophie. Sophie, too, is the youngest of the women and finds a metanarrative, a call and response, within of the mythic narrative of Oshun's relationship to civilization and, in particular, the birthing of humanity. As one of Oshun's representative colors is yellow, Sophie and the color yellow exist within Haiti. Before departing to New York, Atie says to Sophie who is dressed in a yellow robe: "Everything you own is yellow, wildflower yellow, like dandelions, sunflowers."[27] In particular, "As a flower [Oshun] is represented by the sunflower."[28] To the listing of flowers Sophie adds daffodils, which are yellow too. However, daffodils are a European derived flower that because of the Haitian sun have become bronzed, "as though they had acquired a bronze tinge from the skin of natives who had adopted them."[29] Oshun and Sophie both share attributes of a daffodil as both, as the flower, grow in a soil foreign to its origins but still prospers in displaced foreign lands. Although the slave trade was meant to completely sever Africans from Africa, Oshun powerfully finds a place within those who traveled the middle passage and occupies a space in any landscape where Africans exist, only fitting for the protector and guardian of both Ifá and humanity.[30] Daffodils, Martine's favorite blooms, are reminiscent of Martine's disconnect and dislocation from Sophie and Haiti, but also plants the seed for Sophie's impending dislocation from Haiti and Atie. Daffodils, which represent rebirth, further symbolize Sophie's movement to the next phase in her life, and the death of Sophie's nurturing and isolated existence with Atie in Haiti. Sophie travels to a physical new world of New York to join Martine, a mother she has only seen in pictures, and seemingly cutting short her growth and development. However, like Oshun and daffodil's translatability on both sides of the water, Sophie, the youngest of the Caco women, germinates in the new soil where she finds herself planted. Thus, the next section of this chapter will focus on how Sophie transforms into an Oshun like figure and restores the creation narrative of the Caco women through her progression through the cosmogram.

Revisiting Isis' role in remembering Osiris' dismembered body and creating a myth of origin, Edwidge Danticat, in *Breath, Eyes, Memory*, re-members the dismembered lineage of the Caco women who, through Ayajo, reconstruct and create a textual topography within the spiritual realm in order to engender, procreate, and birth, a new narrative body within the physical realm. As Isis conceives and gives birth to Horus, Danticat empowers the women in her novel to conceive of and birth their own narratives. Within the context of Ayajo, a diviner's role is to re-member the textual body, or the corpus of the Odu, to return to the original sacrifice by summoning supernatural powers through myth. In a performative chant or prayer, "myth-incantation," a diviner returns both client and narrative back to the origin of origins or to the narrative origins and site of the problem/solution creation. The invocation of the old within the context of the seemingly new, intertwines the two into one. As a result, this allows several things to occur simultaneously. First, the intertwining of texts creates a space at the center of the old and the new, spiritual and physical, lending itself to the concept of the crossroads. Second, the intertwining of texts creates a textual crossroads, or a story within a story, a metanarrative where myth and reality meet. Third, the intertwining of texts creates a space for the divine and ancestors to interact with the client and/or their progeny and provides a context for corporal healing to occur. Fourth, the intertwining of texts creates a double crossroads where myth and legend merge with the reality of the physical realm and space, place, and time exist immemorial and in continuum.

Utilizing Myriam Chancy's theory culture-lacune as representative points of the cosmogram, the aim of this last section is to demonstrate how Danticat creates a surrogate womb to birth diasporic subjectivity, which acts as healing and cultural regeneration for the Caco women.[31] Through the concept of culture-lacune and the development of bodily senses, the novel's form acts as a lexical womb and fertile ground for the gestation and maturation of a spiritual body and text that corresponds with Sophie's movement through and position, at a particular point, on the cosmogram. As such, each point of the cosmogram represents an aspect of the novel's title, representative órisha or spiritual force, and culture-lacune that represents each section respectively. The last four sections of this chapter will use these labels to demonstrate the movement through these four points and how the intersection between the points connotes the double crossroads that position Sophie and the Caco women in a space of liminality. Beginning with death, the section will follow the counterclockwise motion of the cosmogram, ending with the high consciousness of Tukula.[32]

BREATH, OYA, DEATH AS "EMPTY
SPACE WITHIN THE BODY"[33]

Breath signifies life, but, as Oya represents "the change of a person from being alive to being dead, that is represented by the person's last breath," breath can also represent death.[34] In a traditional sense, death means absence and grief, an unfillable void for the living left behind. And while death is certainly an absence for the living within the physical realm, it begs the question of what death is within the spiritual realm, for "One does not want to face the ultimate truth of Oya, which is, with each breath, a person is both alive and teetering on the edge of death; and could, from one moment to the next, die."[35] A death of a person is a transformation of human materiality into a spiritual entity. The perfect counterbalance between the realms, death takes on new form and substance according to one's positionality. In the context of the Africana diasporic corporal body, death creates the liminality that has become sign and signpost for the diaspora, an existence between two realms. In order for one to pass from the physical realm into the spiritual, a space must exist to hold both simultaneously. Thus, death on the cosmogram creates a functional and liminal space, or crossroads, for the passing of the material into the immaterial. As previously mentioned, the erasure and silence that Black women experience creates a social death and that death creates a space within a space, the space of life and death, that when read cosmographically points back to the origins of origins. Sharon Holland discusses Hortense Spillers' "Interstices" in her text and provides two examples, one of symbol making and the other of the missing word or "interstice," to construct the liminal space of Black women's existence. Holland posits: "What Spillers accomplishes in these two examples is astonishing. Black female bodies serve as a passage between humanity and nonhumanity as well as the articulation of that passage [which] encompasses the terrain between the living and the dead, between the ancestral and the living community."[36] In other words, what Holland suggests of Spillers' text is that within the "lexical gaps" of life and death exists liminal space where those not readily seen as a part of the living, corporal body of humanity, construct topographically conducive space for a life beyond survival, a life of healing and thriving within one's own subjectivity. Taken together with Chancy's first definition of the culture-lacune, death creates "empty space within the body" and functions not only as the liminal space of Black women's subjectivity, but also signifies upon the movement within and outside of the realms of the cosmogram.[37] A textual example is Sophie leaving Haiti and creating an absence, or a space, within the corporal body of the motherland. Mirroring the relationship between the motherland and diaspora, Sophie leaving Haiti represents her physical absence and movement into another space or realm and creates a refrain that mimics the breath within the body of the diaspora and functions to form spaces to heal the trauma of sexual violence that plagues the matriarchal line of the Caco.

Death works on two levels within the novel, to construct Ayajo. First, the death of the Caco patriarch creates a matriarch and, secondly, creates a space for healing within the context of female subjectivity outside of the context of patriarchy. The novel begins with the death of Sophie's grandfather, who suddenly dies in the cane field and the Caco women—Grandma Ifé, Martine, and Atie—try to resurrect him through wails and tears, but to no avail, nothing or no one could bring him back to life.[38] In this moment, the Caco women become a matrilineal bloodline, and the death of the patriarch in the family of women creates a call and response to the Oshun question. What is the role of women within the narrative body of the Caco women after the death of patriarchy? How are women present and respected, even in the absence of men? The empty space that the death of the patriarch constructs provides a new narrative space, a textual womb and body for the Caco women to contemplate and create a new subjectivity. However, while the Caco women try to save the patriarch, they are negligible when it comes to their own survival. Sophie's birth further complicates the Caco women's survival and Oshun question, as she is the result of Martine's rape and subsequent pregnancy. Sophie's faceless father physically mirrors the death and erasure of the patriarch but does not spiritually erase the societal and communal power of paternity and patriarchy. Although Sophie's conception is marred by sexual violence and trauma, her birth sends forth into the physical realm the answer to the Oshun question: Brigitte, the salvation Sophie births for the Caco women and humanity. For Sophie, the death of her existence in Haiti creates a space for the growth and development of her identity and consciousness. Although not a literal death, Sophie's abrupt removal from Haiti calls her forth from the spiritual land of her ancestors to New York the land of the living. Sophie's calling forth from one realm to the next symbolizes movement on the cosmogram and gives breath to the Caco's new narrative body.

EYES, ÒSÓÒSI, REBIRTH AS "A TEXTUAL INTERRUPTION"[39]

Within the midnight of existence lies the point of Musoni, the position of rebirth and the cycle of death's transformation back into life, where the death of the old births a new vision. Death produces space for a lexical womb to hold, within the liminality of the crossroads, the narratives of the Caco women, and Sophie in particular. The space also formulates a new topography to place the narratives within and, hence, rebirth a space and narrative conducive to feminine subjectivity, transforming what was once spiritual back into the materiality of the physical realm. What comes to light in the darkness of midnight are two operable levels of rebirth in the afterlife. But to see in the dark requires sensory skill that no human possesses without the assistance of artificial optical equipment, except in utero.

The development of a baby in and out of utero sheds light on the spiritual movement of the cosmogram. Reminiscent of the darkness of midnight and the position of Musoni, the sensory development of fetuses and newborns illuminate the liminality of possessing sight within darkness. For a fetus, breath begins life and comes before sight. However, to see is a heterogenous and complex notion to ponder. Many studies show fetuses can perceive light and movement, so, while in darkness, they are not blind. Technically, in utero sight is a sense that cannot fully develop because of the darkness that envelops the fetus, and after birth sight continues to develop and sharpen. Discussions of sight, however, typically relate to what one can see in light, and does not presume to utilize darkness as a parameter. Outside of the womb, newborns shield their eyes from light, and it takes months for a baby to adjust to the light of the physical realm and to be able to perceive color. As the clarity of their vision develops, so does the body. Similarly, on a spiritual level, one's vision develops before the body develops, a new vision precedes a new form. In fact, it is spiritual sight that forms the spiritual body. To have faith in the unseen rebirths the spiritual idea of the body into a physical entity.

Under the watchful eye of Òsóòsi, who "defends women," Sophie can function with clear vision, possessing sight in both the darkness of midnight and in the light of the physical realm.[40] The novel connects Sophie with Òsóòsi on two levels, creating a call and response between what the name of the matrilineal line, Caco, represents. In the "Afterword" of the novel, Danticat writes to Sophie: "This family of yours, the Cacos, named after a bird whose wings look like flames, and named after revolutionaries who fought and died in flames."[41] Caco represents distinct characteristics of Òsóòsi who "is associated with birds because of his elevated mental ability."[42] Similarly, the Caco fighters who originated in the Haitian Revolution battled the occupation of Haiti by US government and troops and fought any other opposition to freedom.[43] "Òsóòsi [also] represents all institutions that restrict one's freedom, [and] is known to kill his disobedient children or he drives them crazy and puts them in institutions. Òsóòsi locks up your bird in a cage by putting you away in an asylum."[44] Thus, there is an internal battle between the physical materiality of nature and ethereal immateriality of nature. In other words, the nature of the Caco bird is to imitate the materiality of flames, life, at death—their wings intensify in color at death—so the intensity of color in their wings disrupts the actuality and nature of their death. However, the physical bird is still dead. In contrast, the flames the Caco soldiers die in rebirth them into national heroes and transforms the fixed nature and narrative of death. Hence, death serves as a textual interruption for both bird and soldier as their identity and subjectivity are rebirthed within the midnight and cosmic womb of Musoni.

Textually, the struggle between Martine and Sophie over bodily possession further illuminates the representations of fixed nature and the transformation of nature their name suggests. Through "testing," Martine attempts to deny Sophie the freedom to develop and possess autonomy. The first occurrence of testing happens after Sophie goes out with Joseph and arrives home at three in the morning to find Martine "rocking herself, holding a belt in her hand."[45] Sophie sneaking out to see Joseph defies her mother's narrative and ideas of who is an acceptable suitor for Sophie and proper dating etiquette. However, in the darkness of midnight, Sophie is able to envision a life and existence beyond what Martine's dictates. As if punishing herself, Martine illuminates the reddening plumage of a dying Caco, striking her hand with the belt she intends for Sophie as "her lifelines becoming more and more red."[46] The physical violence takes the form of testing, as Sophie attempts to distance herself from Martine's act of violence with pleasant memories. However, Martine violates Sophie further by striving to control her spiritually. While testing Sophie, Martine recalls the story of the Marassas, asking Sophie to think of them, mother and daughter, as the Marassas: "You would leave me for an old man who you didn't know the year before. You and I could be like Marassas. You are giving up a lifetime with me. Do you understand?"[47] Sophie cannot envision Martine's narrative disruption of the violent testing, and the testing continues, even as Joseph is away on tour.

Joseph returns to inquire of Sophie's desire to be or not to be with him. And, even in her denial of Joseph, Sophie knows she cannot live her life with Martine and testing any longer. In her greatest act of agency, Sophie decides to break her hymen with the pestle she uses to make her mother's favorite dishes and would also mark the death of testing. As a textual interruption, the mortar and pestle symbolize the womb and penis. The pestle is often used to crush herbs and other medicinal plants for medicine to heal. However, in this context the pestle, the instrument of healing, is used to break the hymen, the symbol of the cycle of violence against the women in the Caco's family line. Thus, the pestle is both pain and healing. The pain is the memory, and the healing resides within the destruction of the source of that memory. The breaking of her hymen with the pestle creates a new site of pain and trauma, one caused by her mother/rapist. Through this act, Sophie becomes the mortar, or cosmic womb, that rebirths and frees herself and narrative.

As Sophie uses the pestle to break her hymen, the symbolic barrier between good and evil, wholeness and fragmentation, she re-members the myth of the bleeding woman: "The story goes that there was once a woman who walked around with blood constantly spurting out of her unbroken skin. This went on for twelve long years. . . . After consultation with Erzulie, it became apparent to the bleeding woman . . . if she wanted to stop bleeding, she would have to give up her right to be a human being."[48] Like the bleeding woman, Sophie realizes that the only way she would be able to transform her static and traumatic life would be through metamorphosis. The bleeding woman becomes a butterfly, and Sophie becomes an autonomous woman. Thus, Sophie's insertion of the myth of the bleeding woman interrupts Martine's narrative of subjectivity, and allows Sophie to create a narrative, which rebirths and transforms her into a new form. Void of a hymen, Sophie rebirths her subjectivity outside of her mother's narrative of violation and erasure.

Harkening back to the earlier reference of the relationship between Sophie and Erzulie, when Grandma Ifé gives Sophie Erzulie as healing, Martine is unable to provide Sophie with a pathway to healing. Martine inquires if she is the mother Sophie imagines. However, Sophie imagines her ideal mother as: "the lavish Virgin Mother. She was the healer of all woman and the desire of all men. . . . She never had to work for anything because the rainbow and the stars did her work for her."[49] No of which is Martine. As a failed Erzulie, Martine, instead of sustaining the pain like Erzulie, inflicts pain onto Sophie. Martine becomes a rapist like Sophie's father, in essence, she becomes the father, a failed mother and father figure. Martine's inability to heal from her own sexual trauma inhibits her ability to guide Sophie on a path of healing. Ultimately Martine, instead of protecting Sophie from the physical violation of body that caused her pain and shame, performs the testing, while trying to liken them, mother and daughter, to the Marassa. Essentially, Martine is condemning Sophie to the same space and site of trauma that she exists within. This act of violence and violation pushes Sophie to destroy her hymen with a pestle, attempting to destroy the site of trauma. As Sophie's site continues to inflict physical pain, the emotional trauma Martine experiences through the nightmares that follow her and during her pregnancy do not plague Sophie. Sophie is able to create a new life with the birth of Brigitte, while Martine's pregnancy leads her to insanity and death. The pregnancy locks Martine up in her own personal prison and asylum, as she is so afraid of what others would do to her if they knew her thoughts and nightmares.

MEMORY, OBATALA, BIRTH AS "THAT WHICH IS MISSING TO COMPLETE A PERSON, PLACE, OR THING."[50]

In between spiritual and physical existence, memory functions as a point of connection which births the ability to exist in multiple spaces simultaneously. Memory serves as a caption, a picture, which compels rememory, or the convergence of places, spaces, times, and people. In *Beloved*, Sethe describes rememory as, "Places, places are still there. If a house burns down, it's gone, but the place—the picture of it—stays, and not just in my rememory, but out there, in the world."[51] Hence, the creation of memory produces an additional space of existence "out there, in the word" as Sethe describes. Neither in the past or present nor here or there, the space and place of memory is liminal and multidimensional. Memory, then, acts as a bridge to the past and present and also as a passageway between the two. Without memory, many occurrences would occupy crevices within the mind but not the space and place within the memorial of existence. The concept of memory relates closely to the term and idea of Ayajo, as the memory of the ancient in a modern context is what initially creates Ayajo. Returning to the origins of origins, in an Ayajo context, places a modern narrative within the memorial spaces of an ancient problem or context, and the merging of the two spaces and places births new ground within memory. Further, the integration of storytelling and myth within the intersection of time constructs a narrative ground necessary to situate memory. Earlier discussions of Ayajo demonstrate how the intersection of the ancient and modern create a textual crossroads and *Breath, Eyes, Memory* provides a storehouse of examples.

At the intersection of her own trauma, Sophie visualizes Tante Atie while recalling Atie's screams of resistance to testing told to Sophie through stories. Sophie re-members both instances during her own testing, as Martine attempts to bind mother and daughter into the Marassa through her retelling a myth of the Marassa. Firmly situated between the past and present is the narrative memory of Atie's screams and the myth of the Marrassa, which creates a textual crossroads. Sophie's recollection of Atie's memory, while being tested by Martine, symbolizes a return to her origins and beginnings and the values and lessons that continue to guide her in life. As a surrogate in Sophie's formative years, Atie functions textually as an Obàtálá figure. Representing the head and the domain of memory, "Obàtálá is the revered old man who is symbolic of honored maturity, [and] Obàtálá demands and sanctions high morality."[52] It is important to note that, Obàtálá "is represented as both male and female because reason and good judgment come from both sexes. There is even a theory that Obàtálá could have been a hermaphrodite."[53] Tante Atie's regenerative powers exist within the memory of her African ancestry and her living presence. As her name illustrates, a tie, Tante Atie binds Sophie to a cultural lineage that surpasses the biological lineage of her mother or father, which is steeped in sexual violence and trauma. The cultural heartbeat of the novel, Sophie is essentially motherless and fatherless. Without tangible knowledge of her mother's rape, and the violent, nonmaterial memory of her father—who is only manifest in Martine's nightmares which Sophie attempts to wake or "save" her from—Sophie's parentage, through Atie, is inextricably linked to her ancestry rather than her direct parental biology. Notably, "Obàtálá is the creator deity . . . and shaper of human beings which he forms out of clay. . . . He is the one who shapes the fetus in the womb."[54] Atie gives Sophie, an Oshun like figure in the making, the maternal, cultural educational, and nutritional care she lacks from Martine. In her surrogacy, Atie teaches Sophie lessons of love and self-worth and births a space for Sophie to contemplate her own subjectivity, memory.

As Obàtálá lives in high places, representative of higher consciousness, Sophie must find higher ground to contemplate her subjectivity. Leaving New York with Joseph not only offers Sophie the love and shelter she seeks, but also offers her the space and place she needs for contemplation, Providence: "I was bound to be happy in a place called Providence. A place that destiny was calling me to. Fate! A town named after the Creator, the Almighty. Who would not want to live there?"[55] Hence, the location of Providence operates on two intersecting levels within the novel: one the actual city in Rhode Island and, two, the place of divine destiny. At the crossroads between the physical and spiritual realms, Sophie resides in the liminal and multidimensional space of memory. Somewhere between here and there and the past and present, this new ground births a clean slate, tableau rasa, for Sophie to rewrite her narrative. As in an Ayajo context, rewriting or revision requires a return to the ancient problem within a modern context. Thus, Sophie must return to the origin, which for her is the Oshun question.

Returning to the central tenets and philosophical ideologies of the Oshun question, the novel sends Sophie to the creation of humanity in Ifé: "known in the oral tradition as the original site of human habitation."[56] Providence functions as Ifé, the scared space where Sophie writes and rights her narrative. Reconstructing Providence as Ifé in turn reconstructs the form of Sophie's writing or righting of the past. For Sophie to return to the origins of humanity and the Oshun question, she must also, then, return to the sacred text of Ifá. Being with Joseph and conceiving Brigitte in love begins to rewrite the fixed narrative of sexual violence and trauma that plague the lives of the Caco women. And while the legacy of sexual violence and trauma is a physical and constant reminder for Sophie because of the injury she suffers from breaking her hymen, she attempts to reconcile the memory of violence and trauma through therapy and a sexual phobia group. However, it is Sophie's return to the high plateau of Haiti and the mother of mothers, Grandma Ifé, that leads to the answers she needs to heal and transcend. Sophie begins the spiritual journey of healing and fulfilling her role as an Oshun figure.

SPIRITUAL BODY, ANCESTORS, ÒRUNMÍLÀ, HIGH CONSCIOUSNESS AS "THE ABSENCE OF A LEVEL OF SOIL IN A STRATIGRAPHIC SAMPLE"[57]

Forming breath, eyes, and memory into one entity requires a container to hold within it the essence of what the novel constructs, a corpus. Danticat deconstructs the physical body to reconstruct the spiritual body that Sophie writes through the righting of the sexual violence and trauma the Caco women face throughout the novel. In addition, existing in both the physical and spiritual simultaneously enables Sophie to exist in and function between the two, mirroring Oshun's relationship as a divine entity who is responsible for the creation of humanity. As Ifá's composition of a corpus of narratives serves as a spiritual body of knowledge, the most salient narrative to this discussion is the creation of humanity, the birth of Brigitte functions as a body on which the rewriting of the creation story for the Caco women can exist. Sophie as both writer and creator, births a new textual landscape between the spiritual and physical realm in the form of new life, Brigitte. Through Brigitte, Sophie is able to redefine the narrative of mothers and daughters, and the generational violence inflicted on the female body, by rewriting the creation narrative through a matrilineal perspective, thus liberating and healing the Caco women.

Brigitte, as her name suggests, functions as a "bridge" between the living and their land of origin and also the ancestral spiritual realm. As the fleshly reincarnation of her ancestors, Brigitte returns the mother of mothers, Grandma Ifé, to her origins. It is for this reason that Grandma Ifé can see the reflections of all of her ancestors in Brigitte's face: "The tree has not split one mite. Isn't it a miracle that we can visit with all our kin, simply by looking into this face?"[58] The intersection of time, space, and place not only create a call and response but also an Ayajo crossroads. The spiritual connection with the ancestral realm, as Brigitte's face reflects, garners emphasis by the specific locale it also represents. Said differently, the connection between Brigitte, the youngest of the Caco women, and Grandma Ifé, the eldest, centers Brigitte within a specific lineage and place. As discussed earlier, Grandma Ifé functions as a symbol for the land of Ilé Ifé, the home and birthplace of Ifá. Brigitte functions as the corpus of Ifá that the people of Ifé rely upon and utilize for spiritual healing in their physical lives. Further, the connection between the youngest and eldest draws another parallel between the physical and spiritual realm—as the young come forth from the spiritual to the physical realm the elders are called to the spiritual realm from the physical. Their proximity to the respective realm positions places both elder and youth at intersecting points of existence. Mimicking the dynamic movement through the cosmogram, from one point to the next, the intersecting points the elder and youth experience creates moments of contact where ancestral knowledge and consciousness can transfer. In the text, Grandma Ifé reads into Brigitte, the blank slate of Ifá, her ancestral knowledge, visiting all her "kin" while tracing lines on the face of her granddaughter.

However, in order for the Caco women to heal, they must abide by the edicts of Ifá and get to a place of higher consciousness. Òrunmílà, acts as the spiritual guide and is the "patron and guardian of Ifá, the extensive oral tradition of Yourba knowledge and thought, a responsibility given to him by Olodumare."[59] As a spiritual guard of Ifá, Òrunmílà is known as a both the "second to the Creator . . . [and] witness to creation and destiny."[60] It is important to note that one of Òrunmílà's wives is said to be Oshun—also named "Spirit of divine origin—who creates the human population who seeks Ifá divination for answers to life's questions."[61] Oshun's role in the creation of humanity and their story and Òrunmílà's role as guardian of Ifá serve as part and parcel of Ifá divination, and this relationship serves an integral role within the novel.

Sophie's journey throughout the novel follows the points of the cosmogram and the representative ideas that each point represents. For example, the breaking of her hymen is the beginning of Sophie's freedom from a fixed narrative of female subjectivity within a patriarchal framework, and also signifies a breaking loose from the grip of Martine's sexual trauma and violence that ends up haunting both of them. Although liberatory, the severing of ties functions as a death. Sophie's use of the pestle, but not the mortar, in the violent but liberatory act of breaking her hymen, reserves the mortar as a space and place that is void of sexual violence and trauma. The mortar represents the divine and physical power of the womb when in the service of female subjectivity. Thus, through her own cosmic womb, Sophie is able to rebirth herself in the city of destiny, Providence. Brigitte's birth intertwines the realms, as the duality of Providence represents, and Sophie must navigate the liminality between the two on her journey to higher consciousness and complete freedom.

As earlier discussion reveals, Sophie's first trip back to Haiti, with Brigitte, is fraught with tension and unanswered questions, which prevent her from healing and freedom from the sexual trauma now physically and spiritually plaguing her marriage. Returning to her place of origin gives Sophie the narrative and spiritual space her sexual phobia group cannot, and she engages in a quest for answers to her own version of the Oshun question. Grandma Ifé provides what she can in terms of answers, but also gives Sophie something of much more value, healing through the pierced heart of Erzulie. Passing through the spiritual crossroads of Erzulie's heart, Sophie is able to mend her relationship with Martine and return to Joseph in Providence.

In the final chapter of the novel, as Sophie attempts to navigate the remaining aspects of her healing, Martine's fight with sanity, and the voice of the baby within her womb, ends. Martine's final act of liberation is stabbing herself seventeen times in the stomach. Sophie is tasked with ushering Martine from the physical realm into the spiritual realm, with her first act being to choose Martine's burial clothes. Sophie choses a crimson suit for Martine to wear in eternity. The color represents the dual nature of their surname, Caco. Although Martine loses the battle, she fights valiantly like the Caco soldiers. At the same time, Martine illuminates the plumage of the Caco bird that turns bright red in death through her burial suit. For Sophie, Martine also becomes the intersection, or crossroads, of Erzulie's wounded heart, where "she is the dream impaled eternally upon the cosmic cross-roads where the world of men and the world of divinity meet, and it is through her pierced hear that 'man ascends and the gods descend.'"[62] Similarly, for Sophie, Martine, in death becomes the "hot-blooded Erzulie who feared no men but rather made them her slaves, raped them, and killed them. She was the only woman with that power."[63] As Marc tries to dissuade Sophie of the suit's color choice, saying that "Saint Peter won't allow your mother into Heaven in that," Sophie's response centers both the mother and daughter's destiny, freeing them from a prefixed narrative: "She is going to Guinea . . . or she is going to be a star. She's going to be a butterfly or a lark in a tree. She's going to be free."[64] Both women reside within the spiritual landscape that locates the Caco matrilineal and ancestral lineage; Martine is an ancestor, and Sophie is consciousness. The juxtaposition of mother and daughter forms yet another crossroads between here and there. Sophie's final act of liberation occurs during Martine's internment. The burial becomes too much for Sophie, and she runs to the cane field. It is there, in the site of trauma, that Sophie constructs new ground by tearing down stalks of cane. Both Grandma Ifé and Tante Atie call out to Sophie asking, *"Ou libéré?* Are you free?"[65] Reflecting Sophie's first act of liberation, the breaking of her hymen, Sophie breaks new ground in the cane field and rewrites the site of trauma as a site of liberation. Unlike the first act, which separates her from Martine, the destruction of the cane unites mother and daughter in a new narrative space where they can both be free. Fittingly, Grandma Ifé ends the novel telling Sophie a new story:

> There is a place where women are buried in clothes the color of flames, where we drop coffee on the ground for those who went ahead, where the daughter is

never fully a woman until her mother has passed on before her. There is always a place where, if you listen closely in the night, you will hear your mother telling a story and at the end of the tale she will ask you this question *"Ou libéré?* Are you free, my daughter?" Now . . . you will know how to answer.[66]

NOTES

1. Horus avenges his father's death against Set.

2. Hortense Spillers, "Interstices a Small Drama of Words." *Black, White, and in Color: Essays on American Literature and Culture* (University of Chicago Press, 2003), 153.

3. Sojourner Truth, "Ar'n't I a Woman." In *The Norton Anthology of African American Literature*, edited by Henry Louis Gates and Valerie A. Smith (W. W. Norton & Company, 2014), 178.

4. Sharon Patricia Holland and Donald E. Pease, *Raising the Dead Readings of Death and (Black) Subjectivity* (Duke University Press, 200), 4–5.

5. For further explanation of the concept of "rememory," see Toni Morrison, *Beloved: A Novel*. First Vintage International (New York: Vintage International, 2004), 35–36.

6. This references the line "It was not a story to pass on" from Toni Morrison's *Beloved* (275).

7. Venertria Patton, *The Grasp That Reaches Beyond the Grave: The Ancestral Call in Black Women's Texts* (New York: State University of New York (SUNY) Press 2013), 28–31.

8. Molefi Asante and Ama Mazama, *Encyclopedia of African Religion* (Thousand Oaks: Sage, 2009), 336.

9. Ibid., 329.

10. For a deeper understanding of Ifá seek the Asante's Encyclopedia of African Religion and *Ifá Divination, Knowledge, Power, and Performance*.

11. Ayo Opefeyitimi, "Ayajo as Ifá in Mythical and Sacred Contexts." In *Ifá Divination, Knowledge, Power, and Performance*, edited by Jacob K. Olupona, and Rowland O. Abiodun (Indiana University Press, 2016), 18.

12. Andrew Apter, "Recasting Ifá Historicity and Recursive Recollection in Ifá Divination Texts." In *Ifá Divination, Knowledge, Power, and Performance*, edited by Jacob K. Olupona, and Rowland O. Abiodun (Indiana University Press, 2016), 44–45.

13. Opefeyitimi, "Ayajo as Ifá," 27.

14. Ibid., 18.

15. bell hooks, *Sisters of the Yam: Black Women and Self-Recovery* (Boston, MA: South End Press, 1993), 6.

16. Edwidge Danticat, *Breath, Eyes, Memory* (New York: Vintage Books, 1994), 154.

17. Ibid., 155.

18. Ibid., 154.

19. Ibid., 155.

20. Ibid., 156.

21. Ibid., 157.

22. Asante, *Encyclopedia of African Religion*, 331.

23. Maya Deren, *Divine Horsemen: Voodoo Gods of Haiti* (New York: Chelsea House, 1970), 144.

24. Ibid., 145.

25. Asante, *Encyclopedia*, 477.

26. Edwards and Mason, *Black Gods*, 99.

27. Danticat, *Breath, Eyes, Memory*, 21.

28. Edwards and Mason, *Black Gods*, 99.

29. Danticat, *Breath, Eyes, Memory*, 21.

30. Asante, *Encyclopedia*, 509.

31. See Chapter 2 for more explanation and an integrated image of the culture-lacune and the cosmogram.

32. See Chapter 2 for more explanation and an integrated image of the culture-lacune and the cosmogram.

33. Myriam J. A. Chancy, *Framing Silence: Revolutionary Novels by Haitian Women* New (Brunswick: Rutgers University Press, 1997), 17.

34. Edwards and Mason, *Black Gods*, 92.

35. Ibid., 94.

36. Sharon Patricia Holland and Donald E. Pease, *Raising the Dead Readings of Death and (Black) Subjectivity* (Duke University Press, 2000), 43.

37. Chancy, *Framing Silence*, 17.

38. Unlike the way Isis re-members Osiris to resurrect him, the Caco women are unsuccessful in their attempts. In addition, the underlying use, even in the context of failure, of the myth creates Ayajo.

39. Chancy, *Framing Silence*, 17.

40. Edwards and Mason, *Black Gods*, 33.

41. Danticat, *Breath, Eyes, Memory*, 235.

42. Edwards and Mason, *Black Gods*, 33.

43. Charles Phillips and Alan Axelrod, "Haitian Revolt, 1918–1920." *Reference Guide to the Major Wars and Conflicts in History: Wars in the Early 20th Century (1900 to 1950)*, Charles Phillips, Facts on File, 1st edition (2015).

44. Edwards and Mason, *Black Gods*, 33.

45. Danticat, *Breath, Eyes, Memory*, 84.

46. Danticat, *Breath, Eyes, Memory*, 84.

47. Ibid., 85.

48. Ibid., 86–88.

49. Ibid., 59.

50. Chancy, *Framing Silence*, 17.

51. Toni Morrison, *Beloved: A Novel*. First Vintage International (New York: Vintage International, 2004), 36.

52. Edwards and Mason, *Black Gods*, 42.

53. Ibid., 46.

54. Ibid., 43.

55. Danticat, *Breath, Eyes, Memory*, 89.

56. Asante, *Encyclopedia*, 507.

57. Chancy, *Framing Silence*, 17.

58. Danticat, *Breath, Eyes, Memory*, 105.

59. Asante, *Encyclopedia*, 507.

60. Ibid., 507.

61. Ibid., 509.

62. Deren, *Divine Horsemen*, 145.

63. Danticat, *Breath, Eyes, Memory*, 227.

64. Ibid., 228.

65. Ibid., 223.

66. Ibid., 234.

Conclusion

Existing Beyond the Gaze: Finding Home in the Works of Edwidge Danticat

Describing Africana women's subjectivity, Marita Bonner contends:

> Motionless on the outside. But on the inside? . . . with a smile, ever so slight, at the eyes so that Life will flow into and not by you. And you can gather, as it passes, the essences, the overtones, the tints, the shadows; draw understanding of yourself. And then you can, when Time is ripe, swoop to your feet—at your full height—at a single gesture. Ready to go where? Why . . . Wherever God motions.[1]

Hurston echoes Bonner: "She pulled in her horizon like a great fish-net. Pulled it from around the waist of the world and draped it over her shoulder. So much of life in its meshes! She called in her soul to come and see."[2] Shange completes the triplicate refrain: "I found god in myself & I loved her/I loved her fiercely."[3] Taken together, these quotes illuminate the evolution of Black women writing into existence their subjectivity within an Africana diasporic context and outside of Occidental discourse fraught with hegemonic myths and images meant to devalue and relegate blackness and Black women, specifically, to spaces and places of silence and devaluation. Marita Bonner etches out her own subjectivity in the image of Buddha, who she surmises is a Black woman. At the end of Zora Neale Hurston's magnus opus, Janie Crawford becomes a divine entity imbued with the nature of being she seeks in the beginning of the novel. What Janie calls her "soul to come and see" is her own divine image of being that has come to fruition. While Shange, through the woman in red and all the other colored girls, veritably and boldly, finds God within herself and loves her, not only deeming God as a Black woman, but a God that Black women find within themselves and the hands that lay on healing.

The narratives surrounding Black women, their bodies, and their value is not only a familiar tale, but it is one entrenched and encrusted into the historical and modern imagination and myth of Black women's subjectivity. Deborah Gray White in *Ar'n't I a Woman*? posits that, "The black woman's position at the nexus of America's sex and race mythology has made it most difficult for her to escape the mythology. . . . If she is rescued from the myth of the Negro, the myth of woman traps her. If she escapes the myth of woman, the myth of the Negro still ensnares her."[4] While this quagmire of mythology still attempts to enslave Black women to a given identity, it also creates a space of liminality which Black women utilize in service of their own voice and subjectivity. Famously, Sojourner Truth in 1851 addresses, from which White borrows the title of her text, the gendered and racialized discourse that constitutes the myths and legends of Black women and their subjectivity. The disapproval of Truth speaking her truth from both white men and white women finds its genesis in the same conundrum that White defines. Truth should not be able to speak or give voice to her lived experiences because she is a woman and because she is Black. The intersection of being a Black woman seems to doubly bind Truth to the borders and boundaries of the vision of Black women and their subjectivity permeating the white imagination. However, within the manacles of history attempting to re-enslave her to an object position, Truth flips the narrative script through her famous interrogative refrain, Ar'n't I a Woman? Truth's version of her existence creates a space within the dominant narrative discourse because of the insertion of her voice through the audible rhetoric of a speech, but also creates a space outside of the narrative discourse because her experiences do not fit within the parameters of the white imagination. Truth exists beyond even the definitions of the white men and white women who attempt to define and limit her existence. Truth argues: "Nobody eber help me into carriages, or over mud puddles, or give me any best place, and ar'n't I a woman? Look at me! Look at my arm! I have plowed, and planted, and gathered into barns, and no man could head me—and ar'n't I a woman?"[5] One cannot deny Truth is a woman, nor can one deny that she is Black. So, where is it that Truth's truth resides? The truth resides in the unspoken answer to Truth's rhetorical question. In the essay "Interstices" Hortense Spillers gives nomenclature to the space where Truth's answer resides. Spillers posits: "The missing word—the interstice— both as that which allows us to speak about and that which enables us to speak at all—shares, in this case, a common border with another country of symbols—the iconographic."[6] The missing word, or in Truth's case the missing answer, creates the liminality that Black women possess and utilize to engender new grounds and landscapes conducive to their subjectivity and that symbolize the enduring and refraining voice uttered within and out of that space. In other words, the interstice is the place where Black women's narratives and discourses reside. Although Spillers concentrates her examination of the subversion of discursive silence within non-fiction texts like Truth's, this framework also extends to the interstices Black women create when writing fiction through a racialized and gendered perspective. Toni Morrison in "Home" discusses the ways in which language and writing can be both a liberator or an enslaver, but how she uses language to give substance to a raced voice and perspective. Morrison posits:

> Only in fiction writing. In that activity alone did I feel coherent, unfettered. There, in the process of writing, was the willed illusion, the control, the pleasure of nestling up ever closer to meaning. There alone the delight of redemption, the seduction of origination. It became increasingly clear how language both liberated and imprisoned me.[7]

Even the idea of obscuring Truth's language by Gage to, we assume, be more accepted as palatable and "realistic" is an attempt to reinscribe the myths of Black women back onto Truth.

Nevertheless, in a world that continually diminishes the value and worth of Black women, the task falls upon her to find worth when no one, not even her own community of men at times or instances, sees her, the Black woman, as a living, breathing, and spiritually endowed entity. Through language and narrative spaces, liberation occurs not only for the Black woman, but also, in some cases ironically, her community. Hortense Spillers, discussing the idea of Black women's bodies being captive even when liberated, argues:

> The captive body, then, brings into focus a gathering of social realities as well as a metaphor for value so thoroughly interwoven in their literal and figurative emphases that distinctions between them are virtually useless. Even though the captive flesh/body has been "liberated," and no one need pretend that even the quotation marks do not matter, dominant symbolic activity, the ruling episteme that releases the dynamics of naming and valuation, remains grounded in the originating metaphors of captivity and mutilation so that it is as if neither time nor history, nor historiography and its topics, shows movement, as the human subject is "murdered" over and over again by the passions of a bloodless and anonymous archaism, showing itself in endless disguise . . . just as the retrieval of mutilated female bodies will likely be "backward" for some people. Neither the shameface of the embarrassed, nor the not-looking-back of the self-assured is of much interest to us [Black women], and will not help at all if rigor is our dream. We might concede, at the very least, that sticks and bricks might break our bones, but words will most certainly kill us.[8]

Thus, survival for Black women is in the words they create and craft in the service of subjectivity. Only then, amid words autochthonous to Black women's subjectivity, can true liberation of the Black body occur. Otherwise, as Spillers outlines, death is eminent. Black women's fiction through the structure, symbol, and iconography of a divine container covert narrative spaces, plots primed for discourse, as places of origin and existence. As Alice Walker searches for what can be found in her mother's garden, the expression of her mother's spiritually endowed being, she expresses that, "I went in search of the secret of what has fed that muzzled and often mutilated, but vibrant, creative spirit that the black woman has inherited, and that pops out in wild and unlikely places to this day."[9] And what did Walker find when she was searching for her mother's garden? The origin of the origin. The space and place of creation where the myths, legends, and folklore passed down for generations seen and unseen are planted. Perhaps, she witnessed Isis re-membering Osiris and giving birth to both the story of creation and the salvation of humanity in the form of her son Horus. Perhaps, it was Isis breathing in the symbol of life, the Ankh, Djhuti hieroglyphically holds to her nose. The myth of Osiris follows the motion and meaning of the cosmogram—death, rebirth, birth and higher consciousness—and becomes the ethos that would inspire the biblical trinity, however, not without the narrative prowess of Isis to reconstruct a body for the narrative to reside within.

Hence, this book is a project of reclamation, as the general field of Africana studies is an interdisciplinary reclamation, of space and place to study and examine Africana subjectivity within a cultural canon utilizing African-ness as the given apparatus. This work aims to highlight the depth and breadth of Africana subjectivity as written, crafted, and birthed through the literary tradition of Africana women. In fact, the research within these pages attends to the textual topography diasporic authors, like Danticat, create in order to contemplate Africana subjectivity and consciousness. The primacy of this liminal and uncolonized landscape and conversation remains an imperative aim in the field and has importance in the cultural production of prose. These landscapes reflect Africana people's craving and desire for these spaces and places, as well as people and characters that reflect their lived and embodied histories, experiences, and higher consciousness. One may argue that Edwidge Danticat's fictional works invite engagement in the imperative and important project of cultural and cosmological reclamation by utilizing ritual and its modern articulations. Integrating ancient practices of healing and restoration into the modern landscapes of novels, Danticat's texts transcend the limitation of time and space and create liminal places for modern diasporic people to return to. This return regenerates a timeless practice where ancient practices impact present day negotiations of Africana consciousness.

Thus, this book like that of Africana Studies is a Sankofa—a looking back to origins and ancient beliefs and practices to reorient the present and inform the future of literary expressions and Africana consciousness. Like Asa Hilliard's argument, in *SBA: The Reawakening of the African Mind,* the primacy of liminal and uncolonized landscapes and discourses is imperative to building and rebuilding of Africana consciousness. Specifically, Hilliard argues: "Before any substantial healing can take place, we Africans must 'begin at the beginning' and peruse the wisdom of our ancestors."[10] Hillard's argument as an intellectual enterprise summons the ancestors as the proprietors of cultural awareness, knowledge, and consciousness, while his argument as a cultural enterprise cultivates ancestral veneration as the root and pathway to the healing and restoration of Africana peoples. Both the intellectual and cultural argument Hilliard produces highlight the importance and impact that ancestors and ancestral knowledge have on its progeny. In particular, practices of healing and restoration, such as ritual, require ancestral presence, and knowledge as a functional element. Indeed, Edwidge Danticat's utilization of ritual, and by virtue ancestral presence, have precisely accomplished Hilliard's directive by centralizing ancestors and ancestral knowledge amid modern-day people.

Ritual remains an important and culturally significant trope in Africana literary productions. Although a liminal articulation, ritual provides a stability for the Diaspora, as it maintains a connection to the ancestral realm and reifies a space and practice of transformation. Ritual is a passageway for the Africana spirit even when the physical reality of the flesh is steeped in a hellish or nightmarish reality. Ritual provides movement between the spiritual and physical realms for the Africana spirit to traverse, even in novel form. Danticat helps to fill-in the literary need of analytical expansion for liminal and ritual spaces for Africana peoples to contemplate and consider their own subjectivity. Her commitment to healing and transformation of the Africana subject is formidable. Ritual returns to the origins of Africana cosmological and philosophical notions and the building blocks of Africana consciousness to establish a text of divination transposed in a space and place congruent for the negotiation of Africana consciousness. Danticat's fictional corpus extends beyond the rearticulation of a problem and issue and works toward the transformation of a person or a people. Within Africana-based narratives, ritual extends the narrative beyond page and plot and creates textual ground that functions as a divine container of Africana consciousness. Ritual reifies communal ideological beliefs and practices and creates the space and place to tell the often unheard and, or, misshapen narratives of Africana consciousness. Ritual in literature engenders textual spaces to stories often denied, rejected, or subsumed, and allows them to speak truths into existence. In an Africana and diasporic context this is of particular import because of the historical and systemic attempts to dismiss these narratives. Thus, ritual provides the space to revise this glaring omission and to contemplate Africana subjectivity and identity beyond the borders, boundaries, and limitations of prescribed identity construction and politics. Hence, within the darkness and absence of continual erasure, ritual engenders space congruent to rebirth Africana subjectivity and identity within the parameters of Africana consciousness. Ritual not only sheds light on the Africana subject, but it shifts the Africana subject as the center of the Africana world.

Danticat's fiction is a project of healing, and her body of work speaks to her mission of deliverance and freedom for the Diaspora. Danticat's use of ritual within her fictional texts centralize not only the ancient practices necessary for the healing and restoration of Africana peoples, but it also centralizes the Africana peoples who need to utilize the ancient practices, such as ritual, for healing and restoration of consciousness. Danticat's recognition and identification of the power inherent in Africana traditions and practices function in her literature as an act of reclamation of Africana consciousness. Her fiction provides not only space but function for ritual using the cosmographic symbol of the cosmogram. Although the principles and practices associated with the cosmogram have been discussed in previous chapters, it is imperative to express the potency of the symbol in textual form. The inscription of the cosmogram not only inscribes the text with the symbol's ideology, but it also inscribes its ritualistic function. As the cosmogram also denotes movement, as one reads and moves through the text, they also move through the cosmogram. Thus, ritual seamlessly permeates through the chapters and passages, occurring as a simultaneous performance by the characters as well as readers. Through ritual, Danticat's work restores, centers, and heals.

Collectively the novels under examination in this inquiry—*The Dew Breaker, The Farming of Bones, Claire of the Sea Light,* and *Breath, Eyes, Memory*—etch the cruciform symbol of the crossroads and extend the principles of the cosmogram beyond the pages of the novels. Reading these texts in an asynchronous, yet thematic, sequence allows one to move through these texts without the limitations of time and space, as if textually moving through the cosmogram. In fact, if these four texts are read in the same counterclockwise movement of the cosmogram, following its points, readings render a cosmographic framework for interpreting these texts collectively, and, perhaps, ultimately Edwidge Danticat's fictional oeuvre. The cosmogram within a cosmogram creates the ultimate textual crossroads whereby ritual becomes the form and function of the body of work and the container for its application. Thus, the cosmographic rendering of the ultimate crossroads this quadrilateral of novels engenders could be applied as a literary praxis.

Similar to the way the symbol of the cosmogram functions as a world within a world in an unadulterated space, where access is gained by utilizing an ancient practice like ritual, Danticat's texts provide a world within a world for its readers. Edwidge Danticat instinctively and consistently creates spaces for the contemplation of Africana subjectivity in her fiction, excavating corridors of existence, subjectivity, and identity between the static and invariable renderings and images of Africana people employed to regulate and relegate Blackness to something other than its own articulation. However, the container for the world within a world is not a physical locale. Many of the places and spaces within Danticat's works, created by the use of the cosmogram, maintain the appearance of the functional realities of the people who live within them, but, all the while, harken to something greater if only readers shift their visual lens and focus toward the great beyond. While the idea of a world within a world has ancient articulations, it requires reconstruction in a modern context. Conceptually and theoretically this book constructs an edifice to house the merging of the conceptual idea of the cosmogram within fictional works firmly entrenched in the cosmological articulations of the symbol. Conceptualizing the idea through an Africana spiritual lens and envisioning the texts through an ancient concept without essentializing Africana concepts within the text and the places and people the texts address, create the cosmographic paradigm for the books to be sifted through and was a creative endeavor for this project, for which the blueprints can be found in the introduction and framework. But what will be found here? Holistically vibrant living beings engaging in rich and full lives in wondrous landscapes beyond the view of the white gaze, beyond the reach of those who do not know or cannot comprehend the secret of its existence. Like the myths and legends her fictional texts often employ, Danticat's texts attend to the liminal spaces of diasporic life, which provide healing balm to fabricated and fractured identity constructions. Danticat's works exist outside of our perceived realities of the world. They defy gravity, space, and time. The novel itself is creating alternative realities and spaces for people to consider and to contemplate existence. Her fiction is the vehicle that transports her readers to a space, a place, where one can transform into a being that embodies one's own definition of identity and reality. Individually, each of the texts under examination in this book utilizes the cosmological signification of ritual to create textual space extended through the employment of ritual to contemplate Africana subjectivity through the cosmological and philosophical lens of the cosmogram. Thus, her texts create new ground, and Danticat follows in the footsteps of her literary ancestors.

As one of Danticat's self-proclaimed literary mothers, Toni Morrison's ascension to the spiritual realm, joining the great reign of ancestors, leaves a palpable absence here in the physical and literary realm. Morrison will continue to bless us with the resounding refrain of the words she left and the incredible reach and span of her intellectual and critical projects within the discipline of Africana studies. In the wake of this seismic earthquaking loss, whose reverberations will be felt by generations of Africana people worldwide, the question of who will inherit the role of literary mother is in the undercurrent of every conversation about Morrison after her death. This is not to say who will replace Morrison, as only Toni Morrison is Toni Morrison, but it is to question how the literary and critical seeds that she planted and cultivated will still grow. Stated in another way, whose words will continue to water and grow Africana consciousness? While the great mother, Toni Morrison, leaves behind many literary heirs, Edwidge Danticat stands out as an exceptional example of Morrison's rearing and teaching. As one of Morrison's most successful heirs, Edwidge Danticat extends the call Morrison makes in *Playing in the Dark*. In this work Morrison argues that textual space beyond the Occidental gaze is an imperative project for literature that includes the Africana subject within the terms and turf of Africana consciousness. Specifically, Morrison posits: "These chapters put forth an argument for extending the study of American literature into what I hope will be a wider landscape. I want to draw a map, so to speak, of a critical geography and use that map to open as much space or discovery . . . without the mandate of conquest."[11] To this end, Morrison stresses the import of Africana space, and, moreover, the importance of Africana space within literature. In all of Morrison's literature, she created ground for the multiplicity of iterations of the Africana subject.

Similarly, Edwidge Danticat creates fertile ground where the seeds of life sprout new growth, new images, and new consciousness steeped in blackness. Organically and ethically sustainable crops meant for spiritual consumption and edification of the Africana body, for all those who dare to, as Danticat's book is titled, *Create Dangerously* spaces and places of existence free of constraints and limitations. Spaces and places beyond the borders and boundaries of what Toni Morrison deems the dark presence whose function and purpose in literary spaces and imaginations is merely to define whiteness. Instead, at the behest of her literary mother's call, Danticat summons and communes with the ancestors to build, to create, what the Africana needs to exist and survive. For example, in the *New Yorker* article "Black Bodies in Motion and Pain," written in the wake of the Emanuel African Methodist Episcopal Church shooting, Danticat recalls Morrison as a segue to negotiate the concept of home for Africana people all over the world, even those who are citizen and at "home" like those killed in the shooting. Danticat muses:

> We are not always welcomed, especially if we are viewed as different and dangerous, or if we end up, as novelist Toni Morrison described in her Nobel lecture, on the edges of towns that cannot bear our company. Will we ever have

a home in this place, or will we always be adrift from the home we knew? Or
home we have never known?[12]

In her fiction, Danticat poses a solution to the questions posed at the end of
this quote and creates a home for those "adrift" and seeking a home. The
spaces she creates within her texts give way to fertile textual landscapes.
Moreover, Edwidge Danticat's reference of Morrison iterates Danticat's mission in continuing and extending the work of Toni Morrison. As Morrison's
literature textually constructs the path, land, and structure providing the
blueprint for the replication of home, Morrison teaches other wordsmiths and
architects how to build safe houses along the literary underground for the
Africana fugitives seeking safe passage to freedom. Danticat learned well,
and her literature builds home on the textual landscapes she crafts.

Edwidge Danticat's writing creates a home from the tools and materials
left for her by her literary mothers. Danticat takes her place among those
who boldly construct edifices where Africana peoples can warm their spirits
before an endless fire in a soft cushioned chair. A home where the ancestral
drums beat day in and day out while libations flow like the "ancient dusky
rivers" of Langston Hughes's poem "The Negro Speaks of Rivers."[13] A home
that is shrouded in the elders' blessings and wisdom, of lessons of protection,
of words creating agency and breathing life into voices, spirits, and stories
silenced and all but forgotten by the world. A home, not a house, full of the
soft underbellies of mourning doves. A home surrounded by the protection
of Heru's watchful eye and fortified by the Hawk's battle cries reverberating
through the pine's breeze. A home that is a space and place of peace, rest, and
healing and hidden from the outside world. A home that one can only get to
by traveling ancient roads covered by the shade of trees and overgrown brush.
A home where one finds self. A home where the weary can find respite and
the injured can find healing balm. A home where the thinker can think, the
singer can sing, the dreamer can dream.

Word by log, sentence by nail, passage by shingle, Danticat seamlessly
creates home on the textually cultivated ground hidden and laid bare by
her literary foremothers, deep within a thicket. Danticat creates a home for
the weary travelers wandering in the wilderness searching for the promised
land, a place to call home. A place to finally lay one's burdens down as
Baby Suggs instructs Sethe to do in Morrison's *Beloved.*[14] What Danticat
does within the Africana Diaspora is not only fresh but ancestral. Danticat
expands the projects of her literary foremothers, especially, Toni Morrison.
In fact, Nikki Giovanni names Danticat, in the *Democracy Now* interview
reflecting on Morrison's death, as the heir apparent for the Noble Laureate.[15]
Giovanni seemingly is also alluding to something else, that Danticat is firmly
entrenched in the path where Morrison left off, standing in the footsteps of

one of greatest foremothers and storytellers of all time. Edwidge Danticat's construction of home is a place where the Diaspora find individual and collective truths in stories that speak to them and with them creating an endless dialogue.

Where this project ends, is also where it begins. The merging together of a spiritual and literary enterprise creates a new and revolutionary critical lens to examine the fictional texts of Danticat and, perhaps, other Africana women authors. This approach creates a space for the examination of Africana women writer's articulations of self, identity, and subjectivity. Specifically, this approach creates the space for the healing and restoration work on a communal level that Africana women engage in their daily and lived experiences. These spaces, not found in traditional modes, align with the discipline of Africana studies by centering what is typically left to the margins. This project was an ambitious attempt to merge mixed methodologies in order to illuminate Africana Women's literature as an instinctive and instructive space for exploring the healing and restoration of Africana consciousness. Subsequently, more exploration into the cosmological and philosophical offerings of Danticat, and other diasporic authors is needed. Specifically, frameworks that extend the borders and boundaries of physical reality and incorporate liminal spaces as textual landscape are of import.

NOTES

1. Marita Boner. "On Being Young—A Woman—and Colored." *Double-take: A Revisionist Harlem Renaissance Anthology*, edited Venetria K Patton, and Maureen Honey (New Brunswick, NJ: Rutgers University Press, 2001), 112.

2. Zora Neale Hurston. *Their Eyes Were Watching God* (HarperCollins, 2006), 193.

3. Ntozake Shange. *For Colored Girls Who Have Considered Suicide When the Rainbow Is Enuf: A Choreopoem* (Collier Books, 1989). 63.

4. Deborah Gray White. *Ar'n't I a Woman?* (W.W. Norton & Company, 1999), 28.

5. Sojourner Truth. "Ar'n't I a Woman." *The Norton Anthology of African American Literature*, edited by Henry Louis Gates and Valerie A. Smith (W.W. Norton & Company, 2014), 180.

6. Hortense Spillers. "Interstices a Small Drama of Words." *Black, White, and in Color: Essays on American Literature and Culture* (University of Chicago Press, 2003), 156.

7. Toni Morrison. "Home." *The House That Race Built: Black Americans, U.S. Terrain*, edited by Wahneema H. Lubiano, 1st ed. (New York: Random House, 1997), 3.

8. Hortense Spillers. "Mama's Baby, Papa's Maybe: An American Grammar Book." *Black, White, and in Color: Essays on American Literature and Culture* (University of Chicago Press, 2003), 68.

9. Alice Walker. *In Search of Our Mothers' Gardens* (Harcourt, 1983), 239.

10. Asa G Hilliard. *SBA: The Reawakening of the African Mind.* Revised (Gainesville: Makare Publications, 1998), 2.

11.Toni Morrison. *Playing in the Dark: Whiteness and the Literary Imagination* (First Vintage Books. New York: Vintage Books, 1993), 3.

12.Edwidge Danticat. "Black Bodies in Motion and in Pain." The New Yorker, 2015.

13.Langston Hughes. *Selected Poems of Langston Hughes* (Vintage Classics. New York: Vintage Books, 1990), 4.

14.Toni Morrison. *Beloved: A Novel* (First Vintage International. New York: Vintage International, 2004).

15.Amy Goodman. "Toni Morrison Will Always Be with Us": Angela Davis, Nikki Giovanni, and Sonia Sanchez Pay Tribute Democracy Now! (Organization, 2019), dir. 2019. *Democracy Now!* Democracy Now!

Bibliography

Ameka, Felix. "Access Rituals in West African Communities an Ethnographic Perspective." In *Ritual Communication*, edited by Senft, Gunter, and Ellen B Basso. Wenner-Gren International Symposium Series. Oxford: Bloomsbury Publications (2010): 127–152.

Anderson, Benedict R. *Imagined Communities: Reflections on the Origin and Spread of Nationalism.* Rev. ed. London: Verso, 2006.

Anzaldúa Gloria. *Borderlands: La Frontera.* 2nd ed. San Francisco: Aunt Lute Books, 1999.

Apter, Andrew. "Recasting Ifá Historicity and Recursive Recollection in Ifá Divination Texts." In *Ifá Divination, Knowledge, Power, and Performance*, edited by Jacob K. Olupona and Rowland O. Abiodun. Indiana University Press (2016): 43–49.

Asante, Molefi K. *Afrocentricity, the Theory of Social Change.* Buffalo, NY: Amulefi Publications, 2003.

Asante, Molefi K., and Ama Mazama. *Encyclopedia of African Religion.* Thousand Oaks: Sage, 2009.

Boner, Marita. "On Being Young—A Woman—and Colored." *Double-take: A Revisionist Harlem Renaissance Anthology*, edited by Venetria K. Patton and Maureen Honey. New Brunswick, NJ: Rutgers University Press (2001): 109–112.

Brøndum, Lena. "The Persistence of Tradition." In *Black Imagination and the Middle Passage*, edited by Maria Diedrich, Henry Louis Gates, and Carl Pedersen, W.E.B. Du Bois Institute. New York: Oxford University Press (1999): 153–163.

Browder, Anthony T. *Nile Valley Contributions to Civilization: Study Guide.* Exploding the Myths, Vol. 1. Washington, DC: Institute of Karmic Guidance, 1994.

Brown, Karen McCarthy. *Mama Lola: A Vodou Priestess in Brooklyn.* Updated and expanded. Comparative Studies in Religion and Society, 4. Berkeley: University of California Press, 2001.

Budge, E. A. Wallis. trans. *The Book of the Dead: The Papyrus of Ani in the British Museum.* New York: Dover Publications, 1967.

Candelario, Ginetta E. B., Edwidge Danticat, Loida Maritza Perez, Myriam J. A. Chancy, and Nelly Rosario. "Voices from Hispaniola: A Meridians Roundtable with Edwidge Danticat, Loida Maritza Perez, Myriam J. A. Chancy, and Nelly Rosario." *Meridians: Feminism, Race, Transnationalism* 5, no. 1 (2004): 68–91.

Chancy, Myriam J. A. *Framing Silence: Revolutionary Novels by Haitian Women.* New Brunswick: Rutgers University Press, 1997.

Christian, Barbara T. "Ritualistic Process and the Structure of Paule Marshall's *Praisesong for the Widow.*" In *Black Feminist Criticism: Perspectives on Black Women Writers.* Pergamon Press, 1985.

Clark, VèVè A. "Developing Diaspora Literacy and Marasa Consciousness." *Theatre Survey* 50, no. 1 (2009): 9–18.

Danticat, Edwidge. "Black Bodies in Motion and in Pain." The New Yorker, 2015.

———. *Breath, Eyes, Memory.* New York: Vintage Books, 1994.

———. *Claire of the Sea Light.* New York: Alfred A. Knopf, 2013.

———. *Create Dangerously: The Immigrant Artist at Work.* Princeton: Princeton University Press, 2010.

———. *Krik? Krak!* New York: Soho Press, 1995.

———. *The Dew Breaker.* New York: Vintage Books, 2005.

———. *The Farming of Bones.* New York: Soho Press, 1998.

Danticat, Edwidge, and Garnette Cadogan. "Edwidge Danticat." *Bomb* 126, no. 126 (2013): 104–110.

Dash, Julie. *Daughters of the Dust: The Making of an African American Woman's Film.* New York: New Press, 1992.

Davies, Carole Boyce. *Black Women, Writing, and Identity: Migrations of the Subject.* London: Routledge, 1994.

Dayan, Joan. *Haiti, History, and the Gods.* Berkeley: University of California Press, 1998.

Deren, Maya. *Divine Horsemen: Voodoo Gods of Haiti.* New York: Chelsea House, 1970.

Dove, Rita. "Parsley." In *The Norton Anthology of African American Literature*, edited by Henry Louis Gates and Valerie A. Smith. W.W. Norton & Company (2014): 1360.

Drewal, Henry John, Marilyn Houlberg, and Fowler Museum at UCLA. *Mami Wata: Arts for Water Spirits in Africa and Its Diasporas.* Los Angeles: Fowler Museum at UCLA (2008): 60–83.

Drewal, Henry John, et al. *Yoruba: Nine Centuries of African Art and Thought.* Center for African Art in association with H.N. Abrams Inc., Publishers, 1989.

Edwards, Gary, and John Mason. 1998. *Black Gods—Òrìṣà Studies in the New World.* Rev. 4th Brooklyn, NY: Yorùbá Theological Archministry.

Fu-Kiau, Kimbwandènde Kia Bunseki. *African Cosmology of the Bântu-Kôngo: Tying the Spiritual Knot: Principles of Life & Living.* 2nd ed. Brooklyn: Athelia Henrietta Press, 2001.

Gates, Henry Louis. *The Signifying Monkey.* New York: Oxford, 1998.

Goodman, Amy. "Toni Morrison Will Always Be with Us": Angela Davis, Nikki Giovanni & Sonia Sanchez Pay Tribute Democracy Now! (Organization), dir. 2019. *Democracy Now!* Democracy Now!

————. Interview with Edwidge Danticat. *Novelist Edwidge Danticat: "Haitians are Very Resilient, But it Does Not Mean They Can Suffer More Than Other People."* Democracy Now! (Organization), dir. 2011. *Democracy Now!* Democracy Now!

Graw, Knut. "Beyond Expertise: Reflections on Specialist Agency and the Autonomy of the Divinatory Ritual Process." *Africa (Pre-2011)* 79, no. 1 (2009): 92–109.

Griffin, Jasmine, Farah. "Textual Healing: Claiming Black Women's Bodies, The Erotic Resistance in Contemporary Novels of Slavery." *Callaloo* 19, no. 2 (1996): 519–536.

Gundaker, Grey. "The Kongo Cosmogram in Historical Archaeology and the Moral Compass of Dave the Potter." *Historical Archaeology* 45, no. 2 (2011): 176–183.

Haitian Studies Association, and University of California, Santa Barbara. Center for Black Studies. *Journal of Haitian Studies* 7, no. 2 (Fall 2001): 1–173.

Headlee, Celeste. "Dominicans, Haitians Remember Parsley Massacre": Julia Alvarez and Edwidge Danticat. dir. 2012. *Tell Me More.* NPR News.

Hilliard, Asa G. *SBA: The Reawakening of the African Mind.* Revised., Gainesville: Makare Publications, 1998.

Holland, Sharon Patricia, and Donald E. Pease. *Raising the Dead Readings of Death and (Black) Subjectivity.* Duke University Press, 2000.

Holloway, Karla F. C. *Moorings & Metaphors: Figures of Culture and Gender in Black Women's Literature.* New Brunswick: Rutgers University Press, 1992.

hooks, bell. *Sisters of the Yam: Black Women and Self-Recovery.* Boston, MA: South End Press, 1993.

Hudson-Weems, Clenora. *Africana Womanism: Reclaiming Ourselves.* 4th rev. Troy: Bedford, 2004.

Hughes, Langston. *Selected Poems of Langston Hughes.* Vintage Classics. New York: Vintage Books, 1990.

Hurston, Zora Neale. *Their Eyes Were Watching God.* HarperCollins, 2006.

Jahn, Janheinz. *Muntu: The New African Culture.* New York: Grove Press, 1961.

Jennings, Theodore W. "On Ritual Knowledge." *The Journal of Religion* 62, no. 2, (1982): 111–127.

Johnson, E. Patrick, and Mae Henderson. *Black Queer Studies: A Critical Anthology.* Durham: Duke University Press, 2005.

Karenga, Maulana. *Maat, the Moral Ideal in Ancient Egypt: A Study in Classical African Ethics.* Los Angeles: University of Sankore Press, 2006.

Katz-Hyman, Martha B. *World of a Slave: Encyclopedia of the Material Life of Slaves in the United States.* Vol. 1: A - I. Santa Barbara: Greenwood, 2011.

Kirby, Mandy. *The Language of Flowers: A Miscellany.* London: Macmillan, 2011.

Kolawole, Mary E. M. *Womanism and African Consciousness.* Trenton: Africa World Press, 1997.

Levine, Lawrence W. *Black Culture and Black Consciousness: Afro-American Folk Thought from Slavery to Freedom.* 30th ed. New York: Oxford University Press, 2007.

Mbiti, John S. *African Religions & Philosophy.* New York: Praeger, 1969.

Mihas, Elena. *Upper Perené Arawak Narratives of History, Landscape, and Ritual.* Lincoln: University of Nebraska Press, 2015.

Minh-Ha, Trinh, T. *Woman, Native, Other: Writing Postcoloniality and Feminism*. Bloomington: Indiana University Press, 1989.

Mirabal, Nancy Raquel. "Dyasporic Appetites and Longings: An Interview with Edwidge Danticat." *Callaloo* 30, no. 1 (2007): 26–39.

Moraga, Cherríe, and Anzaldúa Gloria. *This Bridge Called My Back: Writings by Radical Women of Color*. Fourth. Albany: State University of New York (SUNY) Press, 2015.

Morrison, Toni. *Beloved: A Novel*. First Vintage International. New York: Vintage International, 2004.

———. "Home" *The House That Race Built: Black Americans, U.S. Terrain*, edited by Wahneema H. Lubiano, 1st ed. New York: Random House, 1997.

———. *Playing in the Dark: Whiteness and the Literary Imagination*. First Vintage Books. New York: Vintage Books, 1993.

———. "Rootedness: The Ancestor as Foundation." *The Norton Anthology of African American Literature*, edited by Henry Louis Gates and Valerie A. Smith, W. W. Norton & Company (2014): 1067–1071.

Morrison, Toni, and Carolyn C. Denard. *What Moves at the Margin: Selected Nonfiction*. Jackson: University Press of Mississippi, 2008.

Munro, Martin. *Edwidge Danticat: A Reader's Guide*. Charlottesville: University of Virginia Press, 2010.

Nkrumah, Kwame. *Consciencism; Philosophy and Ideology for Decolonization and Development with Particular Reference to the African Revolution*. New York: Monthly Review Press, 1964.

Okpewho, Isdore. *African Oral Literature.* Bloomington: Indiana University Press, 1992.

Okpewho, Isidore, Carole Boyce Davies, and Ali A. Mazrui, The African Diaspora: African Origins and New World Identities. Bloomington: Indiana University Press (2001): xv.

Opefeyitimi, Ayo. "Ayajo as Ifá in Mythical and Sacred Contexts." In *Ifá Divination, Knowledge, Power, and Performance*, edited by Jacob K. Olupona and Rowland O. Abiodun. Indiana University Press (2016): 17–31.

Patton, Venertria. *The Grasp That Reaches Beyond the Grave: The Ancestral Call in Black Women's Texts*. New York: State University of New York (SUNY) Press, 2013.

Phillips, Charles, and Alan Axelrod. "Haitian Revolt, 1918–1920." *Reference Guide to the Major Wars and Conflicts in History: Wars in the Early 20th Century (1900 to 1950)*. Charles Phillips, Facts on File, 1st edition (2015).

Pryse, Marjorie, and Hortense J. Spillers. *Conjuring: Black Women, Fiction, and Literary Tradition*. Indiana University Press, 1985.

Roth, Ann Macy. "Fingers, Stars, and the 'Opening of the Mouth': The Nature and Function of the Nṯrwj-Blades." *The Journal of Egyptian Archaeology* 79 (1993): 57–79.

Scheel, Charles W. "From J. S. Alexis' 'Claire-Heurese' in 'Compère Général Soleil' to Edwidge Danticat's 'Claire of the Sea Light': What Fate for Haitian Marvelous Realism?" *CLA Journal* 59, no. 2 (2015): 177–193.

Schiller, Nina Glick, Linda Green Basch, and Cristina Szanton Blanc. 1995 "From Immigrant to Transmigrant: Theorizing Transnational Migration." *Anthropological Quarterly* 1 (1995): 48–63.

Shange, Ntozake. *For Colored Girls Who Have Considered Suicide When the Rainbow Is Enuf: A Choreopoem.* Collier Books, 1989.

Somé, Malidoma. *Ritual: Power, Healing, and Community: The African Teachings of the Dagara.* African Teachings of the Dagara. New York: Penguin/Arkana, 1997.

———. *The Healing Wisdom of Africa.* New York: Putnam, 1998.

Spillers, Hortense. "Interstices a Small Drama of Words." *Black, White, and in Color: Essays on American literature and culture.* University of Chicago Press (2003).

———. "Mama's Baby, Papa's Maybe: An American Grammar Book." *Black, White, and in Color: Essays on American Literature and Culture.* University of Chicago Press (2003).

Thompson, Robert Farris. *Flash of the Spirit: African and Afro-American Art and Philosophy.* First Vintage Books. New York: Vintage Books, 1984.

Truth, Sojourner. "Ar'n't I a Woman." In *The Norton Anthology of African American Literature,* edited by Henry Louis Gates and Valerie A. Smith. W. W. Norton & Company (2014): 178–180.

Ulysse, Gina A, and Robin D. G. Kelley. *Why Haiti Needs New Narratives: A Post-Quake Chronicle.* Translated by Ménard Nadève and Trouillot Évelyne. Middletown: Wesleyan University Press, 2015.

Walker, Alice. *In Search of Our Mothers' Gardens.* Harcourt, 1983.

Wardi, Anissa J. *Water and African American Memory: An Ecocritical Perspective.* Gainesville: University Press of Florida, 2011.

Washington, Teresa. *Our Mothers, Our Powers, Our Texts: Manifestations of Àjé in Africana Literature.* Bloomington: Indiana University Press, 2005.

———. "Mules and Men and Messiahs: Continuity in Yoruba Divination Verses and African American Folktales." *Journal of American Folklore* 125, no. 497 (2012): 263–285.

Welsh-Asante, Kariamu. *The African Aesthetic: Keeper of the Traditions.* Westport: Greenwood Press, 1993.

White, Deborah Gray. *Ar'n't I a Woman?* W. W. Norton & Company, 1999.

Wolkstein, Diane, and Elsa Henriquez. *The Magic Orange Tree: And Other Haitian Folktales.* New York: A. A. Knopf, 1978.

WuDunn, Sheryl. "In Japan, a Ritual of Mourning for Abortions." *New York Times* (1996): 145.

Yudice, George. *"Testimonio* and Postmodernism." *Latin American Perspectives* 18, no. 3 (Summer 1991): 15–31.

Index

About the Author

Joyce White is assistant professor of Gullah Geechee Literature and Cultures at Georgia Southern University. She received her PhD in Humanities with a primary focus in African American Studies from Clark Atlanta University and earned a BA and MA in English, with a focus in creative writing and literature, from Florida State University. Her research interests include 19th, 20th, and 21st century African American and diasporic literature, as well as African cosmological and spiritual continuities in diasporic literature and cultural productions.

Lightning Source UK Ltd.
Milton Keynes UK
UKHW040851141022
410422UK00036B/109

9 781793 646637